Farewell in June

Contemporary Russian Writing
General Editor: Kevin Windle

Also in this series:
The South American Variant by Sergei Zalygin

Money for Maria & Borrowed Time by
Valentin Rasputin

His Battalion & Live Unit Dawn by Vasil Bykov

second play, "Twenty Minutes with an Angel", is set in the same hotel as "The Compositor", and describes the disbelief and suspicion with which a generous gesture is met and the danger of making such gestures to strangers. Both the "Provincial Anecdotes" make telling points about Soviet society, the first evoking comparisons (via Gogol) with Russia in the early 19th century and suggesting that little has changed in people's ways of thinking. Both plays, however, have wider applications, particularly the latter, and both have universal appeal for audiences other than Soviet.

"Duck-Shooting", which introduces a Soviet anti-hero, is to the Soviet theatregoer, the most provocative of the plays. It concerns Zilov, an egocentric, vain, manipulative, and embittered young man who maltreats his wife and his mistress and alienates his friends. The friends decide to teach him a lesson by sending him a wreath for his own funeral. The action recounts the reasons for this by a series of flashbacks. The title has been interpreted by directors of the play as symbolizing a lust for power.

All four plays make excellent reading as well as being suitable for stage presentation.

The general editor of this series, **Kevin Windle**, graduated from Liverpool University (B.A. in Russian), McMaster University (M.A. in Soviet Literature), and McGill University (Ph.D. in Slavonic Studies). He has been a lecturer in Russian at the University of Queensland, and in Russian and Polish at the Australian National University. An experienced translator, his work includes novels and short stories translated from Russian, Polish, Portugese, and Czech.

Co-translator **Amanda Metcalf** spent 10 months in Moscow while researching her Masters thesis — a study of the Russian playwright Evgenii Shvarts. An adaptation of this research, for which she received her Masters from the Australian National University, was published as "Evgenii Shvarts and Fairy-Tailes for Adults", Birmingham Slavonic Monographs, 1979. While in England working towards her Ph.D. at the University of Hull she was asked to return to the Australian National University's Department of Slavonic Languages where she is currently a temporary tutor.

Farewell in June
FOUR RUSSIAN PLAYS
A. Vampilov

translated by Kevin Windle
and Amanda Metcalf

University of
Queensland Press

ST LUCIA • LONDON • NEW YORK

Originally published in Russian, 1966, 1968, 1970, 1971

English translation © University of Queensland Press, St Lucia, Queensland 1983

This book is copyright. Apart from any fair dealing for the purposes of private study, research, criticism, or review, as permitted under the Copyright Act, no part may be reproduced by any process without written permission. Enquiries should be made to the publishers.

Typeset by University of Queensland Press
Printed and bound by Hedges & Bell Pty Ltd, Melbourne

Distributed in the United Kingdom, Europe, the Middle East, Africa, and the Caribbean by Prentice-Hall International, International Book Distributors Ltd, 66 Wood Lane End, Hemel Hempstead, Herts., England.

Published with the assistance of the Literature Board of the Australia Council

National Library of Australia
Cataloguing-in-Publication data

Vampilov, Aleksandr, 1937–1972.
  [Proschanie v iiune. English].
  Farewell in June.

  ISBN 0 7022 1862 6.

  I. Windle, Kevin, 1947–. II. Metcalf, Amanda J., 1951–. III. Title. (Series: Contemporary Russian writing).

891.72'44

Library of Congress Cataloguing in Publication Data

Vampilov, Aleksandr Valentinovich.
  Farewell in June.

  (Contemporary Russian writing)
  Translation of: Proshchanie v iiune.
  Contents: Farewell in June — The elder son — Duck-shooting — Provincial anecdotes.
  I. Title. II. Series.
PG3489.3.A45A28   1983   891.72'44   82-11161
ISBN 0-7022-1862-6

Contents

vii	Introduction
1	Farewell in June
63	The Elder Son
135	Duck-Shooting
219	Provincial Anecdotes

Introduction

Aleksandr Vampilov was born in 1937 near Irkutsk, in Siberia. He began writing in 1958, during the post-Stalin "Thaw", while he was still at university. He published short stories and plays in journals during the sixties, but the first collected edition of plays was not published until 1975, three years after his death by drowning while fishing on Lake Baikal. He was thirty-four when he died. *Farewell in June* was first published in 1966, *The Elder Son* in 1968, *Duck-Shooting* in 1970 and the *Provincial Anecdotes* in 1970 and 1971.

In understanding Aleksandr Vampilov, it is necessary first of all to recognize his greatest fear. In his dramas and comedies, death is not only a presence, but also a participant in the development of the action. Although in none of his plays does the hero die either a natural or a violent death, nevertheless, death, if not actually present on the stage, gives continual reminders of its existence: the wreath which Zilov receives in *Duck-Shooting*, the cemetery fence which Koliosov has to take down in *Farewell in June*, the heart-attack suffered by the unfortunate hotel-manager Kaloshin, overwhelmed by the consequences of his own ignorance, in *The Compositor*. Even in his brightest, most cheerful comedy, *The Elder Son*, Vampilov strikes a mournful note — the musician Sarafanov, who has dreamed all his life of playing in a symphony orchestra, earns a subsistence-wage with a third-rate band playing at funerals. It is as though the thought of death continually haunts the author; as though he forsees that his own life will be cut short by an unexpected chance, shortly before his thirty-fifth birthday. Perhaps for this reason, his plays, which often begin like comic vaudeville sketches, suddenly acquire a tone of impending tragedy.

Another of the dramatist's fears is loneliness, the loneliness of the man who surrounds himself with an insurmountable wall, but forgets to make a door in it, not realizing that sometimes he himself may need to emerge from his refuge to see the people who bore him so much.

The third fear which oppresses Vampilov is homelessness: not because, in the course of the action, his heroes have to live in hostels, hotels and hastily-rented rooms — after all, Zilov in *Duck-Shooting* has even got a new flat and is celebrating his housewarming. Homelessness is not the absence of a roof over one's head, it is the mental state of not having a place where one can feel at home. The loneliness and homelessness of Vampilov's characters is akin to the homelessness of Chekhov's wanderers, even though the latter live on their own estates. Both groups are searching for acceptance somewhere. Vampilov has a lot in common, not only with Chekhov the playwright, but also with Chekhov the short-story writer. Like Chekhov, he proceeds from unusual, surprising happenings to ordinary, prosaic events; from the improbably absurd to the everyday absurd. Like his great predecessor, Vampilov comes to tragicomedy through comedy and farce, and dilutes potentially exciting events in the routine of everyday life. Chekhov's influence is felt, not only in similarities of dramatic construction, motifs and dialogue, but in the dissimilarities, in the obvious literary caricaturing of some of Chekhov's situations. The duel between Bukin and Frolov in *Farewell in June* clearly echoes the duel between Tuzenbach and Soliony in *Three Sisters*. The comic fire in *The Elder Son* can call up associations with the tragic fire in the same Chekhov play. It is unlikely that the young playwright was consciously parodying motifs and characters borrowed from Chekhov. More probably, Chekhov's influence on Vampilov was so deep that it was reflected unconsciously. Vampilov shares with Chekhov the same constant horror of the ordinary, dull, every-day existence, which leads to spiritual anaemia. The main dilemma confronting Vampilov and his heroes is a choice — not of "life or death", "to be or not to be", "to love or not to love"; but "the real person or the shell", "empathy or apathy".

Vampilov's last play, *Last Summer in Chulimsk*, appeared in 1972. The hero, Shamanov, is a young lawyer who is thirty-two — almost the same age as his author — and who, after an idealistic youth, disillusioned by his failure to change the world by his own efforts, has given up, run away from people, places and responsibilities, and now finds himself in Chulimsk, a small, forgotten town somewhere in Siberia — the end of the line.

Only six years separate this play from the earlier comedy *Farewell in June*, Vampilov's first full-length play. Only six years separate the creation of the lawyer Shamanov, marking time as he waits for a pension, from that of the young, energetic Koliosov, the hero of *Farewell in June*. In age they could almost be father and son.

It is characteristic of Vampilov to investigate father-son relationships within his plays. One aspect of this is a search for lost roots, an overcoming of "fatherlessness" as the hero seeks somewhere to shelter, as in *The Elder Son*. Another aspect is the son's admission of his guilt, in that he has, of his own free will, cut the threads connecting him with his father, his past and his origins, for which he now yearns, like Zilov in *Duck-Shooting*. Lastly, the relationship is a reflection of the young and the old. Like a magnifying glass, it shows what the younger man may become if he follows in his father's footsteps. Such a reflection is given of the young Koliosov in the person of the old man Zolotuev, a man with the philosophy that anything in the world can be bought, if the price is right. Once, many years before, Zolotuev, a salesman in a butcher's shop, was caught cheating the customers. He tried to bribe the inspector, but the latter would not take the money and, when offered a larger bribe, simply had Zolotuev imprisoned. Since then, Zolotuev has been tortured by one single thought — he did not offer enough. It simply does not enter into his view of the universe that there might be even one unbribable man in the world. With fanatical determination he collects twenty thousand rubles to prove his point, however belatedly, confident that the inspector will not stand out against such an offer. Here, funnily enough, Zolotuev is quite disinterestedly defending the principle of self-interest. At precisely this point he employs as watchman and gardener young Koliosov, who has just been expelled from his institute, and now has neither home nor family. Koliosov jokingly proposes that the old swindler should adopt him. He does not realize that he is indeed Zolotuev's spiritual heir. He professes the same mercenary philosophy, only on a more elevated level. When the Vice-Chancellor of the institute proposes a deal to Koliosov — successful graduation, a degree, a postgraduate place — if the latter will renounce Tania, the Vice-Chancellor's daughter, Koliosov accepts. Giving up the girl is both difficult and ignoble, but the budding scientist, like Zolotuev, has an obsession. However, whereas the old man's obsession was in the cause of self-preservation, Koliosov's extends to other people; he intends to improve the lot of humanity with his discoveries, and there is no place for the individual in this broad programme.

Although the author seems to think better of allowing his hero to commit an ignoble act, and makes him tear up his diploma at the end, nonetheless, despite Vampilov's wish to reform Koliosov, the play is, in the final analysis, not about spiritual renewal, but about a person subjecting himself to a cold-blooded plan.

Vampilov's attitude to this play was mixed. He rewrote it several times — there are three versions of *Farewell in June*. In the second version, Vampilov was already making this light comedy of student life end with the parting of the hero and heroine. The new finale served as a key to an understanding of the title. The "farewell" is not only the sad end of the love between Koliosov and Tania, but also a parting with the hopes of youth and an entry into the world of conflicts: it is the author's farewell to his hero, both as he would have liked to have written him: ardent, ungovernable, incorruptible; and as he wrote him in fact: a young dogmatist, creating his own design for life.

Despite all Vampilov's efforts to regenerate his hero, he cannot succeed in rehabilitating Koliosov, because a person's desire to serve the common good has to be a spiritual necessity, and if it springs from theoretical considerations, they eventually stifle him, and his end is spiritual boredom and apathy.

In his early works the playwright assumed that the young dreamers, the "sons", if they allow themselves to be bought, turn into "fathers", of the Zolotuev type, money-grubbers who do not care what they collect: money, houses, cars, or science degrees. Later, Vampilov probably came to the conclusion that the Koliosovs cannot become Zolotuevs, because they are "bought" not by material things, but by ideas of the highest, noblest kind. Later, unable to bear the burden of imaginary great deeds, they suffer a spiritual collapse and wander aimlessly around, spreading disillusionment and apathy.

In his mature works, Vampilov follows precisely this path of gradual transformation of the energetic "sons" like Koliosov into the "old" young men like Shamanov from Chulimsk.

Vampilov is always worried that such shells of people, boring and sleepy, serve as wonderful fertilizer for the growth of Russian philistinism. The heroes of his plays, despite their loss of faith, still have something left in their hearts: unfulfilled hopes, memories, a faded desire for regeneration. The true philistine has only one feeling left, which replaces all others for him: suspicion. Suspicion is his *raison d'être*, and he is most energetically and inventively ready to expose his neighbour. Besides, suspiciousness gives the philistine absolution from his sins: if everyone else is a villan, why should he be any better than the rest? It is precisely this sort of philistine which Vampilov presents in his *Provincial Anecdotes*. The action of these tragicomic episodes takes place in a second-rate hotel with the symbolic name "Taiga", referring to the wild forests of provincial Siberia. In one of the anecdotes, *Twenty Minutes with an Angel*, two hung-over workers on a business trip are in search of a few rubles in order to get drunk again. No one in the hotel will give them any money, so one of them opens the window and shouts "Who will lend us a hundred rubles?" — and the miracle happens: a man appears and sadly offers them a hundred rubles. The existence of a man who is willing to help his neighbour for no reason is outside their comprehension and brings on an attack of sudden suspiciousness, which is all the more frightening in that it infects all the other guests of the "Taiga". In the heat of their interrogation of him, the philistines suppose all kinds of things about the man. Perhaps this stranger is a speculator, a scoundrel, a thief; perhaps he has delusions of grandeur. In the end, they are prepared to tie the "angel" up and drag him off to the police station. The philistine is not satisfied without a sacrifice, and the more innocent the sacrifice, the more satisfaction for the philistine, because he has brought him down to his own level.

Vampilov was always struck by the psychology of philistinism. Those who knew him, bear witness that whenever he came into contact with things he detested, he would say helplessly: "philistines, absolute philistines . . ." As soon as he gained strength and experience, he let fly with a salvo of biting, malicious *Provincial Anecdotes*.

The philistine is on the attack, the intelligentsia is half-asleep, death and loneliness are becoming steadily more inevitable — one by one the playwright sets traps around his contemporary hero. But the author is only just over thirty years old, the forces of youth are up in arms against hopelessness, and he is desperately searching for some way to get his hero out of this dead-end. Sometimes he takes him off into the fields and forests, intending to cleanse him by means of nature; sometimes he tries to rehabilitate him by means of love. But Vampilov is a mocker, and deals mercilessly with provincial lyricism. A fascination with nature suddenly becomes a parody on the hero's every-day existence. Zilov, in *Duck-Shooting*, yearning for mists and quiet mornings, declaims his monologue about the beauty of the new-born world and the flight of ducks across the water, like a professional recitation artiste. Meanwhile, he has already done his "duck-shooting". Wandering through life as if through a mist, seeing nothing and hearing nothing, he has, in passing, "shot down" and crippled those nearest him. The day-dream about the hunt turns into murderous reality.

Vampilov's young heroines, too, undergo sad transformations. From one play to another the author produces variations on one and the same type of fresh young girl, still in her teens. With a stubborn persistence he keeps drawing his ideal woman, impulsive, emotional, unreserved. However, the dramatic paradox of almost all Vampilov's plays lies in the fact that, although his heroes are sincerely attached to their chosen girls, they often betray them through cowardice. Their self-destruction extends to their girl-friends. It becomes a vicious circle. The girls in his plays, instead of representing "the light", become merely the feminine embodiment of the fate of their men. It is no coincidence that the first version of *Last Summer in Chulimsk* ended with the suicide of the girl who loves the lawyer Shamanov. What should have happened to the hero, happened instead to the young girl who could not adjust herself to the cruelties of life. Afterwards, Vampilov changed that ending. The girl remains alive, but turns into the image and likeness of Shamanov. She only wants to be left in peace. The spirit has gone — the shell is left.

Vampilov wrote three one-act and five full-length plays. A sixth play remained unfinished, still in the planning stage, at his death. One can only speculate as to the further development of his work. Perhaps he would have gone off into the field of romantic lyricism as an escape from reality, as has happened with other talented playwrights, or perhaps he would have continued to create variations on the theme of modern philistinism. Perhaps he would have become a dealer in paradox, playing with theatrical situations; or perhaps continued to study the withering of the human soul. Everything is possible, because lyricism, satire and the ability to juggle with hypotheses were all equally at his command. He was talented. Perhaps for this reason his plays, which, during his lifetime had been published mainly in local provincial periodic anthologies, were collected into a book and published in Moscow only after his death, when he had ceased to be a developing personality, when one could no longer expect any surprises from him. Nonetheless, Vampilov remains a dangerous author — with a sharp, bold and talented pen he described in detail problems which no one before him had even mentioned, tracing their development and illustrating their persistent and disturbing topicality.

Elena Fortescue
September 1982
Canberra

Farewell in June
A comedy in two acts

translated by Amanda Metcalf

CHARACTERS

TATIANA (TANIA) a student
NIKOLAI KOLIOSOV (KOLIA) a biology student
VASILY BUKIN (VASIA) a geology student
MARIA (MASHA, MASHENKA) his bride
GOMYRA (BORIA) his friend and fellow-student
GRIGORY FROLOV (GRISHA) a biology student
THE CHEERFUL ONE)
THE SERIOUS ONE) other male students
THE PRETTY GIRL)
THE KOMSOMOL ORGANIZER) other female students
THE STUDIOUS GIRL (ALLA))
VLADIMIR ALEKSEEVICH REPNIKOV Vice-Chancellor, Tania's father
POLICEMAN
ZOLOTUEV amateur horticulturist
MRS REPNIKOV Tania's mother

ACT ONE
SCENE ONE

A Street

Spring. A painted fence, a large board covered with advertisements and posters. The corner of an old two-storey house, a pole marked "Bus-stop". Scales can be heard: in the old house someone is learning the piano. TANIA *is reading the posters. Enter* KOLIOSOV.

KOLIOSOV: Good evening.
TANIA: [*without turning round.*] Good evening.
KOLIOSOV: How long is it since the last bus?
TANIA: I don't know. [*Turns round.*]
KOLIOSOV: A-ha! Good evening!
TANIA: What does "A-ha" mean?
KOLIOSOV: A compliment.
TANIA: Oh. [*Turns back to the posters.*]
  [*For some time they both read the posters in silence.*]
KOLIOSOV: [*moves closer to* TANIA.] Excuse me, where are you going, if it's not a secret? [*Standing by the poster.*] The cinema? . . . No? Must be a concert then . . . Not that either? . . . Well where *are* you going? Not the theatre? . . . I see. Even you don't know where you're going. In which case, come with me.
TANIA: Are you pestering me?
KOLIOSOV: No. I'm inviting you . . .

TANIA: [*interrupts*] Thanks, but go and invite someone else . . . And anyway, I haven't time to talk to you.
KOLIOSOV: That's not true . . . How many times have you read through those posters? Be honest.
TANIA: [*after a pause.*] Three. So what?
KOLIOSOV: You see, you're bored.
TANIA: [*shrugging her shoulders.*] I'm just deciding where to go tomorrow.
KOLIOSOV: And what about today? Where do you want to go? To a dance? A concert? A fête?
TANIA: That's all tomorrow. Read the posters. And the fête in the park is a week away.
KOLIOSOV: Rubbish! We'll make them all happen today. I'm inviting you.
TANIA: What are you inviting me to?
KOLIOSOV: A wedding. To start with, I'm inviting you to a wedding.
TANIA: A wedding? You mean now?
KOLIOSOV: Immediately. What's your name? Haven't you got a name?
[*Silence*]
TANIA: Yes I have, but what's it to you? If I told you, you'd probably forget it straightaway.
KOLIOSOV: Why?
TANIA: Well if you're always in such a hurry, you must forget everything.
KOLIOSOV: I have a good memory.
TANIA: Don't boast.
KOLIOSOV: No really, I do have a fairly good memory. Do you want me to prove it?
TANIA: Okay. Let's prove it . . . Turn your back!
KOLIOSOV: How's that?
TANIA: Right . . . And now tell me who it is who's on tour here.
KOLIOSOV: Zhanna Goloshubova, popular singer.
TANIA: And who's with her? So you don't know . . . And did you notice her picture? What does she look like?
KOLIOSOV: Lovely. She's smiling.
TANIA: Do you like her?
KOLIOSOV: She's a good-looking woman.
TANIA: Then invite her to the wedding.

KOLIOSOV: And what about you? . . . Do you refuse?

TANIA: Are you serious?

KOLIOSOV: What?

TANIA: Well, inviting me to a wedding . . .

KOLIOSOV: I know what I'm doing. [*Looks at his watch.*] You see, my friend's getting married and I promised to come to the wedding reception with the most attractive girl in town. I've been looking for you all day. Surely you won't let me down. Well? . . . They're expecting us.

TANIA: Us? . . . Well, you know, you . . . And just where are they expecting "us"?

KOLIOSOV: Number eighteen Chapaev Street, room forty-two. Well? . . . Say yes! I promise you won't be bored.

TANIA: No . . . and anyway, I'm expected somewhere myself.

KOLIOSOV: What a pity . . . Well, never mind . . . I'll just have to invite Miss Goloshubova . . . Enjoy yourself.

TANIA: Have a good party.

KOLIOSOV: [*starts to leave, comes back.*] Listen, let's introduce ourselves before we part. [*Holds out his hand.*] Nikolai. Nikolai Koliosov.

TANIA: [*shakes hands.*] Tania.

KOLIOSOV: All the same, Tania, you shouldn't miss out on this wedding. You'll regret it, Tania.

TANIA: Never mind, I'll survive.

KOLIOSOV: I hope so. Or else do come if you change your mind. Room forty-two remember.

TANIA: What? Are you inviting *me* again now? And what about Miss Goloshubova?

KOLIOSOV: I'm inviting you *and* Miss Goloshubova. What's wrong with that? [*Leaving.*] There's room for everyone — it's a wedding. [*Exit.*]

SCENE TWO

A student hostel

In a big room the beds have been removed and the tables moved together. The wedding feast. BUKIN *and* MASHA *(the bride and groom), and* FROLOV. *Among the guests one stands out for his immoderate spontaneity —* BUKIN's *friend and classmate, nicknamed* GOMYRA. *The others, seated round the table, are best referred to as: the* KOMSOMOL ORGANIZER *(female), the* CHEERFUL ONE, *the* SERIOUS ONE, *the* PRETTY GIRL. *The gaiety is at its height.*

KOMOSOL ORGANIZER: Comrades! Attention please, comrades!
GOMYRA: [*interrupting her.*] Let me speak! [*Gets up.*] Quiet! I want to say a few words . . .
BUKIN: [*encouragingly*] Go on, Boria, say it. Speak up.
GOMYRA: In a minute, Vasia. Don't rush me . . . Okay. So . . . We have sitting here today in his capacity as bridegroom and man-in-love my friend and geologist Vasia Bukin. What did I want to say? . . . Vasia is the sort of chap who, if he makes up his mind to do something, goes straight to it, honestly and openly. No beating about the bush. He is incapable of beating about bushes . . . And there's no reason for certain people to snigger either. I've been on all sorts of journeys with Vasia, and if you don't know what sort of fellow he is, I do. He's never chickened out of anything, never left a friend in the lurch. I'm saying this so that, since he's got himself into a situation like this, he'll know . . . [*Turns to* BUKIN.] In other words, if anything happens, Vasia, you know you've got friends who won't just leave you to your fate. That's all I've got to say. Let's drink to it.
MASHA: Wait a minute. I don't quite understand. [*To* GOMYRA.] Could you make that a bit clearer?
BUKIN: It's quite clear, Masha. He's proposing a toast to friendship. Isn't that right, Boria?
GOMYRA: Vasia, you have understood me perfectly.
SERIOUS: To friendship.
 [*All, except* MASHA *and* FROLOV, *drink.*]
GOMYRA: [*to* FROLOV.] And what about you? Why aren't you drinking?
 [*To* BUKIN.] Vasia, why isn't he drinking?
BUKIN: Don't worry, he will.
KOMSOMOL ORGANIZER: Comrades! May I have your attention please . . .

SERIOUS: [*interrupting*] Not another toast? You can't start again so soon after the last one. Give us time to eat something first.

MASHA: Yes you really should, lads. Eat something, or you'll all be under the table.

CHEERFUL: Why don't we sing something, eh? I think this is just the right time for it. Something really new.

KOMSOMOL ORGANIZER: [*breaking through the noise.*] Friends! Listen, friends. Today we are celebrating an event which is a happy one for all of us. Just think, in our fifth-year biology class there are only eighteen girls and, would you believe, eleven of them are married by now. Today we're marrying off Masha — she's our twelfth, don't you think that's an achievement? In the chemistry department it's much worse, that's for sure. On behalf of the girls on our course, I heartily wish the young couple happiness and joy. And one more thing. May Bukin here value Masha as highly as she is valued by the rest of us. Mashenka, give me a kiss!

[KOMSOMOL ORGANIZER *and* MASHA *kiss. Noise.*]

GOMYRA: [*picks up a bottle, examines it.*] Champagne, eh? . . . Aren't we getting sentimental! . . .

KOMSOMOL ORGANIZER: And the most important thing, comrades! A surprise for the newlyweds! As a wedding present our committee and the trade union have allotted them a room in hostel number one.

[*Shouts of approval, the clink of glasses, cries of "Kiss her!"* BUKIN *and* MASHA *kiss each other.*]

BUKIN: Thank you . . . Masha and I drink to the health of the committee and the trade union. And also to the rank and file members present here. To you.

SERIOUS: Hey, where's Koliosov got to?

PRETTY: That's true, why isn't Koliosov here?

MASHA: [*laughing*] He's coming, don't worry. He's probably still rushing round the streets.

SERIOUS: What for?

MASHA: He promised to come to our wedding with the prettiest girl in town.

[*Shouts of "What vanity!" "He'll find her!" "He'll bring her!" "We'll see!".*]

CHEERFUL: That's nothing new.

BUKIN: There's no point in trying. I told him so straightaway. The most beautiful girl in town is here already. She's my bride. [*Embraces* MASHA.]
GOMYRA: Champagne . . . How are the mighty fallen!
[*Noise,* CHEERFUL *whispers something to* PRETTY.]
PRETTY: Be quiet, that's just boring.
CHEERFUL: I'm quite serious . . . [*Gets up.*] Your attention for one moment!
SERIOUS: What, again? We can't go on like this. You're setting a ridiculous pace.
GOMYRA: I agree, give a man time to get some food down.
CHEERFUL: Your attention for one moment! I refer to the quest for the best girl. The bridegroom is right, your Koliosov has made a grave miscalculation. Today the prettiest girls are all sitting round this table. Let's drink to their health, and leave Koliosov to run round the streets. To you, ladies!
[*Noise. All drink except* GOMYRA, *who ostentatiously pushes away his glass.*]
GOMYRA: [*to* FROLOV] Oh, so you drank that one? So you'll drink to the ladies but not to friendship amongst men? What do you mean by that? [*to* BUKIN.] Vasia, what does he mean by that?
BUKIN: It's no use nagging at him. Stop it, Boria.
[*Noise.* FROLOV, *who has been silent till now, gets up. Silence falls.*]
FROLOV: I can see that I'll have to say a few words. It's unavoidable . . . You people gathered here are basically pretty knowledgeable and, I hope, understand that this evening is extremely important to me too. You all know why: I've loved this girl for five years, and for all five of those years she hasn't loved me. Masha, I wouldn't have brought the subject up, but I think one or two people here are in need of some information, so . . . I have nothing to thank the bridegroom for, but, after all, this same evening relieves me of all hope, and believe me, after five years I'm rather sick of hoping. I want you all to know: I came to this wedding to sincerely congratulate the bride and groom and wish them all the best. I wish you happiness.
MASHA: Thank you, Grisha.
SERIOUS: Well said.

GOMYRA: [*suspiciously*] Very pretty.
BUKIN: [*to* FROLOV.] Your health.
GOMYRA: [*gets up.*] I propose a toast to geologists.
BUKIN: Hang on, mate. Sit down and have something to eat. Go on, eat something, please.
GOMYRA: What is geology? . . . Do you know? . . . You don't know. Geology is like this . . . it's when we go away on a trip and you stay behind with our women.
BUKIN: Please, that sort of thing is unnecessary.
GOMYRA: Vasia, let's face the truth. Are you and I going away? We are. And they're staying. Isn't that true? . . . They can't wait for us to go.
BUKIN: [*gets up and pushes* GOMYRA *into his seat.*] Sit down, mate . . .
SERIOUS: And behave yourself better.
GOMYRA: Better? . . . Well yes, I suppose so. Champagne, of course, how should we . . . well, never mind. We're going away soon, and there are bears there. Nothing but polar bears.
CHEERFUL: Hey, how about a song, eh?
[*Noise.* MASHA *gets up, moves away.* BUKIN *follows.*]
MASHA: I'm sick of your Gomyra.
CHEERFUL: Don't be angry. He's taking it rather hard. It's a purely alcoholic reaction. I'm sure you'll get to like him later.
MASHA: What for? Why should I get to like him?
BUKIN: But he's my friend, he's not just anyone . . . And, you see, at the moment he thinks I'm putting my head in a noose.
MASHA: A noose? And what do you think?
BUKIN: Me? I'm happy to put my head in it. [*Kisses her*]
[*Noise and jollity around the table.*]
Anyway, what do you think of it all . . . the ceremony and everything? Is it all right?
MASHA: It's okay . . . It's not at all how I imagined it.
BUKIN: What do you mean? Don't tell me you're not enjoying it!
MASHA: It could be more enjoyable.
BUKIN: You think so?
[*A knock at the door. Enter the* STUDIOUS GIRL.]
STUDIOUS: Good evening. I wouldn't have interrupted you, but as a member of the student council I ought to warn you that the Vice-Chancellor is in the hostel.

CHEERFUL: That's a new one!

PRETTY: What's he come here for?

STUDIOUS: Nothing in particular, just because. As a rule he visits us once a semester . . . I don't know but I think you ought to invite him.

BUKIN: Any objections? [*Gets up.*]

KOMSOMOL ORGANIZER: Sit down bridegroom, I'll take care of it. [*Exit.*]

MASHA: [*to* STUDIOUS.] Sit down, Alla. Be our guest.

PRETTY: Sit here.

STUDIOUS: Oh no I couldn't.

VOICES: "Go on", "sit down".
[*Gomyra is dozing.*]

STUDIOUS: I don't know, I never thought . . . but, as a member of the student council . . . [*Sits down.*]

BUKIN: So, we'll have the Vice-Chancellor at our wedding feast. [*To* MASHA.] Are you pleased?

MASHA: I'll say! Now we really will enjoy ourselves.

PRETTY: Koliosov obviously isn't coming now. Well, all the better.

CHEERFUL: [*jealous*] Strange. One minute you're sorry he's not here, the next you're pleased about it. All very mysterious . . . [*To everyone.*] Well, so how about it — are we going to sing or not? Let's have a sentimental ballad, eh? Something new.

BUKIN: No, no ballads. I want something a bit more cheerful. [*Gets up.*] One moment please . . . I propose a new addition to the programme. Something new in the wedding repertoire. Bukin saying farewell to Bukin. Just a minute . . . [*Puts the half-asleep* GOMYRA *into his own seat.*] He doesn't look like me but that's irrelevant. Imagine that he is Bukin, i.e. I am sitting in my seat, not standing over here. [*Goes to the opposite end of the table.*]

STUDIOUS: [*suspiciously*] Interesting . . .

BUKIN: [*with a glass in his hand.*] Ladies and comrades! Friends, I know Bukin very well. I have been personally acquainted with him for twenty-four years. If all the bottles of vodka that he and I have drunk together were put on this table, we would all be drinking for days.

CHEERFUL: That's a new one!

BUKIN: I know him very well. He was a cheerful lad. I honestly never thought he was about to take it into his head to get married. I just didn't expect him to do anything so stupid.

STUDIOUS: This is a farce.

BUKIN: Even tomorrow he'll go out on the street, he'll see lots of pretty girls there, he'll be sad, and he'll understand what an idiot he is.

CHEERFUL: That's new too.

[*Laughter.*]

STUDIOUS: I say, this isn't a wedding, it's . . . I don't even know what it is.

GOMYRA: [*wakes up suddenly. To* MASHA.] A woman . . . there's nothing but bears out there. Nothing but polar bears . . .

MASHA: [*to* BUKIN.] That's enough. Take this scarecrow away and sit down in your own seat. Before it's too late.

BUKIN: You wanted more jollity.

MASHA: Well now there's too much of it.

PRETTY: [*to* BUKIN.] No, go on, it's interesting.

CHEERFUL: Yes, go on, it's original.

BUKIN: In short, it's all up with Bukin. He's a hopeless case. Before our very eyes he is setting off on his furthest and, one might say, his most dangerous journey . . . He's buckled on his pack, taken a compass reading and . . . he's off! The course is set for married life. Goodbye Bukin, old man! Have a good trip and may you not be weighed down by the extra burden. Kiss her!

[*Laughter.*]

GOMYRA: [*gets up.*] Vasia! Friend! . . . Everything's okay. Wonderful. [*Gloomily*] But there's a woman mixed up in it.

MASHA: [*to* BUKIN.] Listen, that'll do, okay?

BUKIN: [*takes* GOMYRA *back to his seat.*] That's all, Boria, the comic turn is over, back to your own seat.

MASHA: He needs to go for a walk.

GOMYRA: [*to* MASHA.] Women! Let's face it: you're all the same. As soon as we go away . . .

BUKIN: [*shakes* GOMYRA.] Be quiet, Boria, be quiet . . .

STUDIOUS: What a lout!

GOMYRA: You're all the same. All of you!

MASHA: Is that so? . . . Get out.

[*Silence.*]

Get out!

GOMYRA: Vasia, I'm being invited to withdraw.

BUKIN: [*with restraint.*] Be quiet, Boria . . . You can stay, but be quiet.

MASHA: He's not going to stay. He's going to get up and leave.

FROLOV: [*gets up.*] He can't get up. He needs helping.

STUDIOUS: Disgraceful!

FROLOV: He needs a change of air.

GOMYRA: Rubbish! All I need is a drink.

[FROLOV *and* SERIOUS *move in on* GOMYRA. BUKIN *stops them.*]

BUKIN: He's staying.

MASHA: He's leaving.

BUKIN: I beg your pardon. Yours and everyone's. But he's staying.

GOMYRA: Vasia, don't demean yourself. If you don't mind, I think I'll go.

BUKIN: Sit still and shut up.

MASHA: Then I'm leaving.

BUKIN: Sit down, please. Are you or are you not my wife?

MASHA: Either he goes or . . . go on, let him leave!

BUKIN: [*firmly*] He's staying.

MASHA: As you wish . . . [*Loudly to everyone.*] Well then, dear guests . . . Listen and don't be angry. I hereby declare this marriage null and void.

BUKIN: Masha . . .

PRETTY: Maria! Don't!

MASHA: It was a joke, not a wedding . . . We [*Points at* BUKIN] that drunkard over there and I — we were joking. That's all. [*Goes out quickly.*]

[PRETTY *follows* MASHA *out.*]

FROLOV: [*to* GOMYRA *and* BUKIN.] Are you enjoying yourselves? You clowns!

[*Silence.*]

GOMYRA: [*gets up. Goes over to* FROLOV.] Vasia, let me make my point.

BUKIN: [*shouting.*] Sit down, I tell you!

[GOMYRA *stops.*]

FROLOV: [*sarcastically*] Well? . . . I don't suppose you're going to fight a duel about it?

[*Stands for a minute, then leaves.*]

BUKIN: No, there won't be a duel. He's right. Please — drink up, have something to eat.
GOMYRA: Vasia! What's this? What sort of talk is this? It's . . . it's champagne, not a serious conversation, Vasia! This isn't like you.
BUKIN: How can you tell anyway? You've had a lot to drink today.
GOMYRA: Fair enough . . . I'm just drinking the last one. To civilization. [*Drinks and goes out, followed by* SERIOUS.]
STUDIOUS: Why did you invite that hooligan?
BUKIN: He's my friend . . . And he's a bit depressed today.
[PRETTY *returns*. BUKIN *leaves*.]
PRETTY: Imagine backing out of a wedding. That's what I call really irresponsible.
STUDIOUS: I don't know, of course, and it's not my business, but I must say I don't understand Masha. Frolov is a serious chap, he's loved her for a long time, but Bukin, where did he spring from? One minute he meets her and the next . . .! And then there's this hooligan Gomyra. I heard that someone walked off with his fiancée last summer. Well, so what? That's his problem. He doesn't have to take it out on the rest of us, does he?
CHEERFUL: Well that's that. And we never did sing anything.
STUDIOUS: No, I don't understand Masha.
PRETTY: Oh I don't know, these geologists aren't bad . . . They're entertaining lads.
CHEERFUL: And what about Koliosov? Have you forgotten him already?
PRETTY: Koliosov? Yes . . . It *is* a pity he didn't come.
[*Enter* KOMSOMOL ORGANIZER *with a tape-recorder*.]
KOMSOMOL ORGANIZER: Comrades! The Vice-Chancellor is in the next room. He'll be here in a minute.
CHEERFUL: What a time to pick.
KOMSOMOL ORGANIZER: I've brought some music . . . But where are the others? What's happened?
CHEERFUL: The wedding is over.
PRETTY: The honeymoon has begun.
KOMSOMOL ORGANIZER: They haven't quarrelled?
STUDIOUS: It wasn't a wedding, it was a brawl.
KOMSOMOL ORGANIZER: But how come? . . . We've invited the Vice-Chancellor . . .

STUDIOUS: [*gets up.*] As a member of the student council . . . This is embarrassing. I'm going. [*Exit.*]
KOMSOMOL ORGANIZER: He's coming . . . Whatever will we tell him?
PRETTY: Don't worry, we'll lie our way out of it somehow. He won't know the difference.

[*A knock at the door. The* KOMSOMOL ORGANIZER *opens it.*]

REPNIKOV: [*entering*] May I?
KOMSOMOL ORGANIZER: Come in, Vladimir Alekseevich.
REPNIKOV: Good evening.
ALL: Good evening.
KOMSOMOL ORGANIZER: Do sit down, Vladimir Alekseevich.
REPNIKOV: [*taking in the situation.*] I would seem to have come at the wrong time . . . Where are the guests?
PRETTY: The guests? . . . They're outside . . . They've gone for a walk.
REPNIKOV: I see . . . [*To* CHEERFUL.] You must be the bridegroom? [*Sits down.*]
CHEERFUL: Me? . . . Well, yes . . . In a way . . .
REPNIKOV: You're a geologist, aren't you? I've heard about you. I dropped in to congratulate you. Congratulations.
CHEERFUL: Me? . . . Oh well, thank you.
REPNIKOV: And the bride? Which of you is the bride?
KOMSOMOL ORGANIZER: She . . . She went out . . .
PRETTY: A slight mishap. She spilt some wine on her white dress.
REPNIKOV: Oh, that's nothing to worry about.
PRETTY: No, of course not!

[*Enter* GOMYRA.]

GOMYRA: And if anything's wrong you can hit me one . . . [*Notices* REPNIKOV.] No, I . . . Nothing of the kind . . . Just bears, nothing but polar bears . . .
REPNIKOV: But why so gloomy? No songs, no dances. Don't tell me students have forgotten how to enjoy themselves?
PRETTY: No of course not. We're just sort of . . . having a breather.
CHEERFUL: Well, perhaps we could sing something anyway?

[KOMSOMOL ORGANIZER *muttering "hang on" turns on the tape-recorder. Music plays softly — something very jolly.*]

GOMYRA: [*to* REPNIKOV.] A geologist decides to get married — and, as you see . . . Let's drink a toast, Vladimir Alekseevich, to geology. You know, geology is such a subtle subject . . .

REPNIKOV: You're right there. Once upon a time I thought of doing geology, but I'm a stay-at-home and so . . .
GOMYRA: You stay at home. And you're quite right, by the way . . . But Vasia is a geologist, and he's still young . . . it doesn't matter, he'll thank his friend yet, you'll see. Well, I was against it from the start . . .
REPNIKOV: Against what?
GOMYRA: Against everything. Mainly against female personnel . . . You mean you don't know what's been happening?
REPNIKOV: Apparently not. [*To everyone.*] And what has actually been happening here? . . .
[*Silence*]
PRETTY: They weren't suited to each other. The usual story . . .
REPNIKOV: Usual? . . . At the wedding they found out that they weren't suited? . . . Curious . . .
GOMYRA: [*sobering up.*] No, whatever happened it wasn't Vasia's fault, remember that. It was all because of me . . .
REPNIKOV: Because of you? . . . All sorts of things could happen because of you, I don't doubt it.
[*To everyone.*] Well, tell me the whole story.
PRETTY: Oh well, it was all pretty calm and dignified really.
KOMSOMOL ORGANIZER: Vladimir Alekseevich, we'll see they make it up.
PRETTY: Oh yes, of course. And there wasn't really anything bad in it.
KOMSOMOL ORGANIZER: And there won't be.
[*Suddenly the window bursts open and* KOLIOSOV *jumps into the room.* REPNIKOV *is sitting with his back to the window, so that* KOLIOSOV *doesn't recognize him and perhaps doesn't even notice him.* KOLIOSOV *dives for the light switch. Darkness.*]
KOLIOSOV: Begging your pardon. Lock the door and sit quiet. If anyone knocks — this is a room full of girls and they've all undressed and gone to bed. Got that? . . . Don't open the door under any circumstances. I'm sorry I'm late.
REPNIKOV: What's all this . . . What's going on?
KOLIOSOV: Nothing in particular. The police are after me.
REPNIKOV: Turn on the light.
KOLIOSOV: Not on your life! There are girls asleep here, remember. And turn that tape-recorder off.

[*Someone inadvertently turns the tape-recorder up. Everyone cries out.*]

REPNIKOV: Turn on the light!

KOLIOSOV: Shush! . . . Who's this bass voice that's suddenly appeared amongst you?

REPNIKOV: Turn on the light, I said!

KOLIOSOV: And I said shut up, you! What's the matter with you? Scared of the dark or something?

REPNIKOV: Turn on the light this minute!

KOLIOSOV: Listen, are you going to shut your trap or not?

KOMSOMOL ORGANIZER: Kolia, stop it!

[*There is a scrimmage at the light switch. Something falls over. Noise. Music.*]

REPNIKOV: Light! . . .

KOLIOSOV: Gomyra, take your friend, or . . .

GOMYRA: Don't touch him, Kolia! Don't touch him!

PRETTY: Oh how awful!

[*The* KOMSOMOL ORGANIZER *manages to switch on the light.* KOLIOSOV *and* REPNIKOV *are holding each other by the arms. Outside the window stands a policeman. A pause.*]

REPNIKOV: Oh, so it's you?

KOLIOSOV: Vladimir Alekseevich?

REPNIKOV: [*to the* KOMSOMOL ORGANIZER, *about the tape-recorder.*] Switch it off.

[*The* KOMSOMOL ORGANIZER *switches off the tape-recorder. The policeman outside the window disappears.*]

KOLIOSOV: I'm sorry, Vladimir Alekseevich, but in the dark . . .

REPNIKOV: You didn't recognize me. I hope.

KOLIOSOV: Honestly . . .

REPNIKOV: All right, we'll sort that out later. Now you'd better tell us who's after you and why.

[*Enter the policeman.*]

POLICEMAN: Good day. [*Goes up to* KOLIOSOV *and stretches out his hand.*] Your papers.

[KOLIOSOV *hands over his papers.*]

POLICEMAN: [*takes them, looks through them*] What's the booze-up for?

REPNIKOV: This, believe it or not, is a wedding feast!

POLICEMAN: [*to* REPNIKOV.] What was your problem with the offender?

REPNIKOV: Don't worry, we'll sort that out ourselves.
POLICEMAN: As you like. You must be a lecturer?
REPNIKOV: Yes. And what's he been up to with you?
POLICEMAN: An uproar in a hotel. Your student burst into the room of Miss Goloshubova, the singer.
KOLIOSOV: I knocked.
POLICEMAN: Burst in and caused an uproar.
KOLIOSOV: I invited Goloshubova to the wedding and she accepted . . .
POLICEMAN: And, moreover, caused bodily harm to one Shafransky, a musician.
KOLIOSOV: That character burst into the room and started shouting. He insulted a woman and he insulted me. I showed him his mistake . . .
POLICEMAN: With a fist. Moreover, he tried to escape. Anyway, you'll be getting a copy of the charge-sheet. [*To* KOLIOSOV.] Come on.
KOLIOSOV: [*with a sigh*] Okay. Let's go. [*To everyone.*] See you later. [*to* REPNIKOV.] See you later, Vladimir Alekseevich.
[KOLIOSOV *and the* POLICEMAN *leave.*]
REPNIKOV: He's a fine lad! . . . Last year the biology students were agitating for non-compulsory attendance at lectures. If my memory serves me right, Koliosov was the ringleader . . . I'm afraid he's got what he was after . . .
[*Silence.*]
PRETTY: This would happen . . .
KOMSOMOL ORGANIZER: Now what's going to happen?
REPNIKOV: By the look of it, they'll take him to court.
PRETTY: It would happen now: just before the state exams! Would they really, just for that . . .
REPNIKOV: [*interrupts her.*] He'll get what he deserves. No less. But no more, either.
[BUKIN *appears.*]
BUKIN: [*with a sigh.*] Hullo . . .
REPNIKOV: Hullo . . .
[*A short pause.*]
BUKIN: [*shrugging his shoulders.*] It's my fault, I admit it. . . . I beg your pardon . . . But what can you do? And anyway, who's suffered most? Me of course.
REPNIKOV: And why you in particular?

BUKIN: Who else?
REPNIKOV: Sorry, but who are you? A relative of the bride? Of the groom?
BUKIN: What do you mean a relative?
REPNIKOV: Well, who are you?
BUKIN: How do you mean "who"? The bridegroom . . . unfortunately.
REPNIKOV: The bridegroom?
[*A short pause.*]
Well, my friends. Thank you for the invitation. Thank you. Allow me to return the compliment. I invite the bride and groom to my office tomorrow. By ten o'clock . . . [*To the others.*] and you lot as well.
[*A knock at the door.*]
PRETTY: Come in.
[*Enter* TANIA.]
TANIA: Excuse me, can I see Koliosov?
PRETTY: Who?
TANIA: Koliosov.
CHEERFUL: You'd better come back later. In about fifteen days time.
REPNIKOV: [*turns round.*] Tatiana?

SCENE THREE

Outside the town

Sunlight. Young birch trees, the fence of an old cemetery. In the foreground, asphalt, far away new building sites. Enter KOLIOSOV, ZOLOTUEV *and the* POLICEMAN. KOLIOSOV *is carrying a crowbar,* ZOLOTUEV *a spade. They stop.*

ZOLOTUEV: But sergeant, this is a cemetery.
POLICEMAN: Well, so what?
ZOLOTUEV: How do you mean — so what? I'm fifty-eight and I've got a weak chest. I don't get this kind of joke. I object.
POLICEMAN: [*shaking the fence.*] Please do.

ZOLOTUEV: I'm against such methods. It's illegal. I should be getting the normal ten days.

KOLIOSOV: Calm down, the sergeant has brought us on an excursion.

POLICEMAN: Listen, you hooligans. It's a simple job: you're going to take this fence to pieces. Break it up and dig out the posts. And then drag it all over there [*points*] well away from the road.

ZOLOTUEV: What for, for God's sake?

POLICEMAN: None of your business. By order of the town council.

KOLIOSOV: No, really, what are they going to put here?

POLICEMAN: Tramlines. You'll be able to ride through here on a tram. Unless, of course, they put you in prison before then.

ZOLOTUEV: And you're making an old man destroy a cemetery! Is that fitting?

KOLIOSOV: Yes, it really is a bit tactless.

POLICEMAN: Get on with it.

KOLIOSOV: [*to* ZOLOTUEV.] A picturesque corner, don't you think? Do you like it here? . . . [*To the* POLICEMAN.] Sergeant, we wouldn't mind getting a plot here ourselves, on the side, through some useful contact. Eh, sergeant?

POLICEMAN: They don't bury anyone here now. And start working. Get moving. I'll just go and get a few smokes. You've got to get as far as that post over there today. And remember, you won't leave till you've done it.

ZOLOTUEV: Sergeant, I really do protest.

POLICEMAN: Please do. [*Goes off.*]

KOLIOSOV: What kind of a protest can you make? You've lived it up, you've broken the law — that's enough from you already.

ZOLOTUEV: If you were only my son! I'd give you a proper hiding!

KOLIOSOV: Well, adopt me then.

ZOLOTUEV: You? What for? I could take you on as a watchman. I need a watchman. For my holiday cottage.

KOLIOSOV: No. I'd rather you adopted me. You're an orphan, so am I, if it comes to that — there'll be two orphans less in the world. So, you've got a holiday cottage? . . . That's interesting. And a pension? Will you have a pension?

ZOLOTUEV: I won't need a pension, I've got a weak chest.

KOLIOSOV: A holiday cottage and a weak chest, I like you more and more every minute . . . But I wonder what you're suffering out here for?

ZOLOTUEV: What for? . . . That's the point; I don't know what for.
KOLIOSOV: Oh come on!
ZOLOTUEV: I tell you I don't know . . . I dug up an orchid — real vandalism, eh?
KOLIOSOV: What sort of an orchid?
ZOLOTUEV: An ordinary one. In the town square I dug up an orchid. Just a flower . . . Is that really vandalism?
KOLIOSOV: It's an unheard-of liberty. In the town square, under the very noses of the police. What was the matter with you? Couldn't you find one anywhere else?
ZOLOTUEV: No I couldn't.
KOLIOSOV: Well what did you want an orchid for?
ZOLOTUEV: I like flowers.
KOLIOSOV: Yes, but why dig it up? After all, it'd be less noticeable if you picked it.
ZOLOTUEV: I like live flowers.
KOLIOSOV: Did you want to give it to someone?
ZOLOTUEV: I wanted to admire it myself. Personally.
KOLIOSOV: Well, yes, you've got a cottage and beside the cottage, of course, a kitchen-garden . . . Is it a big garden?
ZOLOTUEV: Listen, what are you pestering me for?
KOLIOSOV: I'm intrigued. A hooligan who grows orchids. A freak. Why not dill, why orchids?
ZOLOTUEV: I've got my own bit of land. On my own land, young man, what I want to do, I do. That's enough chat, let's get working. Didn't you hear what the sergeant said? I don't want to be here all night.
KOLIOSOV: Why not? I don't see what it is you don't like about this place.
[*They work. Enter* MASHA *and* TANIA.]
MASHA: Hi, Kolia. Still alive?
TANIA: Good morning.
KOLIA: Hullo, hullo.
MASHA: Do you know what they told us at the police-station? At the moment, they said, he is in the cemetery. But that, they said, is a secret, for you alone. Not a bad joke, eh? [*To* ZOLOTEUV.] Greetings!
KOLIOSOV: That's Zolotuev. He's another delinquent. We're a pretty desperate crew.

ZOLOTUEV: Nonsense, I'm a peaceful man. [*Goes off to one side along the fence.*]
KOLIOSOV: [*to* TANIA.] Come over here. You can sit down here.
MASHA: And where's your guard?
KOLIOSOV: The police escort has gone off somewhere.
TANIA: What do you have to do here, anyway?
KOLIOSOV: We're breaking up the fence.
TANIA: What for?
KOLIOSOV: By order of the town council. This world is being widened, the hereafter is being reduced.
MASHA: Great!
KOLIOSOV: Sit down and tell me everything. How was the wedding? Where's your husband?
MASHA: Where indeed? A good question . . . I left him, Kolia, I left him at the wedding.
KOLIOSOV: How do you mean — at the wedding? Why?
MASHA: Oh it wasn't a wedding! Weddings aren't like that. I don't want to talk about it. The others will tell you. Other people always know more about things.
KOLIOSOV: Just give it to me in a nutshell.
MASHA: It all started because of Gomyra. They're such great friends, why doesn't Vasia marry *him*? Imagine — they gave us a room, and now Vasia's moved Gomyra into it. He's laughing at me . . . And then Frolov, yesterday in the hostel. You can teach me how to live, he says. And now they're always together.
KOLIOSOV: Don't get upset, old girl. You're our most marriageable girl.
MASHA: But he doesn't want to be married to me, Kolia, so . . . We had to see the Vice-Chancellor. Bukin, Gomyra and I each got a warning. But that's nothing . . . Your case is worse. We couldn't do anything.
KOLIOSOV: Make it short.
MASHA: You're being expelled from the University.
KOLIOSOV: Expelled? Now? . . . Is it official?
MASHA: Not yet, but the Vice-Chancellor says it's all decided.
KOLIOSOV: I see.
MASHA: That musician. You dislocated his arm, and he's a guitarist.
KOLIOSOV: Just my luck . . .

MASHA: He went to the Vice-Chancellor and said if you weren't punished he'd sue. That singer, Goloshubova, she rang the dean.
KOLIOSOV: And?
MASHA: Well, she said you had behaved politely and invited her to a party . . . Kolia, we'll all go to the Vice-Chancellor, all our year.
KOLIOSOV: So, it's expulsion, is it? . . . He really must be foaming at the mouth.
MASHA: Steady on. This lass happens to be Vladimir Alekseevich's daughter.
KOLIOSOV: You're his daughter?
TANIA: I can't help it.
KOLIOSOV: It gets worse all the time.
MASHA: But I think Tania's on your side.
TANIA: I don't yet know whose side I'm on.
MASHA: Oh yeah? Think I can't tell? . . . Kolia, perhaps all is not yet lost . . . Don't worry too much.
KOLIOSOV: I'm not worrying . . . Although I do think he could have stopped short of expulsion.
MASHA: All our year, and the dean's office too, are sticking up for you . . .
KOLIOSOV: [*interrupting*] Okay, okay.
MASHA: Well, anyway, see you later. I must run. I've got heaps of other things to do, and a divorce to see to as well. I'll send the lads to see you tomorrow.
KOLIOSOV: Tell them to bring some cigarettes.
MASHA: All right. [*Goes.*]
TANIA: I'll bring you some cigarettes, do you want some?
KOLIOSOV: What? Daddy's cigarettes? No thank you.
TANIA: You think he wouldn't want to share his cigarettes with you?
KOLIOSOV: No, he wouldn't.
TANIA: Nonsense, he's not greedy. Listen, he's so busy. He always tries to be fair.
KOLIOSOV: Oh yes of course! He hasn't got time to be fair. I understand perfectly.
TANIA: But he's not doing it for revenge. You do understand he's not doing it for revenge?
KOLIOSOV: Of course. Revenge is a feeling unworthy of a leader.

TANIA: And anyway, my father is a kind man. I think I'd say that, even if I wasn't his daughter.
KOLIOSOV: Tania, you are not mistaken in your dad. You have a good dad. Kind, serious, authoritative.
TANIA: If Father is wrong, I don't intend to defend him. But I would like to clear something up . . . [*Stops*]
KOLIOSOV: Clear what up?
TANIA: I've quarrelled with my father. About you.
KOLIOSOV: You shouldn't have bothered. Your father and I are both responsible adults. It doesn't matter what happens between us. We'll probably meet and have a chat about it some time . . . If I were you I'd wash my hands of the whole thing and go out to the pictures.
TANIA: It's easy to say that when you know the whole story, but I've got to make some kind of sense of it.
KOLIOSOV: Why, you funny girl? Look at that lot lying on the other side of the fence. They wanted to make sense of everything too. I promise you they ended up not understanding anything.
TANIA: Nothing at all?
KOLIOSOV: Probably each of them had so many adventures . . . They just didn't have time to understand anything.
TANIA: You're judging them by your own standards. Not everyone is in such a hurry as you. Some people think, meditate . . .
KOLIOSOV: No, Tania. Either you live or you meditate about life — one or the other. You have to choose from the beginning. There's not enough time for both. That's what I think anyway . . . Their life [*Points at the fence.*] is over, and it's easier for us, the living, to make sense of their lives. And then others will judge us. After all, you always get a better view from the outside.
[ZOLOTUEV *reappears.*]
ZOLOTUEV: I'm fifty-eight years old. I'm tired.
KOLIOSOV: Listen . . . You just said you needed a watchman.
ZOLOTUEV: So?
KOLIOSOV: I'm looking for work.
ZOLOTUEV: I'm not taking you on, so forget it.
KOLIOSOV: But why not? You just offered it to me.
ZOLOTUEV: I've changed my mind. You're vulgar and I don't like that.

KOLIOSOV: Vulgar? Well what sort of watchman do you want then? One with good manners? With a degree from the conservatorium?

ZOLOTUEV: Of course not. I need a quiet chap, hard working . . . You don't need an education for watering flower beds. I need a watchman who knows how to hold a watering-can and a pair of shears.

KOLIOSOV: A common interest. I'm keen on gardening. Can't you see how lucky you are?

ZOLOTUEV: Well, I don't know, young man. I don't know . . . The sergeant's coming!

TANIA: Oh well . . . I'd better be off . . .

KOLIOSOV: I'm sorry, Tania. But you can see for yourself — the setting is all wrong. Maybe we'll meet again. Have a talk.

TANIA: You haven't explained anything properly . . . you've just confused me even more. Good-bye.

KOLIOSOV: So long, Tania . . . Don't upset your dad.

[TANIA *goes out. The* POLICEMAN *appears.*]

POLICEMAN: I see . . . Slacking, eh? I trust you, and what do you do?

KOLIOSOV: We trust you too.

POLICEMAN: So I trust you, and you let me down? . . . You're clever and I'm a fool, eh?

KOLIOSOV: Sorry about that, sergeant, we'll reform. Can I have a smoke?

SCENE FOUR

A Flat

A large room in the REPNIKOVS' *house. Ground floor. Two large windows, beautiful curtains. Judging by the decor this room is intended as a room for receiving guests and also for festive meals. It is getting on for evening.* TANIA *and her mother are putting an elegant white cloth on the table which stands in the middle.* MRS REPNIKOV *is wearing an apron,* TANIA *is in a house-dress.*

TANIA: [*laying the table.*] Always such a ceremony. We could eat just as well in the kitchen.
MRS REPNIKOV: Sunday is Sunday. Don't grumble.
[REPNIKOV *appears with a bouquet of flowers and a bottle of wine. He is in an excellent mood.*]
REPNIKOV: Well? [*Stops.*] Mmm . . . Smells divine! How is it? It's cooked already isn't it?
MRS REPNIKOV: Not yet.
REPNIKOV: [*puts the bottle on the table, hands the flowers to his wife.*] How come?! It's been a full hour and a half.
MRS REPNIKOV: Another fifteen minutes.
REPNIKOV: [*horrified*] Fifteen? . . . Are you sure it won't burn? [*Heads for the door leading to the kitchen.*] And what about the sauce?
MRS REPNIKOV: [*not letting him pass.*] No, no, there's nothing for you to do there.
REPNIKOV: [*trying to get past.*] I'll just take a look, just a look . . .
MRS REPNIKOV: Go into your study and wait there.
REPNIKOV: Listen, it's sizzling . . . It's hissing like a live one . . . It's ready!
MRS REPNIKOV: Go on with you [*Pushes him towards the other door.*]
REPNIKOV: If it's not on the table in fifteen minutes, I warn you, I'll die [*Goes into the study.*]
MRS REPNIKOV: [*looking at the clock.*] Yes, we are a bit late with dinner today.
TANIA: Well we can't do anything about it now.
REPNIKOV: [*appearing in the doorway.*] What about the onion? I can't smell any onion!
MRS REPNIKOV: [*laughing and shutting the door.*] Oh stop it, do.
TANIA: It's always the same.
MRS REPNIKOV: Are you grumbling again? I don't understand what's bothering you.
TANIA: We always overeat like I don't know what, and then spend the whole evening digesting . . .
MRS REPNIKOV: Well don't eat then, no-one's forcing you.
TANIA: What, not eat your cooking? Very likely! Even the smell's worth a million. And anyway, Daddy would tease me.
MRS REPNIKOV: [*puts the vase of flowers on the table.*] Nice ones . . .

And look, buds. These ones will wilt but the buds are only just about to open . . . But then they'll wilt too.

TANIA: Oh I wish it would all hurry up and be over with! Everything's lovely in spring except for exams.

MRS REPNIKOV: Typical! Everyone's in a hurry. You want the spring to hurry, the exams to hurry, the summer to hurry. Hurry, hurry, hurry. But where to? High blood pressure? Sclerosis?

TANIA: [*puts her arms round her mother.*] And what's bothering *you*, then? You're young, you're pretty . . . You should live, not philosophize. You can meditate as much as you like — you still won't understand anything. You'll just be letting time pass you by.

MRS REPNIKOV: What's this? Wherever did you get these ideas from?

TANIA: [*smiling*] From a textbook. Political economy.

MRS REPNIKOV: Oh yes? Don't try to fool me. I know what textbook you mean . . . I can see your father's right — that lad is a very tricky customer indeed.

TANIA: Mum, don't condemn a person if you don't know him.

MRS REPNIKOV: And what did this person of yours get up to in the hotel, eh? And what about in the hostel?

TANIA: He didn't do anything awful.

MRS REPNIKOV: Well he will, if he's that sort, give him time. If he doesn't come to his senses. [*Going into the kitchen. In the doorway.*] Call your father. [*Goes out.*]

[*The doorbell rings.* TANIA *opens the door. Enter* KOLIOSOV.]

KOLIOSOV: Hullo, Tania.

TANIA: [*confused*] Hullo.

KOLIOSOV: You weren't expecting me?

TANIA: [*after a pause*] Well, I suppose, no, I didn't think . . .

KOLIOSOV: To tell the truth I hadn't reckoned on it either. Yes, well there you are. Stranger things have been known.

TANIA: Has anything happened?

KOLIOSOV: Oh yes. There's a scandal in Panama, a revolution in Zanzibar. Some sections of the Bratsk Hydroelectric Station have begun operating — haven't you heard? . . . And we're sweeping the roadway. Here in the next street.

TANIA: They haven't let you go yet?

KOLIOSOV: Yes, for half an hour. On parole.

TANIA: Come in, sit down for a minute . . .
KOLIOSOV: I actually . . . I've come to see Vladimir Alekseevich.
TANIA: I thought you had.
KOLIOSOV: Is he at home?
TANIA: Yes.
   [MRS REPNIKOV *appears with a large platter in her hands. On it is a large brown goose, garnished with salad.*]
KOLIOSOV: Good evening.
MRS REPNIKOV: Hullo.
TANIA: Mum, this is . . .
KOLIOSOV: Koliosov.
MRS REPNIKOV: Really? . . . Well, yes, how interesting to meet you. [*Puts the platter on the table.*]
KOLIOSOV: Perhaps I've come at the wrong time, but . . .
MRS REPNIKOV: Of course not! . . . Do stay and have dinner with us.
KOLIOSOV: Thanks very much, but I've had dinner already.
MRS REPNIKOV: Do sit down . . . Tania, give the guest a chair.
KOLIOSOV: Thank you [*Sits down on the very edge of the chair.*]
   [*Silence.* TANIA *also sits down on a chair near* KOLIOSOV. *Enter* REPNIKOV. *Not noticing* KOLIOSOV *at first, he approaches the table, rubbing his hands.*]
KOLIOSOV: [*gets up.*] Hullo, Vladimir Alekseevich.
REPNIKOV: [*after a pause.*] Hullo there, young man.
KOLIOSOV: I beg your pardon, but circumstances compelled me to come and see you at home.
REPNIKOV: [*after a pause.*] To see me? . . . I see . . . Curious . . .
KOLIOSOV: I decided to come and disturb you because I can't come to the university . . . neither tomorrow nor the day after . . . It is essential that I talk to you.
REPNIKOV: To me? [*To* TANIA *and her mother.*] In that case, you'd better leave us alone. This young man has something to discuss with me.
   [MRS REPNIKOV *goes out to the kitchen.* TANIA *hangs back.*]
REPNIKOV: [*sternly*] Tania, please. [TANIA *goes out.*] Go ahead, I'm listening.
   [*There is a light tap at the window, to which* REPNIKOV *at first pays no attention.*]
KOLIOSOV: It's a request. [*Another tap at the window.*] I apologize for the pretentious-sounding tone but I want to tell you that

long ago I came to a firm decision to devote myself to science and I would not like to have wasted my time . . .
[*The curtain is suddenly pulled back and* ZOLOTUEV's *head appears in the open window.*]
ZOLOTUEV: [*to* REPNIKOV.] My humble apologies, but it's time for your guest to leave. [*To* KOLIOSOV.] Time you were off.
KOLIOSOV: [*goes over to the window, screens it with his back. In a whisper to* ZOLOTUEV.] Disappear!
[ZOLOTUEV *disappears.*]
REPNIKOV: What was that apparition? Who is it?
KOLIOSOV: Oh, it was just this bloke. Don't pay any attention.
REPNIKOV: But what does he want?
KOLIOSOV: He's worried that I may be boring you. He's very protective about me.
REPNIKOV: A relative?
KOLIOSOV: Yes, he's my uncle.
REPNIKOV: [*displeased*] In that case tell him to come in.
KOLIOSOV: Oh no, that's not a good idea. You see he's an unsociable fellow, even anti-social and anyway . . . Vladimir Alekseevich! The point is that for the last two years I've been studying one subject. Grasses. Perhaps you've heard.
REPNIKOV: Yes. And so?
KOLIOSOV: Apparently, Vladimir Alekseevich, that's the whole point. You're an academic and you know what it means for a beginner to lose a couple of years.
REPNIKOV: I see . . . You said I was an academic. That's good. When it comes to attending my lectures I'm not an academic but when you have a favour to ask — suddenly I'm an academic.
KOLIOSOV: Vladimir Alekseevich, the point is . . . I think that what I'm doing is important not only for me . . .
[*At the window, behind* KOLIOSOV's *back,* ZOLOTUEV's *face appears again.*]
ZOLOTUEV: Listen! We're abusing his trust! The sergeant won't forgive us.
KOLIOSOV: [*in a menacing whisper to* ZOLOTUEV.] Get lost, I said!
ZOLOTUEV: If you're not careful we'll be going hungry.
REPNIKOV: [*to* KOLIOSOV.] Listen, what does all this mean, for heaven's sake?

KOLIOSOV: [*pushing* ZOLOTUEV *away from the window with one hand.*] Oh nothing. He just loves eating and talking about food. You know, sometimes, for no reason at all . . .
REPNIKOV: [*annoyed*] You were right, your uncle is a man of strange habits. [*Shuts the window.*]
KOLIOSOV: Vladimir Alekseevich! On Wednesday the exams begin at the university . . .
REPNIKOV: [*interrupting*] And so, Koliosov, you have decided that all you have to do is come and see me at home and all is well — I'll cancel the expulsion order and admit you to the exams.
KOLIOSOV: It seems I've made a mistake in coming to your house. I came to you with a personal request; I apologize once again for disturbing you.
REPNIKOV: You're a fast worker, Koliosov. A very slippery customer.
KOLIOSOV: Meaning?
REPNIKOV: You've set my daughter against me and then decided that this is just the moment to come and see me with a personal request.
KOLIOSOV: I have not set your daughter against you. She and I are acquainted, that's all.
REPNIKOV: I think it's very unfortunate that you are acquainted with her.
KOLIOSOV: My request has nothing do with that circumstance.
REPNIKOV: Oh go on!
KOLIOSOV: I assure you, I am not here as a suitor.
REPNIKOV: [*after a pause.*] Have you talked to her about this?
KOLIOSOV: No. But then she hasn't asked.
  [ZOLOTUEV *unexpectedly appears at the other window.*]
ZOLOTUEV: You do as you like, but I'm off.
KOLIOSOV: [*to* ZOLOTUEV *still in a whisper.*] Get out of here . . . Lunatic! [*Shuts the window.*] I'm sorry, Vladimir Alekseevich . . . You see . . . I have to admit: my uncle is a delinquent.
REPNIKOV: [*greatly annoyed.*] That'll do! [*Draws the curtain.*]
KOLIOSOV: Vladimir Alekseevich! I came here in the hope that you would understand me . . .
REPNIKOV: That'll do, Koliosov. The conversation is over! You didn't just come here — no, you burst your way in. It's a habit of yours! And you didn't come with a request, but with a demand! And do you know what such visits are called?

KOLIOSOV: [*has also lost his temper.*] No I don't know. I came to you with a request, but I have no intention of crawling to you. And even if you don't understand me, it doesn't mean you can shout at me.

REPNIKOV: I see! I hope you don't intend to strangle me? Here, in my own home!

[*Enter* MRS REPNIKOV.]

MRS REPNIKOV: Couldn't you be a little quieter?

REPNIKOV: There he is! Look at him! A very nice young man! Formerly a student, now . . .

KOLIOSOV: [*bowing to* MRS REPNIKOV.] A hooligan.

REPNIKOV: There — just look at him!

MRS REPNIKOV: Well . . . Even if he is a hooligan — do you need to get so upset about it? [*Takes* REPNIKOV*'s arm.*]

REPNIKOV: Consider this conversation finished! And may I request you, young man, to leave my house, myself, and my daughter in peace!

[*His wife drags* REPNIKOV *off to the kitchen.*]

KOLIOSOV: [*goes towards the exit, stops by the mirror.*] A suitor . . . Do I really look like a suitor?

[TANIA *appears.*]

KOLIOSOV: Tell me, Tania, do I look like a suitor?

TANIA: Not in the least! Who would ask a favour in that tone? Who would talk to people in that way? You look like a rooster! A quarrelsome rooster.

KOLIOSOV: Seriously? Well, your father thought I'd come as a suitor.

TANIA: Well . . . That was silly of him. I'm sorry.

KOLIOSOV: Silly? . . . But why? On the contrary, I think that for the first time in his life he has just put forward an interesting hypothesis. [*In the doorway.*] Au revoir, Tania. Tell your dad from me that I like you. That will impress him. [*Goes out.*]

[*Enter* REPNIKOV *and his wife.*]

REPNIKOV: Has he gone?

TANIA: You don't think he'd stay in this torture-chamber?

REPNIKOV: What? What did you say? [*To his wife.*] Did you hear that?

MRS REPNIKOV: Tatiana, you're being impertinent!

REPNIKOV: Do you realize that that scoundrel came here counting on help from you?

TANIA: Oh is that it? So you refused him because of me? Go on, say it! Was it because of me or not?
REPNIKOV: I refused him because he's an insolent lout. And that'll do! I don't want to hear any more about him!
TANIA: And I don't want to see you! [*Puts on her raincoat.*]
MRS REPNIKOV: And where do you think you're going?
TANIA: To get some air!
MRS REPNIKOV: Tatiana!
TANIA: Don't Tatiana me! I don't want Dad doing anything shabby on my account! Do you hear? [*Goes out.*]
REPNIKOV: What's got into her? . . . It's his influence? [*Suddenly shouting.*] Who let that ruffian into my house?
MRS REPNIKOV: [*shrugging her shoulders.*] I did. I opened the door and there was this pleasant-looking fellow . . . What's he done to make you dislike him so much, anyway?
REPNIKOV: What's he done to make me like him? Well what? . . . [*Walks around the table.*] I never did like these characters, these young conquerers with an opinion of themselves as high as the sky! Some genius! He turned up here, convinced that the world was created exclusively for him, whereas in fact the world was created for everyone equally. Yes, he has talents, but so what? You never know what he'll come out with next, and what's the good of that? . . . At the moment he's in the public eye, a hero, a victim of injustice! And that is precisely the bait that Tatiana has swallowed! Oh yes! He's oppressed, he's proud, he's alone — how romantic! Not just Tatiana! There's whole hordes of people wandering round the university making appeals on his behalf! But who are they! Loafers who don't come to lectures, boozers who arrange fictitious wedding parties, lecturers who hang around with that sort of crowd. You see? He's not alone — that's the whole problem. He has support — that's why I expelled him! . . . If I hadn't, just imagine what those smart-Alecs would take it into their heads to do! I'd be a fine one if I hadn't expelled him! . . . In other words, he's a quarrelsome, insolent, irresponsible person and Tatiana is not to go meeting him! That must be stopped once and for all before it's too late!
MRS REPNIKOV: [*after a pause.*] Well, as far as I'm concerned — let her. Let her love a ruffian, a hooligan, the devil himself — let her.

REPNIKOV: I see. That's what you want for our daughter, is it?
MRS REPNIKOV: Yes. And we don't know yet what's better — that or something else.
REPNIKOV: I don't understand you.
MRS REPNIKOV: Nothing difficult about it. For them it's one thing, for us it's another.
REPNIKOV: For us? [*Cautiously.*] What do you mean, for us? . . .
MRS REPNIKOV: For us everything is fine.
REPNIKOV: Then what's the matter? Kindly explain. What, may I ask, is displeasing you?
MRS REPNIKOV: Oh all right then, nothing is displeasing me . . . For heavens sake sit down and eat before everything goes stone cold.
REPNIKOV: No! I won't sit down until I find out what you're hinting at. [*Sits down.*]
MRS REPNIKOV: Calm down. You're the best husband in town . . . And I . . . I'm a good wife . . . Eat up . . . I tell you, everything is fine. We live in perfect harmony. Everybody envies us.
REPNIKOV: I see . . . [*Gets up from the table.*] I must confess, I have been expecting some piece of stupidity or other from you lately . . .
MRS REPNIKOV: "Lately" . . . All our lives you've been expecting stupidity from me. Always. Stupidity and nothing else . . . Don't tell me it's not true. It's always been like that. You were touched by my stupidity, you cultivated it, and all you ever wanted from me was stupidity.
REPNIKOV: If that's so, then I obviously got what I wanted. I just don't understand why I'm supposed to have wanted it, this stupidity of yours, or what good it was to me.
MRS REPNIKOV: For convenience. And so as to have something to feed your vanity. You couldn't look a genius unless compared to an idiot like me . . . Well what am I then? When she was at school, I was a member of the Parents' Association. Now she's grown up, who am I now?
REPNIKOV: [*after a pause.*] You're the wife of an academic, and you really are a good wife. Isn't that enough?
MRS REPNIKOV: But you *aren't* an academic, that's the whole point. You're an administrator and a bit of an academic. Just for prestige.

REPNIKOV: [*deeply hurt.*] No-one's going to write memoirs about me — is that what's upsetting you?
MRS REPNIKOV: No. But I would have justified my existence if you were an academic . . . Well, anyway, that's enough about that. And don't worry, nothing is threatening you: I've understood it all too late . . . You'd better think about your daughter. Can't you see that she's grown up and you can't forbid her anything any more? And listen. What do you want from that lad? Why have you got your knife into him like this? Couldn't you treat him a little less harshly?
[*Silence.*]
REPNIKOV: All right, I'll think about it . . . Just tell me that everything's all right between us. It will be. Tell me!
MRS REPNIKOV: Sit down and eat up.
REPNIKOV: Okay . . . But first I'd like to hear . . .
MRS REPNIKOV: It's all right. Everything's all right.
[*Kisses him on the cheek.*] All's well.
REPNIKOV: I don't want quarrels. I want peace and harmony. Haven't I deserved it? [*Looks out the window. Suddenly.*] What impudence! Just look at him! He's chatting her up under my very nose. How's that for insolence? Now tell me, just tell me. How could you possibly put up with such a man beside our daughter? Never!

ACT TWO
SCENE ONE

A Garden

A garden in spring. A wooden shelter; underneath it, garden tools, a gun hanging up. Also several baskets, one of them full of flowers — daisies. Half of a new-looking summer cottage is visible. KOLIOSOV *is crossing the stage with a watering-can in his hand. He is barefoot and dishevelled. Enter* TANIA.

TANIA: Hands up! Don't move! You're surrounded . . . You're a fine watchman! I just wandered into the garden, and you never even raised an eyebrow. Good afternoon.
KOLIOSOV: Did you have trouble finding me?
TANIA: [*comes nearer.*] No. You explained it all very clearly. [*Looks around.*] Good heavens, what a lot of flowers you've got here . . . Is the owner someone important?
KOLIOSOV: Oh yes, he's a big noise.
TANIA: Peonies, gladioli . . . [*Goes over to the flower beds.*] And what's this?
KOLIOSOV: Delphiniums. And that's galanthus. Red snowdrop. A Frenchman by birth.
TANIA: And what's here?
KOLIOSOV: That's going to be grass.
TANIA: Grass?
KOLIOSOV: Alpine grass. I'm domesticating it.

TANIA: Oh? Is it being difficult?
KOLIOSOV: Yes. The sun here doesn't suit it. Never mind, we'll teach it . . . Look at that hillside . . . Let's be honest, it looks pretty pale, doesn't it? But now, imagine it under this sort of grass [*Points*], an Alpine pasture. Eh? . . . I'd let you run round on it barefoot.
TANIA: I'd love to.
KOLIOSOV: Well, I'll arrange that for you. [*Takes the watering-can in under the shelter.*]
TANIA: And is that the gun you go around the house with?
KOLIOSOV: That's it.
TANIA: I can just imagine . . . Do you know what you look like at the moment?
KOLIOSOV: What?
TANIA: A ruffian. That's what my father calls you. I like it. Ruff-i-an . . . Funny word, isn't it?
KOLIOSOV: Not bad. Expressive, anyway . . . How is your father? What's he doing with himself?
TANIA: I don't know. I haven't seen him today.
KOLIOSOV: Why, has he gone off somewhere?
TANIA: [*unconcernedly*] No. I haven't been home since yesterday.
KOLIOSOV: Is that so? . . . Where did you spend the night?
TANIA: Walking around the town.
KOLIOSOV: All night?
TANIA: Yes.
KOLIOSOV: [*going up to her.*] Why?
TANIA: Because . . . I didn't feel like going home. And I didn't feel like going anywhere else. So I just walked.
KOLIOSOV: Alone?
TANIA: Well I did get pestered occasionally.
KOLIOSOV: Why didn't you spend the night at home? [*Takes her in his arms.*]
TANIA: [*fending him off, although not very energetically.*] Because . . . [*Not very sternly.*] Let me go . . .
KOLIOSOV: Not on your life . . .
TANIA: Let me go . . .
KOLIOSOV: Never . . . Look at me. Answer me . . . Why did you come to the hostel that evening?
TANIA: Because . . .

KOLIOSOV: And why did you come to the cemetery? . . . And what about today?

TANIA: Because . . . Because . . . Because . . .

[*They kiss. Then* KOLIOSOV *sits her down on the bench.*]

KOLIOSOV: So, you didn't spend the night at home? . . . Was that the first time?

TANIA: Yes, the first time.

KOLIOSOV: Well after all, you won't always be spending the night at home.

[*A short pause.*]

TANIA: How quiet it is here . . . Are you here on your own?

KOLIOSOV: My friends call me Kolia. How about you?

TANIA: Okay. Are you here on your own, Kolia?

KOLIOSOV: No. The owner is usually here during the day.

TANIA: What about the evenings?

KOLIOSOV: In the evenings I'm on my own . . . Come and see me if you want to . . . Will you come?

TANIA: Yes.

KOLIOSOV: When will you come?

TANIA: At nine . . . ten . . . whenever you like.

KOLIOSOV: At nine. Or better still, at eight. [*Tries to embrace her again.*] And what about now? Are you rushing off anywhere?

TANIA: Home. To console my parents. Can't you just imagine what's going on there? I should think they've called the police in by now.

KOLIOSOV: What happened, anyway?

TANIA: Father shouted at me, and so . . . Before, we very rarely quarrelled, but now we have scenes every day . . . That's since your visit . . . You know, it turns out that we not only don't understand each other, but don't even know each other as well as we should . . . I'm sorry for my mother . . . Yes, and I'm sorry for Father too . . . You see, it's always his fault, never Mother's.

[*Someone whistles nearby.*]

TANIA: [*jumps up onto the bench, and peers.*] You have visitors. I think it's your friends.

KOLIOSOV: [*half rises.*] So that's who it is! . . . Frolov and Vasia Bukin, retired husband. They go everywhere together now. Friendly rivals. I don't see the point myself.

[*Enter* FROLOV *and* BUKIN.]
BUKIN: [*sings*] "The lilies of the valley say . . ."
FROLOV: Greetings to the hirelings of capitalism!
KOLIOSOV: Shut the gate.
BUKIN: [*sings*] "You should not give your heart away . . ." Nice place you've got here.
KOLIOSOV: It suits me. Let me introduce you. This is Tania.
BUKIN: [*bows*] I'm Vasily.
TANIA: Hullo.
FROLOV: And my name's Frolov.
KOLIOSOV: Give me a light. [*Lights a cigarette.*]
BUKIN: [*sings*] "The lilies of the valley say,
'You should not give your heart away.'
They tell us, friends, the students' life
Is better far without a wife."
FROLOV: [*to* KOLIOSOV.] This is the story so far. Our whole year has been to see the Dean, the trade union, the newspapers, we've made a noise, we've talked about how talented you are. We were going to go to the Vice-Chancellor, but the ranks wavered.
KOLIOSOV: I know.
BUKIN: When the Vice-Chancellor was talking to me about my marriage, do you know what he said? He said: Your year has come so badly unstuck that it would be a crime not to expel one or other of you. You and your friend (that is, Gomyra and me) you, he says, are unmitigated trash, but that Koliosov is the absolute end. You won't believe it, but he even frightened Gomyra. The poor lad's sitting there *studying*. [*To* TANIA.] What a life. What's yours like?
TANIA: Mine? . . . Mine's fine.
BUKIN: Lucky thing. How old are you? Fourteen?
TANIA: You must be joking.
BUKIN: No, seriously.
TANIA: Seriously — nineteen.
BUKIN: I don't believe it.
FROLOV: Kolia, don't lose hope. We've arranged something today. Tomorrow a handful of the brave, together with the Dean, will advance against the Vice-Chancellor.
KOLIOSOV: It's no use . . . You've already done the practicals. It'll be exam-time soon.

BUKIN: [*sings*] "I am seventeen, you are nineteen." [*Picks up the gun.*] Hey, what a musket! Does it go off?
KOLIOSOV: I don't know.
BUKIN: [*sings*] "They're not years, but a string of pearls . . ." [*Walks up and down carrying the gun.*]
TANIA: [*following behind him.*] Be careful, those are snowdrops.
BUKIN: Really? I must have a sniff.
FROLOV: [*to* KOLIOSOV.] I've been told where I'm going to work.
KOLIOSOV: Where?
FROLOV: Out of town. At the plant-breeding station. Do you want me to take you along as a water-carrier?
KOLIOSOV: I'll think about it . . . Hang on, did you say the plant-breeding station? Isn't that where Masha's parents live?
FROLOV: Concidence.
BUKIN: Oh yeah, sure — coincidence. He's stealing my wife. It's obvious.
FROLOV: Masha's diploma isn't tied to an appointment. No one knows where she'll decide to go.
BUKIN: [*to* KOLIOSOV.] Did you hear that? This isn't Grisha, it's a vulture circling around, you know, round and round . . . Kolia, keep an eye on me, or I might just inadvertently wing him.
KOLIOSOV: Listen, jealousy, are you divorced yet?
BUKIN: We're not talking. To get divorced, you have to be at least on speaking terms.
FROLOV: He's still hoping for something.
TANIA: [*goes up to* KOLIOSOV.] Well, shall I be off then?
KOLIOSOV: I'll come a bit of the way with you.
TANIA: [*to* FROLOV *and* BUKIN.] Goodbye.
[KOLIOSOV *and* TANIA *go off.* BUKIN *stands in the middle of the yard with the gun.*]
FROLOV: [*sprawls on the bench.*] I don't see what you can still be hoping for? Do you really think that she'll fly off to the north with you? She knows perfectly well you'll leave her behind in some tatty pub or other. You and your best friend Gomyra.
BUKIN: I understand, Grisha. You're out to break up a marriage.
FROLOV: You've had it. In a month's time I'll put you on a plane and we'll wave each other goodbye, and meanwhile, Masha will be waiting for me at the station. Will that suit you?

BUKIN: Don't, Grisha. I'm a sensitive person. I might up and shoot you.
FROLOV: The gun suits you, you bandit.
BUKIN: "The lilies of the valley say . . ."
FROLOV: Brigand.
BUKIN: " 'You should not give your heart away.' "
FROLOV: You jovial mass-murderer, you.
BUKIN: Grisha, you're well educated, and you know how to behave. On all occasions . . .
FROLOV: Any objections?
BUKIN: Of course not. I like it. I'm even grateful to you. You always managed to stop me in time. Correct me. Hold me back . . . I just envy you. You are an organized person, you're all in one piece. You have surprising tact and a great sense of proportion . . .
FROLOV: It's always from outsiders that you find out you're not a bad chap.
BUKIN: With you around, who would do anything silly? On any occasion you know how one ought to behave. Grisha, tell me, what do you do if you feel like shooting someone?
[*Silence. The game takes on a serious appearance.* FROLOV *gets up and goes over to* BUKIN.]
BUKIN: Isn't that interesting! So you'd never even been able to imagine such a thing.
FROLOV: Give it here.
BUKIN: [*steps back*] Don't come any closer, Grisha. I know this is the silliest joke I've ever made. But don't you come any closer. You'd better tell me what to do.
FROLOV: Give me the gun, you clown.
BUKIN: I'm a clown. Compared to such a serious person as you, I'm a jester. But jesters are dark horses . . . Didn't that ever occur to you?
FROLOV: [*sits down*] Go on, play. Little things please little minds . . .
BUKIN: You won't believe this, Grisha, but sometimes such a serious mood comes over me . . . I'm a wild person, and I have wild thoughts. And now I'm thinking, where I would be without you. After all, it's only you, the sensible one, who knows how one ought to live. And here's me, who's not sensible, living a life that's not the one I want. I'm living the life

you want me to. And sometimes, Grisha, I can't bear to look at you.

FROLOV: What's this rubbish?

BUKIN: And I want to do what *I* like.

FROLOV: Put down the gun.

BUKIN: And today, we'll do what *I* like. Today we'll act sensibly.

FROLOV: Put down the gun, if you want to talk to me.

BUKIN: We're going to shoot it out. However stupid that may seem to you.

FROLOV: Ah, a duel. *I* see . . . Go and sleep it off, fire-eater!

BUKIN: Courage, Grisha. We're going to go outside the garden and draw lots.

FROLOV: [*cheerfully*] What? One musket between the two of us?

BUKIN: It doesn't matter, we'll take turns. When you get there, you'll forget how silly it is.

FROLOV: Yes, but . . . what about the seconds? They're called witnesses these days, by the way.

BUKIN: You won't wriggle out of it, I can promise you that. I won't even let you get cold feet. [*Raises the gun.*]

FROLOV: What the hell . . .? Have you gone crazy?

BUKIN: Let's go!

FROLOV: Wait. Is this supposed to be funny?

BUKIN: If you're going to chicken out, I'll shoot you in the leg.

FROLOV: If you're going to make jokes, you should collect an audience. After all, you don't often see a shoot-out nowadays.

BUKIN: Let's go!

FROLOV: Listen . . . Are you really serious? What if we cripple each other? Just think about it. It'll be a scandal; hospital. And anyway, it's such an undignified affair. We'll be the laughing stock of the town . . .

BUKIN: Get going, I said.

[*They go along the path which leads further into the garden.*]

FROLOV: Stop, Vasia . . . Wait!

[*They stop.*]

FROLOV: Listen, let's have a punch-up, eh? At the worst we'll smash each other's faces in. Why go to extremes?

BUKIN: Stop snivelling! You might be the lucky one.

FROLOV: [*suddenly*] All right then, come on!

[*They go out. Re-enter* KOLIOSOV. *Looks round. Sits down on the bench. The sound of a car horn. Enter* ZOLOTUEV, *in a straw hat and a white embroidered shirt. He looks cheerful and confident.*]

KOLIOSOV: Hi, chief, how's trade?

ZOLOTUEV: I'm not a tradesman, I'm an amateur horticulturist. Kindly distinguish between the two. If you must know, I beautify the earth. I've even been written about in the papers.

KOLIOSOV: That's what you'll say when they come to dispossess you as an over-rich peasant.

ZOLOTUEV: [*sitting down on the bench.*] They'll go away empty-handed if they do. I know the laws, don't you worry. I'm an educated man, mate.

KOLIOSOV: Are you?! And what sort of an education have you got?

ZOLOTUEV: A good one. I got it out east, in a labour camp on the Indigirka.

KOLIOSOV: I see. Well, that *is* a good education. After all, you're within a stone's throw of the University of California out there. What did they send you there for, if I may ask?

ZOLOTUEV: What for indeed! Maybe I don't even know myself what for. To this day I'm still wondering what for.

KOLIOSOV: That's nothing to wonder about. The only wonder is that they ever let you out.

ZOLOTUEV: I'll chuck you out if you're not careful!

KOLIOSOV: Don't be silly. You can't do without your research officer ... You got back quickly today.

ZOLOTUEV: The demand's not bad, but the prices are falling. We'll have to get a move on. [*Gets up, walks around the yard.*] Have you cut a lot? Only two baskets? What have you been doing then? ... And you haven't fixed the tap. You haven't even earned enough to buy cigarettes with.

KOLIOSOV: Talking of cigarettes, did you bring any? [*Stretches out his hand.*]

ZOLOTUEV: Two baskets all morning! Just remember, if it goes on like this, I won't pay you one kopeck. [*Throws him a packet of cigarettes.*]

KOLIOSOV: A packet? Is that all? [*Lights up.*] Listen boss, you be careful how you treat me. And how you talk to me. Where do you think you are? In Argentina, on your own plantation?

... Don't forget yourself. Unless you want your stall to be closed for stock-taking?

ZOLOTUEV: Don't try and frighten me. I've got nothing to fear. I don't go around stealing gold or trading in foreign currency. I pay my taxes on the dot. Don't you worry about me, you worry about yourself ... I need flowers, and what are you doing? You've taken to messing around with these grasses, or whatever they are. This isn't the place! What the hell do I need your grasses for?

KOLIOSOV: To chew. You ought to be chewing grasses. Good for you.

ZOLOTUEV: Huh! Even among the criminal classes I never met such a lout. No wonder they chucked you out of the institute.

KOLIOSOV: And anyway, we agreed: one day I work for you, one day I work for myself. Don't you trust me?

ZOLOTUEV: No I don't. But don't take offence. I don't trust anyone. I'm the only person I can really rely on.

KOLIOSOV: That's not right. You can't be like that ... [*After a pause.*] Hey, boss, did you have a family?

ZOLOTUEV: I've been married. And more than once. No children.

KOLIOSOV: One more nosey question — why do you want so much money? You've got so much already, and you keep on raking it in, grubbing it up, and you hardly spend any of it — it makes me sick to watch you.

ZOLOTUEV: What do I want money for? Well isn't that a stupid question!

KOLIOSOV: But you've got everything already: a house, this cottage, a car. What more do you want, boss? After all, you're an old man.

ZOLOTUEV: Yes, I'm an old man, but what of that? When you've been kicking around the world as long as I have, you won't be asking why people want money. One wants a house, another wants his freedom, another wants a castle in the air, and another one, perhaps, doesn't need anything, because he just likes having money ... It takes all sorts. For example, I know of one case: there's this old man; he, the poor fool, for his own peace of mind, needs to buy one particular person ... [*Unexpectedly.*] Shall I tell you about it?

KOLIOSOV: [*unwillingly*] Go on then, tell me ...

ZOLOTUEV: Okay, listen . . . [*The monologue proceeds calmly at first, then he gradually gets more and more carried away.*] About fifteen years ago, that poor fool worked in this town, in a butcher's shop. His work was interesting, he was working behind the counter. He did no harm to anyone, and, of course, he took care of himself as well. Time went by. Customers came and went, review commissions made flying visits, the auditors made spot checks and our poor fool went on working behind the counter. Of course he slipped up sometimes — who doesn't — but he never actually came a cropper — he knew his business, and he stood firm. He would have gone on standing firm for a long time if this particular person hadn't turned up. He turned up, said hello. Just an ordinary inspector. Youngish, cheerful. The girls started counting up, and our salesman ends up with a surplus. Not a large sum, just middling. Nothing to speak of. But the inspector makes a complaint out of it: how did this happen, comrade? So you're cheating people? So what about this surplus then? Where do we go from here? Where? thinks our salesman — where do you reckon! And so as not to have to fool around with that surplus, he says to the inspector: take it yourself, he says, please, go ahead. Just an ordinary deal. But the other says to him: so, he says, you're not only giving people short weight, he says, you're offering bribes as well. Right, he says, you won't get away with that . . . Okay, thinks our salesman, so I've offered him too little. So I'll add some more on. And he offered him more. But the inspector says to him: you crook, he says. You want to buy me, do you? Well, that's your lookout. And off he goes. And slams the door. Well, thinks our salesman, this is no joke. Still not enough. He found that inspector and he was so frightened he offered him everything he had. Turned out all his pockets. Go on, he says, eat it up!
[*Silence.*]
KOLIOSOV: Well?
ZOLOTUEV: Well nothing! [*After a pause.*] He put that salesman in prison for ten years for the surplus and the bribe together. So that was that. Ten wonderful years, as you can imagine . . . And then our salesman comes out. When he went in he still

had a wife, a nice-looker. Fifteen years younger than him. But when he came back — What's he got? Nothing. Not a thing. Not one person he could turn to. He goes wandering round his home town, tightening his belt. And he runs into the inspector. Who is smiling like he did ten years ago. Welcome back, he says, glad to see you. You bet you're glad, thinks our salesman, and you don't know how glad I am to see you, my lad. [*At this point he starts to accompany the tale with appropriate changes of face and voice.*] Well, says the salesman to him, what's done is done, but now tell me, comrade, frankly: how much should I have given you? What was the figure? He just grins. Oh, he says, a lot; you didn't have that sort of money then, and you never will. No, go on, I said, how much? Don't be silly, he says, it's an absolutely staggering amount. So like what? Thousands, he grins, many thousands, certainly not less than twenty. And, says the former salesman, if I get this money, and bring it to you, will you take it now? What a strange question, he answers. Why should you want to give me money now, and whyever would I take it from you? But the salesman carries on. I'll get you this money, he says, and, he says, you'll take it from me. And in return, he says, I don't want anything from you except for one word. What do you mean? he asks. This, he says: I'll give you twenty thousand and you'll give me just one word, and without even any witnesses . . . What word? he asks. This, he says: I'm a swine, I sent a man to prison for no reason. That word, he says. And I'll damn well see that I get it out of you. Yes, says the inspector, you're a strange man, and you make strange jokes. Farewell, he says. But the salesman calls after him: no, au revoir, we'll meet again, don't worry. And so they parted.
[*Silence.*]

KOLIOSOV: And is that all? Is that the whole story?
ZOLOTUEV: No it's not. The salesman found himself another occupation, and made another pile.
KOLIOSOV: You mean he's really going back to see this inspector?
ZOLOTUEV: You bet he is!
KOLIOSOV: He thinks the inspector will take it?
ZOLOTUEV: Of course he'll take it.

KOLIOSOV: Are you sure?
ZOLOTUEV: Twenty thousand! Who would refuse? Who? I ask you! Who?
KOLIOSOV: [*shrugging his shoulders*] An honest man.
ZOLOTUEV: [*getting carried away*] What honest man? . . . Who's an honest man? . . . An honest man is one who doesn't get offered enough. You only have to give him so much that he can't refuse it and then of course he'll take it. [*Forgetting himself.*] He hasn't long to wait! Another fortnight, a month, and then there'll be enough! He'll give him the lot! The house, the car, the cottage! He'll go out and beg! [*Shouting.*] But he'll take it from him! He'll take it! I tell you, he'll take it!
KOLIOSOV: [*gets up.*] You know, you're a pretty hellish old man . . . [*Silence.*] Steady on, what are you so het up about? What's the matter?
ZOLOTUEV: [*suddenly coming to.*] Eh? . . . You're right, what came over me?
KOLIOSOV: Strange . . . It wouldn't be you, would it — that salesman?
ZOLOTUEV: Of course not . . . God, no, it's not me! No, just an acquaintance, one of my mates! We did our stretch together. You could say he was a friend . . . I'm just getting worked up over a friend . . . And then there's my nerves. At my age, they can't be any good can they?

[*A shot.*]

ZOLOTUEV: [*jumps*] What's that?
KOLIOSOV: No idea. Yes . . . and how's your bad chest?
ZOLOTUEV: Same as ever . . . Stifling me . . .
KOLIOSOV: Well, good luck to it.
ZOLOTUEV: Don't say things like that! . . . Thanks, son, what did I do to deserve you?

[*From the garden,* FROLOV *appears, followed by* BUKIN. FROLOV *carries the gun,* BUKIN *is holding a dead magpie.*]

ZOLOTUEV: [*to* KOLIOSOV] Who's this lot?
KOLIOSOV: Friends.
ZOLOTUEV: There's no such things as friends — only accomplices. Was that you shooting?
BUKIN: Yes, why?
ZOLOTUEV: [*looking suspiciously at* FROLOV] You don't look very happy about it.

BUKIN: We've spilt blood, so now we're repentant.
KOLIOSOV: What's that thing?
BUKIN: A magpie.
ZOLOTUEV: What did you have to kill the poor thing for?
BUKIN: We shot the witness.
FROLOV: We had to shoot something.
ZOLOTUEV: Letting off guns. Who said you could? Go into the forest and shoot there, if you must.
FROLOV: No thanks. We've had enough for today. Not a bad way to spend the time. He wanted to kill me, but fortunately he changed his mind.
BUKIN: Whatever gave you the idea that I might shoot you? . . . I was twice as worried as you. I had to worry about you as well as about myself. But you, Grisha, you only had to worry about yourself.
FROLOV: Loony. You won't catch me getting mixed up with you again! [*Heads out of the yard, but sets off in the wrong direction at first.*]
BUKIN: I just hope he doesn't fall under a tram out of sheer fright. [*Gives the gun back to* KOLIOSOV.] There, take it! You've got a hard job. See you on Saturday.

[FROLOV *and* BUKIN *leave.*]

ZOLOTUEV: Great friends you've got. Pair of cut-throats.
KOLIOSOV: [*picking up the magpie*] Well, *you* won't be hopping round any more, you poor silly bird. [*Takes it under the shelter.*]
ZOLOTUEV: [*has seen someone*] Suddenly the place is crawling with strangers.
KOLIOSOV: Now who have you seen? [*Looks at the gate.*]
ZOLOTUEV: I don't like strangers.
KOLIOSOV: Aha!
ZOLOTUEV: Who is it?
KOLIOSOV: It's for me. A personal matter . . . Don't let me keep you, boss.
ZOLOTUEV: Just remember — I don't like it . . . Don't forget, you were going to fix the tap. [*Goes into the house.*]

[*Enter* REPNIKOV.]

REPNIKOV: May I?
KOLIOSOV: Come in, Vladimir Alekseevich. Come in.

REPNIKOV: [*coming through*] Hullo.
KOLIOSOV: Good evening.
REPNIKOV: Are you wondering how I found you?
KOLIOSOV: Yes, I am.
REPNIKOV: Finding you wasn't difficult. You've become quite a celebrity in the university.
KOLIOSOV: I didn't reckon on that.
[REPNIKOV *sits down on the bench. A short pause.*]
REPNIKOV: I want to ask you something. May I?
KOLIOSOV: Please do.
REPNIKOV: What are you doing with yourself at the moment?
KOLIOSOV: As you see, I'm looking after this cottage.
REPNIKOV: So you're working as a watchman? What for? As a protest? For a joke? For fun?
KOLIOSOV: I didn't get this job on ideological grounds. The work suits me. I study during the day and sleep soundly at night. Thieves only come in the daytime, of course . . . Besides, Vladimir Alekseevich, as they say — if you don't work, you don't eat.
REPNIKOV: And what about science? Are you intending to be a scientist?
KOLIOSOV: And I will be, Vladimir Alekseevich.
REPNIKOV: Judging by your behaviour — not for some time, if ever. I think you're training to be a tight-rope-walker.
KOLIOSOV: Why do you think that?
REPNIKOV: Well, do you think a *scientist* could walk on his head?
KOLIOSOV: I don't know. At the moment I'm not a scientist, but a watchman, and your metaphors are too subtle for me.
REPNIKOV: Now don't get excited. This time we'll keep it cool. Okay?
KOLIOSOV: As you wish.
REPNIKOV: Listen, Koliosov, I admit you have ability. But bear in mind that there are many able people. A great many. A lot more than there are scientists. Isn't that so?
KOLIOSOV: Vladimir Alekseevich, what's all this leading up to?
[*A short silence.*]
REPNIKOV: Last night my daughter didn't come home. Do you happen to know where she spent the night?
KOLIOSOV: She didn't spend it with me.

REPNIKOV: Tell me, frankly, what sort of terms are you on with her?
KOLIOSOV: We're on good terms. I like her.
REPNIKOV: And is that all?
KOLIOSOV: No, Vladimir Alekseevich, I think she likes me too.
REPNIKOV: I see . . . You will leave her alone.
KOLIOSOV: And why is that?
REPNIKOV: Don't you know why?
KOLIOSOV: No, I don't.
REPNIKOV: Stop that, you understand perfectly well. I underestimated you. With people like you, it's better to come to an agreement at once. Listen! You're not to see her, leave her in peace! You like her, I can understand that, but then, surely you like any pretty girl, don't you? So why pick on my daughter? Yesterday she left the house, presumably to come here. I beg you, get rid of her, disappear, think of some way . . .
KOLIOSOV: Vladimir Alekseevich, tell me . . . Doesn't it seem a bit strange to you . . .?
REPNIKOV: What, Koliosov?
KOLIOSOV: All this. Everything that you came here for. Isn't it strange?
REPNIKOV: Not at all. I came here to get you away from my only daughter.
KOLIOSOV: And are you sure that she'll want that . . . I'd like to hear her opinion.
REPNIKOV: You're older than she is, Koliosov: she's nineteen. Which of you do you think is more likely to show some common sense? [*In a different tone*] I've heard that the dean's office is going to put in another plea on your behalf. I won't raise any objections . . . You'll get your degree and leave town. You'll have a job to go to somewhere . . . To Kamenka, to the plant-breeding station if you like . . . Just what you need. [*A short pause.*] What's up? Perhaps you don't want that job?
[*Silence.*]
KOLIOSOV: [*after a pause*] No. That's not what I was thinking about.
[*Silence.*]

KOLIOSOV: [*slowly*] But I ought to be thinking about it now.
REPNIKOV: It was common sense that brought me here to see you. You be sensible as well.
[*Silence.* ZOLOTUEV *appears.*]
REPNIKOV: So there it is . . . I'll be waiting for you to ring me . . . Goodbye for now.
[REPNIKOV *goes off.* ZOLOTUEV *goes past* KOLIOSOV, *then comes back.*]
ZOLOTUEV: Who was that? [*Silence.*] Professor! Who was that who came to see you? . . . You sit there, doing nothing . . . Instead of sitting around, you could be weeding a couple of flower beds.
KOLIOSOV: You know what you can do with your flower beds.
ZOLOTUEV: [*surprised*] What's the matter, don't you want to work for me?
KOLIOSOV: I suppose you thought your herbaceous borders were the limit of my ambitions. You're mad, boss.
ZOLOTUEV: [*anxiously*] You planning to leave? What's the matter, are you sore about something? . . . Listen, I'm not complaining at you. You just carry on as you are. You're a bit of a lout, of course, but you're a good worker as well, and you know about flowers. In fact, to be honest, you're a real expert.
KOLIOSOV: [*grinning*] Recognition at last? So you've learnt to appreciate me, you old spider.
ZOLOTUEV: But where were you intending to go? . . . What was it, a profitable offer? . . . Okay! You can fool around with your damn grass as much as you like! Listen, I'll raise your pay . . . Seventy. You want it?
KOLIOSOV: [*absent-mindedly*] Be quiet, boss.
ZOLOTUEV: Engineers are getting seventy these days. How about it, professor?
KOLIOSOV: Be quiet, I said.
ZOLOTUEV: [*obligingly*] Go on, think it over, I'm not stopping you. But don't do anything silly. Don't be obstinate, work for me. [*Goes off, looking back over his shoulder.*]
[KOLIOSOV *is sitting on the bench. Sound of music; the melody is that of the song "The lilies of the valley say". The lighting grows dimmer and changes direction, there are long dark*

shadows in the garden. It's after eight in the evening. TANIA *appears.*]

TANIA: I'm late . . . [*Goes up to* KOLIOSOV.] Five minutes late . . . Am I forgiven?

[*Silence.*]

TANIA: [*realizes something is wrong*] What's the matter? [*Silence.*] Has something happened?

KOLIOSOV: There's been a scandal in Panama, there's a revolution in Zanzibar. I'm still working as a night watchman . . .

TANIA: You're in a bad mood? . . . Why? Tell me.

KOLIOSOV: Yes, I'll tell you everything.

TANIA: Hang on, can I just interrupt . . .

KOLIOSOV: [*jumps up, nearly falls over the watering-can, throws it to one side.*] No you can't just interrupt!

TANIA: What's the matter with you?

KOLIOSOV: Sorry . . . Just listen. You went off, and I was here thinking, and what I was thinking was: we've got to stop this . . . I'm no Romeo. I just thought I was. Who the hell am I to play Romeo? . . . Well, anyway: let's be honest, it won't do any good . . . That's all! I'm not Romeo. I don't have time for that sort of thing . . . I'm too busy, got that?

TANIA: Why are you saying this to me?

KOLIOSOV: Why? . . . To put it simply: we've got to stop. Or rather, we'd better not start. This afternoon I behaved a bit too . . . familiarly, but that's . . . That's just my way. I apologise.

TANIA: No . . . You're just putting this on . . .

[*Silence.*]

KOLIOSOV: That's all. And if you took all that seriously — then just forget it, you'll get over it . . . That's all I wanted to tell you.

TANIA: That's all?

KOLIOSOV: Yes. Full stop. We're not going to see each other again.

[*Silence.*]

TANIA: You want me to go?

KOLIOSOV: What do you think?

TANIA: Everything you've said is a lie. Why don't you just say straight out that you don't like me?

KOLIOSOV: Yeah, that's it. I don't like you.

[*Silence.* TANIA *goes off.* KOLIOSOV *watches her go. Then he wanders around the courtyard. Stumbles over the watering-*

can for the third time, grabs it, swings his arm back, but
lowers it again — more a comic gesture than a significant one.
Stands in the middle of the yard with the can in his hand.]

SCENE TWO

The University

Graduation dance at the university. A terrace, with the windows of the hall behind, covered with blinds. Several small tables on the terrace. Three entrances; two from the hall and one from the street. From the hall come sounds of laughter. Noise and music.

KOLIOSOV *is sitting at one of the tables. He has a bottle of wine in front of him and several glasses.*
BUKIN *and* GOMYRA *come out of the hall. They stop near the door, without noticing* KOLIOSOV. BUKIN *is absent-mindedly whistling or humming "The lilies of the valley".*
GOMYRA: Vasia, excuse the impertinence, but I want to ask you . . . [BUKIN *goes on whistling.*] I always used to understand you pretty well, but now I don't understand you at all. [BUKIN *goes on whistling.*] Vasia, it's about that woman. After the wedding, you didn't say one word about her, I got the impression that she had ceased to exist. But today, Vasia . . . pardon the liberty, but I thought that . . .
BUKIN: [*quietly*] Listen . . . You can kill me if you like, but I can't live without her.
GOMYRA: [*after a pause, genuinely astonished.*] I'm sorry Vasia, if you put it like that, then . . . well, forgive me . . .
[*They notice* KOLIOSOV, *and go over to him.*]
BUKIN: What are you doing here on your own?
KOLIOSOV: Oh, just enjoying the scenery.
[*Silence. The sound of music from the hall.*]
GOMYRA: Hey, lads . . . Vasia, Nikolai . . .
BUKIN: What is it?
GOMYRA: Fellers . . .
KOLIOSOV: You're not sloshed already are you? That was quick!

GOMYRA: No, lads, that's not it. Just a thought suddenly hit me: that time's just flying past . . . [*In a different tone.*] The shops'll be shut soon.
BUKIN: Shall we have a drink?
GOMYRA: No, I don't want one.
BUKIN: What's this I hear?
GOMYRA: You may not believe it, but I haven't touched a drop today, and I don't want to start now. You never know, fellers, I might want to retain some memory of the evening.
ZOLOTUEV: [*off*] Professor!
[*Enter* ZOLOTUEV. *Dressed in his best, but looking stricken. He is carrying a briefcase.*]
ZOLOTUEV: Hey, lad . . .
KOLIOSOV: That you, boss?
BUKIN: Kolia, come on with us and down one in honour of the geologists.
KOLIOSOV: I'll be along in a minute. Where did you spring from?
ZOLOTUEV: I thought I'd never find you . . . Something terrible's happened, professor. He wouldn't take it.
KOLIOSOV: What's all this? What's your problem?
ZOLOTUEV: He wouldn't take it, I tell you! He chucked me out. Just today.
KOLIOSOV: Who wouldn't take it? What wouldn't he take? What are you on about?
ZOLOTUEV: *He* wouldn't take it! The inspector.
KOLIOSOV: Oh yes. The inspector? I see . . . So he wouldn't take it?
ZOLOTUEV: He wouldn't stoop so low . . . Hell, lad, it's ruined my life . . . But what about you? What are you doing with yourself?
KOLIOSOV: Me? Oh, I'm just . . . having a good time here. I've passed my exams and I'm saying farewell to the university.
ZOLOTUEV: So, that means you've got your education? . . . How did you manage that? How much did you give for it?
KOLIOSOV: [*after a pause, quietly.*] I gave plenty for it . . . [*To* ZOLOTUEV] Plenty, boss, you can't imagine how much . . . Goodbye, then. Off you go.
[ZOLOTUEV *goes off,* FROLOV *and* MASHA *appear.*]
MASHA: [*talking about* KOLIOSOV] So that's where he's been hiding. [*Goes over.*] I don't understand what's the matter with him, everything's sorted itself out, everything's been arranged,

everything's fine. [*To* KOLIOSOV.] Come on, then, tell me, what's worrying you? [KOLIOSOV *doesn't answer.*] Listen, I've been meaning to ask you, where's that girl Tania? Why isn't she here?

KOLIOSOV: Why am I supposed to know where she is? . . . I haven't a clue.

[*A short pause. Music is heard.*]

FROLOV: It's a good party.

MASHA: Yes . . . It's quiet and cool here. I feel like saying something silly.

FROLOV: So what's the problem?

MASHA: I don't know how. I want to, but I don't know how to say it.

FROLOV: [*to* KOLIOSOV] When do you leave town?

KOLIOSOV: I don't know exactly, the sooner the better.

MASHA: I'm going in a few days time. I'm going home, you know.

KOLIOSOV: Yes, I know.

MASHA: And Grisha, there, is going to the same place, my home district. Kolia, perhaps I should just marry him, and stop all this?

FROLOV: You're very kind.

MASHA: Well, he's serious, reliable, understands everything, loves me. [*To* FROLOV.] Do you love me or not?

FROLOV: If you ask in that tone, then no.

KOLIOSOV: Are you preparing to get married again? This looks bad . . . I'm going to join the geologists, perhaps they can make me laugh.

MASHA: They'll make you laugh all right.

[KOLIOSOV *goes into the hall.*]

FROLOV: Masha, yes or no? I've been waiting for an answer for five years.

MASHA: I've already told you many times.

FROLOV: But this time you could say "yes".

MASHA: I could, Grisha. But it would be the sort of "yes" that . . . Wouldn't a "no" be better?

[FROLOV *and* MASHA *go back into the hall. Out of the hall come* REPNIKOV *and his wife.*]

REPNIKOV: They haven't forgotten how to have a good time, have they?

MRS REPNIKOV: I don't know. I was never a student . . . Tell me, how many words has our daughter said to us over the past week? Have you counted them? It wouldn't be difficult. She'll end up running away from us.

REPNIKOV: I don't understand how she managed to fall so much in love with him in such a short time.

MRS REPNIKOV: Instead of asking such silly questions, you could be thinking how to help her.

REPNIKOV: How? I can't force her to be helped. You have to bear that in mind too.

MRS REPNIKOV: I heard they were going to let him stay on as a postgraduate. Everyone's in favour of it except you.

REPNIKOV: Well I should think not! Isn't it enough that he's got through university?

MRS REPNIKOV: But you must admit, he deserves to stay on. Everyone says he deserves it.

REPNIKOV: Listen, the whole town knows this story, and it is generally considered that the incident is closed. And then suddenly we start it all over again? Just think what repercussions it could have. Think of me. Just a little.

MRS REPNIKOV: I don't see how you could be blamed for letting a good lad stay on as a postgraduate.

REPNIKOV: Yes, but then you don't know enough about him. What if he's not the sort of person he pretends he is? . . . And besides, the place has already been offered to another . . .

MRS REPNIKOV: You'll do as I ask you . . . Let's go in. I'm cold.

[*They return to the hall. Enter the* CHEERFUL *one, the* PRETTY *girl, the* KOMSOMOL ORGANIZER, *the* SERIOUS *one, the* STUDIOUS *girl,* FROLOV *and* MASHA . . . THE CHEERFUL *one is carrying a bottle.*]

CHEERFUL: This way, everyone, into the fresh air. [*All go over to a table.*] So, friends, allow me to propose a toast. [*Pours out wine into the glasses.*]

PRETTY: Do we have to have all these toasts? Toasts and toasts — can't anyone just have an ordinary drink?

CHEERFUL: Of course you can. We'll just have an ordinary drink, to skiing in Africa. [*Laughs loudly*].

[*Enter* BUKIN, *followed by* GOMYRA.]

BUKIN: What are you all so cheerful about? Why are you making such a joyful noise? Surely not because you're no longer students? [*Pours wine for himself and* GOMYRA.] You poor things. The outside world is waiting to embrace you in its iron grip. Have a good party, but don't forget that it's really a wake . . .

SERIOUS: Well, that was quite neatly put.

MASHA: Of course . . . On such an occasion, we couldn't do without a comic turn or two.

BUKIN: For the last time this season. Get your tickets now, as you might say . . . By the way, Masha. We're about to go our separate ways . . . But, if you remember, we got married. That's what I call really irresponsible. We didn't think it out properly, we didn't weigh up the pros and cons; just one-two-three and stamps in the passports. And now there's this divorce. It's a bit of a mess.

MASHA: It's not a mess at all. We only have to put in an application form at the registry office — that's all.

BUKIN: And that's all there is to it? . . . The wonders of modern progress. I hope you'll go and put it in?

MASHA: Yes, I was meaning to drop it in, but somehow I just never had time. Don't worry, I'll do it tomorrow for sure.

BUKIN: I knew you wouldn't be stubborn.

GOMYRA: Masha, I have to talk to you.

MASHA: You? . . . To me?

GOMYRA: Confidentially. And may I point out that I'm completely sober.

PRETTY and CHEERFUL: [*together*] What?!
[*Laughter.*]

GOMYRA: I'm as sober as a judge. Please. [*Offers* MASHA *his arm.*]

MASHA: Well, in that case . . . [*Takes* GOMYRA's *arm and they move off in picturesque style.*]

PRETTY: Is that really Gomyra?

CHEERFUL: That's new!

BUKIN: Oh well, that was another disgraceful scene. A farewell appearance. Full evening's programme of Vasia Bukin, comic parody artist . . . [*To* FROLOV.] Grisha, you know what I regret now? For some reason I'm sorry for that magpie. Why did we kill it? What for? The magpie had nothing to do with it.

FROLOV: [*recoiling*] I don't know . . . And anyway, do please spare me these nervous disorders of yours . . .
BUKIN: Nobody knows anything. [*Music from the hall.* PRETTY *and* CHEERFUL *go back into the hall.*] Well, I might as well go to the bar.
[*From the other door to the hall, enter* MASHA *and* GOMYRA. GOMYRA *leads* MASHA *up to* BUKIN *and goes on past.*]
BUKIN: Masha . . . People always feel like making up quarrels before a journey. It's the done thing. Amongst people with nervous disorders.
MASHA: Go away.
BUKIN: What a life . . . Nobody understands anything. The paleolithic period . . . Masha, I've rethought my whole philosophy . . .
MASHA: Shut up, you idiot.
BUKIN: [*beaming*] That's more like it! . . . But why the tears?
MASHA: [*drying her eyes*] Leave me alone. It's because I've been drinking . . . When do you leave?
BUKIN: The third of July.
MASHA: Will you take me with you?
BUKIN: I warn you, it's a permafrost area.
[MASHA *and* BUKIN *go off, oblivious, with their arms round each other's waists.* FROLOV *and* KOLIOSOV *appear.*]
FROLOV: That's it! I think I've had my lot. [*To* KOLIOSOV.] Kolia, I was going to tell you, they've offered me a postgraduate place. It was to have been yours; I have to tell you that . . .
KOLIOSOV: What's the fuss? Here's luck to you, Grisha . . . I don't care.
FROLOV: Really? . . . I kept quiet because I intended to go elsewhere. But now that's finished. I'm staying as a postgrad.
[*Goes off.*]
[TANIA *comes in from the street. Comes up to* KOLIOSOV, *who is sitting at the table.*]
KOLIOSOV: [*coldly*] What did you come here for?
TANIA: To congratulate you on your degree . . . Congratulations.
KOLIOSOV: [*gloomily*] Thank you.
TANIA: I'm sorry if it's the wrong time . . .
KOLIOSOV: Oh no, this is just the right time . . . The right time for congratulations . . .

TANIA: [*after a pause*] Are you going away?
KOLIOSOV: Yes.
TANIA: [*after a pause*] I wouldn't have come. But I knew that you were going away . . .
KOLIOSOV: Did Daddy tell you?
TANIA: Yes.
[*A short pause.*]
KOLIOSOV: Well, how are you?
TANIA: If you were interested to know, you could have rung up.
KOLIOSOV: I rang once.
TANIA: [*joyfully*] You rang me?
KOLIOSOV: I spoke to your father.
[*A pause.*]
TANIA: Your grass . . . Has it grown at all? You remember you invited me . . . barefoot on the meadow.
KOLIOSOV: It isn't a meadow yet . . . But it's grown enough to run barefoot on.
TANIA: I even had this dream that you and I were running through a meadow.
KOLIOSOV: Running? . . . Did you happen to notice if we were both going the same way?
TANIA: Oh yes. Yes, of course.
KOLIOSOV: A pleasant dream . . . idyllic. [*Suddenly.*] But I don't see why you've come. I've told you everything, we've put the full stop at the end, and what more is there?
TANIA: [*agitatedly*] You're going away . . . But I think we will meet again, you and I. Maybe not for a while, maybe in a year, two years . . . And you won't stop me thinking about that! . . . And when we meet again, then . . . Tell me it *is* possible. That's all I need. Tell me it's possible.
KOLIOSOV: [*taking her by the shoulders*] You're raving . . . In a month's time this fairy tale will have flown out of your mind.
TANIA: Never! . . . How can I prove it to you?
KOLIOSOV: [*forgetting himself*] You halfwit . . . [*Pulls her to him. Then remembers.*] You don't know what you're saying . . . You know, it wouldn't hurt you to be a bit more cautious.
TANIA: More cautious?
KOLIOSOV: That's what I said. More cautious.
TANIA: What's that? What sort of weird idea have you got now? What do you mean by caution?

KOLIOSOV: Listen. Do you know who you came to see?
TANIA: [*smiling*] Yes, I know. A ruffian.
KOLIOSOV: That's the point — it's worse than that.
TANIA: You're not glad I came . . . I always . . . It's always me who . . . I've been making the running, haven't I?
KOLIOSOV: No, you're okay. You came just at the right time . . . But forgiving? Do you know how to forgive?
[REPNIKOV *enters from the hall.*]
TANIA: [*softly*] He's turned up . . . Haven't seen him for ages.
REPNIKOV: [*to* TANIA] Have you been here long?
TANIA: Not long. I came to congratulate a few people I know.
REPNIKOV: Yes, well, congratulations are in order.
KOLIOSOV: That's just what I was saying; this is just the right time to congratulate you and me.
REPNIKOV: [*taking* KOLIOSOV *aside*] Why, for heaven's sake, did you have to arrange a meeting?
KOLIOSOV: Because, for heaven's sake, we haven't seen each other for ages. A whole three weeks.
REPNIKOV: But . . . We weren't talking about three weeks, were we, you and I?
KOLIOSOV: We've been missing each other, can't you understand that? Maybe we can't do without each other after all. I think that's worth more. Don't you agree?
REPNIKOV: Don't joke, Koliosov, it doesn't suit you now . . .
KOLIOSOV: Why do you think that? Surely I haven't changed?
REPNIKOV: Is that what you think? Anyone who comes a real cropper once will have a slight limp for the rest of his life.
KOLIOSOV: In that case, you didn't pay me enough. You've given me a degree and now you demand that we don't see each other for the rest of our lives . . . So . . . [*Takes the diploma out of his pocket*] Take it back. [*Throws it onto the table.*]
TANIA: What? What's all this about?
KOLIOSOV: That day, when you came out to the cottage . . .
REPNIKOV: [*shouting*] Tania! Leave the two of us to talk this out.
TANIA: No, I'm not going anywhere.
REPNIKOV: Oh yes you are. [*To* KOLIOSOV.] Can I talk to you alone?
[TANIA *and* KOLIOSOV *exchange glances.* TANIA *leaves.*]
KOLIOSOV: Okay, let's talk. I'm listening.
REPNIKOV: Right, you hate me. But why, exactly? Let's sort it out

... When I was an aspiring scientist, something similar happened to me.

KOLIOSOV: Why are you confessing to me?

REPNIKOV: Surely it's not impossible for you and me to be frank with each other. You must admit, we have got something in common . . . Sit down for a minute . . . And think about whether you have the right to hate me . . . To be quite honest, you're really lucky it was me.

KOLIOSOV: Yeah, sure. You're with me all the way.

REPNIKOV: Maybe I am. . . . The Dean's office is proposing to give you a postgraduate place . . .

KOLIOSOV: And . . . ?

REPNIKOV: And, you know, . . . I don't object.

KOLIOSOV: Aha . . . So you've decided to raise the price? And the conditions?

REPNIKOV: Forget Tatiana, keep your mouth shut. Well, you understand. We'll keep quiet. You and I — we'll both be good little boys. And pick up that document. It's yours . . . That's all. Go and dance, enjoy yourself. We'll see each other again sometime. Unfortunately. [*Leaves. Enter* TANIA.]

TANIA: You haven't been fighting each other?

KOLIOSOV: No, talking.

TANIA: And?

KOLIOSOV: They want to give me a postgraduate place. Your father has no objection.

TANIA: You mean that? You're staying . . . Really?
[*After a pause.*] What's the matter? Aren't you pleased? . . . What else has happened?

KOLIOSOV: Let's sit down.
[*They sit down.*]

TANIA: Everything's improving. Order has been restored in Panama, Zanzibar is now a republic . . .

KOLIOSOV: I have to tell you how I graduated. [*Silence.*] That evening when you came to see me at the cottage, your father was there . . . I had to choose. One of two things.

TANIA: I don't understand.

KOLIOSOV: Just that: one of two things. You or the university.
[*Silence.*]

TANIA: Me or the university? . . . What nonsense . . .

KOLIOSOV: That's how it was.

TANIA: [*after a short silence*] But, you don't really mean to tell me that . . . you swapped me for a degree from my father?

KOLIOSOV: I'm telling you how it happened.

TANIA: Nonsense . . . Tell me it's nonsense . . . Please, tell me it's nonsense.

KOLIOSOV: I couldn't have done anything else. [*Silence.*] I gained some time: you must understand that. [*Silence.*] Would you have wanted me to be a watchman all my life? [*Silence.*] Do you think I did it for fun?

TANIA: [*quietly*] So you came to an understanding with my father . . . And just now? What were you two talking about just now? The postgraduate place? . . . That means my price is going up . . . It's a pity my father's not in the Academy of Sciences . . . Never mind . . . You're doing all right as it is, aren't you? [*After a pause.*] Why did you tell me about it? What for? Or is that done for a purpose as well?

KOLIOSOV: Stop it, let me finish.

TANIA: No, I don't believe you.

KOLIOSOV: Let me finish. You ought to understand me. You of all people.

TANIA: I understand everything. You didn't do it for fun, I understand that. You couldn't have done anything else, I understand that . . . You gained some time, now you'll get what you're after. You'll have your meadow, you'll have everything as you want it. There is nothing in the world that could get in your way . . . You'll have everything the way you like it . . . Without me.

KOLIOSOV: And if I do have a meadow — who will run barefoot on it? I can't do it on my own, you know . . . people will think I'm a lunatic. [*Takes her by the shoulders.*] Stay . . .

TANIA: No, I don't believe you. How do I know you won't trade me in again? In the interests of the cause. I can't live like that. Goodbye . . . Goodbye . . . [*Leaves.*]

KOLIOSOV: Tania! [*Goes after her.*]

[*For a moment* ZOLOTUEV *blocks his path.*]

KOLIOSOV: What are you doing here? What do you want?

ZOLOTUEV: Where are you off to, lad? Why don't you come and live with me? I'm alone, you know that. Alone and friendless. I'll make the house over to you, the cottage, the car . . .

KOLIOSOV: Hang on, boss . . . [*Goes out.*]
ZOLOTUEV: Hey, lad! [*Follows him out.*]
  [*A noisy crowd spills out of the hall: the* PRETTY *girl, the* CHEERFUL *one, the* SERIOUS *one, the* STUDIOUS *girl, the* KOMSOMOL ORGANIZER, GOMYRA, BUKIN, MASHA. *The music from the hall gets louder.*]
CHEERFUL: This way, everyone! . . . Looks like everyone's here?
ALL: [*in chorus*] Give her a kiss! Give her a kiss!
SERIOUS: The Vice-Chancellor's not here.
GOMYRA: They're bringing him, he's coming . . . Give her a kiss!
  [REPNIKOV *appears.*]
REPNIKOV: What's going on?
BUKIN: Vladimir Alekseevich. Do you remember our wedding?
REPNIKOV: And how!
BUKIN: [*to everyone*] Well then. The wedding is still on. As you see.
  [*Noise, laughter.*]
REPNIKOV: Oh, so that's it eh? Everything's turned out all right? I'm glad.
BUKIN: The same show, with the same cast. Look, everyone's here. You were the only one missing.
CHEERFUL: What about Koliosov?
SERIOUS: Yes, Koliosov isn't here yet.
  [*Laughter.*]
REPNIKOV: [*laughing with the rest*] By the way, talking of Koliosov. He's got a postgraduate place for next year.
  [*Noise. Exclamations of approval.*]
MASHA: Where is he then? We must find him! Congratulate him.
SERIOUS: Where's Koliosov?
  [KOLIOSOV *appears.*]
KOLIOSOV: Here I am.
SERIOUS: Congratulations. You deserve it. You are being reserved for science.
KOMSOMOL ORGANIZER: Kolia, our former class . . . What's up, aren't you pleased? What's the matter with you? What's happened?
BUKIN: Say something, speak up!
KOLIOSOV: I haven't anything to say to you. But there is something I have to do. [*Takes his diploma, tears it in half. Throws it on the floor.*]

[*A short pause.*]
MASHA: Whatever have you done?
KOLIOSOV: Don't worry. It's *my* degree . . . I've paid for it. That's all. Goodbye.

SCENE THREE

Back in the Street

The setting from the first scene: the old house, the fence, the pavement, the posters. Late evening in summer. KOLIOSOV *stands near the posters. Walks around the pavement, back to the posters, examines them pensively. It is not clear whether he is waiting for someone, or whether he merely has nowhere to go this evening. He has another little wander, and returns to the posters. In the old house, someone is still learning scales, sounding much more confident than in early spring.* TANIA *appears. Goes past.*

KOLIOSOV: [*stopping her*] Excuse me, where are you going in such a hurry?
[*Silence.*]
Home?
[*Silence.*]
To the park?
[*Silence.*]
To a concert?
TANIA: I'm sorry, I haven't got time. [*Tries to go past, he stops her again.*] I'm in a hurry.
KOLIOSOV: That's a pity . . . I wanted to invite you . . .
TANIA: [*interrupting him*] Invite somebody else.
KOLIOSOV: I can't. I'm inviting *you*.
TANIA: You invited me once before. Don't you remember?
KOLIOSOV: Yes, I remember . . . I have a pretty good memory.
[*Silence.*]
KOLIOSOV: You won't come?
TANIA: No . . . Enjoy yourself.
[*They stand three paces from each other.*]

The Elder Son
A comedy in two acts

translated by Kevin Windle

CHARACTERS

VLADIMIR PETROVICH BUSYGIN, (Volodia)
SEMION SEVOSTIANOV, (Silva)
TWO GIRLS
ANDREI GRIGORYEVICH SARAFANOV
NEIGHBOUR
VASILY SARAFANOV, (Vasia, Vasenka)
NATALIA MAKARSKAIA, (Natasha)
NINA SARAFANOVA
MIKHAIL KUDIMOV

ACT ONE
SCENE ONE

Late on a spring evening. The yard of an apartment building. Gates into yard. Entrance into building. Adjoining is a little wooden house, with a porch and a window facing onto the yard. A poplar and a bench. Voices and laughter are heard from the street.
Enter BUSYGIN, SILVA, *and the two girls.* SILVA *is adroitly, casually strumming on a guitar.* BUSYGIN *is walking arm in arm with one of the girls. All four are obviously feeling the cold.*

SILVA: [*croons*] "Riding in a troika — you can't catch us — Far off something flickers — don't know what..."
FIRST GIRL: Well, here we are, boys, practically home.
BUSYGIN: "Practically"? That doesn't count.
FIRST GIRL: [*to* BUSYGIN.] Would you let go of my arm? [*Frees her arm*] Thank you for seeing us home. We'll go the rest of the way by ourselves.
SILVA: [*stops playing.*] By yourselves? How's that? ... You go that way [*Pointing*], and we go back, you mean? ...
FIRST GIRL: That's right.
SILVA: Well, what do you think of that, pal?
BUSYGIN: [*to* FIRST GIRL.] You're abandoning us in the street?
FIRST GIRL: What do you think?
SILVA: Think? ... I was quite sure you were going to ask us in.
FIRST GIRL: Ask you in? At night?
BUSYGIN: Why not?

FIRST GIRL: Then you were mistaken. We don't have visitors at night.
SILVA: [*to* BUSYGIN.] What do you say to that?
BUSYGIN: Good night.
GIRLS: [*together*] Sleep tight!
SILVA: [*stopping them.*] Think about it, girls. Why hurry? You'll be weeping from boredom in a minute! Reconsider! Invite us in!
SECOND GIRL: Invite you in! You're a fast worker! A bit of a dance, a glass of wine, and he wants to be invited in right away! You've picked the wrong girls for that!
SILVA: Well I never! Did you ever see such perfidy? [*Holds back* SECOND GIRL.] Give us a goodnight kiss, at least.

[SECOND GIRL *breaks free and both walk quickly away.*]

Wait, girls! Wait!

[BUSYGIN *and* SILVA *start off after the girls. Enter* SARAFANOV, *carrying clarinet. An elderly neighbour comes out of the building towards him. He has a sickly look, but is warmly dressed. His manner suggests a middle-rank official, perhaps from the State procurements office.*]

NEIGHBOUR: Hullo, Andrei Grigoryevich.
SARAFANOV: Good evening.
NEIGHBOUR: [*sarcastically*] Home from work?
SARAFANOV: What? . . . [*Hastily*] Yes, yes . . . Back from work . . .
NEIGHBOUR: [*in mocking tone.*] From work? . . . [*Reproachfully*] Oh dear, Andrei Grigoryevich, I don't care much for your new job.
SILVA: [*hastily*] And where are you off to at this time of night?
NEIGHBOUR: Off to? Nowhere in particular. My blood pressure's playing up. Thought I'd come out for some fresh air.
SARAFANOV: Quite so. Take a walk . . . It'll do you good, do you good . . . Good night. [*Tries to get away.*]
NEIGHBOUR: Just a moment . . .

[SARAFANOV *stops.*]

[*Pointing to clarinet.*] Who've you been seeing off?

SARAFANOV: What?
NEIGHBOUR: Who's died, I want to know?
SARAFANOV: [*frightened*] Shh! . . . Quiet!

[NEIGHBOUR *puts finger to lips and nods quickly.*]

[*Reproachfully*] Careful! Didn't I ask you not to? My children might hear you, God forbid . . .

NEIGHBOUR: All right, all right . . . [*Whispers*] Who've you been burying?

SARAFANOV: [*whispers*] A man . . .
NEIGHBOUR: [*whispers*] A young man? . . . An old man? . . .
SARAFANOV: Middle-aged . . .
   [NEIGHBOUR *gives long and sorrowful shake of head.*]
   Excuse me, I'll be going in. The cold's getting to me . . .
NEIGHBOUR: No, Andrei Grigoryevich, I don't care for your new job.
   [*They part.* SARAFANOV *enters the building, the* NEIGHBOUR *goes out into the street. Enter* VASENKA *from the street. He stops in the gateway. His manner betrays great anxiety and uncertainty. He is waiting for something. Footsteps are heard in the street.* VASENKA *runs towards the door.* MAKARSKAIA *appears at the gate.* VASENKA *walks calmly towards the gate, trying to make the meeting look accidental.*]
VASENKA: Well, well, who do I see before me?
MAKARSKAIA: Oh, it's you.
VASENKA: Hullo!
MAKARSKAIA: Hullo there, Muggins. What are you doing here? [*Going towards wooden house.*]
VASENKA: Nothing much. Thought I'd go out for a walk. Shall we go for a walk together?
MAKARSKAIA: Not likely! A walk in this cold! [*Takes out key.*]
VASENKA: [*placing himself between her and the door, detains her on the steps.*] I won't let you in.
MAKARSKAIA: [*unruffled*] Here we go again.
VASENKA: You don't get enough fresh air.
MAKARSKAIA: Go home, Vasenka.
VASENKA: Wait a moment . . . Let's have a chat . . . Tell me something.
MAKARSKAIA: Good night.
VASENKA: Tell me you'll go to the pictures with me tomorrow.
MAKARSKAIA: We'll see about that tomorrow, but now go to bed. Will you let me pass?!
VASENKA: No.
MAKARSKAIA: I'll tell your father, and you'll get what you deserve!
VASENKA: What's there to shout about?
MAKARSKAIA: Oh, you are a nuisance!
VASENKA: Go ahead and shout. Actually I rather like it.
MAKARSKAIA: What do you rather like?

VASENKA: When you shout.
MAKARSKAIA: Vasenka, do you love me?
VASENKA: Do I?!
MAKARSKAIA: You do. You don't show it very well. Here I am, freezing in this jumper, tired, and what do you do? . . . Come on, let me in . . .
VASENKA: [*giving in.*] Are you cold? . . .
MAKARSKAIA: [*unlocking door.*] There . . . Good boy. If you're in love you must do as you're told. [*In doorway.*] And I don't want you waiting for me, following me around, treading on my heels. Because it won't get you anywhere . . . And now go to bed. [*Enters house.*]
VASENKA: [*goes up to door as it closes.*] Open the door! Open up! [*Knocks.*] Open the door for a moment! I've got something to tell you. Do you hear? Open up!
MAKARSKAIA: [*at window.*] Don't shout! You'll wake the whole town.
VASENKA: To hell with the town! . . . [*Sits down on steps.*] Let them all get up and hear what a fool I am!
MAKARSKAIA: Won't they be fascinated? . . . Vasenka, seriously, you must understand that you and I can't have anything in common. Except arguments like this, of course. Think, you silly boy. I'm ten years older than you! And we've different ideas and interests, everything. Surely they tell you these things at school. You ought to be friends with little girls. Love's allowed at school these days, I believe. So you'll be fine. Go and love somebody your own age.
VASENKA: Don't talk such nonsense.
MAKARSKAIA: That's quite enough! I see you don't understand polite requests. I'm sick of you. Sick of you! Is that clear? Get out, and don't ever come back!
VASENKA: [*goes to window.*] All right . . . You won't see me again. [*Mournfully*] Ever.
MAKARSKAIA: The child's lost his head completely!
VASENKA: We'll meet tomorrow! Just once! For half an hour! For the last time! . . . Well? What'll it cost you?
MAKARSKAIA: Oh, sure! And there'll be no getting rid of you afterwards. Do you think I don't know you?
VASENKA: [*suddenly*] Bag! You bag!

MAKARSKAIA: What?! . . . What's that? . . . I like that! As if every lout had the right to shout insults . . . I see you really are up against it in this world if you haven't got a husband! . . . Get out! Out!
[*Silence.*]
VASENKA: Sorry . . . Sorry, I didn't mean it.
MAKARSKAIA: Get out! Time for beddie-byes! Cheeky young whelp!
[*Slams window.*]
[VASENKA *shambles back to his door. Enter* BUSYGIN *and* SILVA.]
SILVA: They gave us the run-around all right, eh?
BUSYGIN: Let's have a smoke.
SILVA: Bit of all right that blonde . . .
BUSYGIN: Bit on the short side.
SILVA: Come on! You fancied her.
BUSYGIN: I don't any more.
SILVA: [*looks at watch, whistles.*] Hey, know what the time is?
BUSYGIN: [*looks at watch.*] Half past eleven.
SILVA: What? Isn't that great?! You and I have just missed the last train.
BUSYGIN: Have we?
SILVA: Yes. The next one's at six in the morning.
[BUSYGIN *whistles.*]
[*Shivering*] Brrr . . . Right pair of chivalrous gentlemen we are! . . . Seeing them home! Suckers!
BUSYGIN: You got far to go?
SILVA: At least twenty kilometres! . . . And all because of those modest maidens! Why the hell did we have to go and get mixed up with them?
BUSYGIN: What part of town's this? I've never been here before.
SILVA: Novo-Mylnikovo. Right out in the sticks!
BUSYGIN: Know anybody here?
SILVA: Not a soul! No relations, and no friendly cops.
BUSYGIN: Right. But where are all the people?
SILVA: They're all asleep. Like in the country. They go to bed before dark.
BUSYGIN: So what shall we do?
SILVA: Look, what's your name? Sorry, I didn't catch it in the café.
BUSYGIN: I didn't catch yours either . . .

SILVA: Here's to our meeting then . . . [*They shake hands.*]
BUSYGIN: I'm Vladimir Busygin.
SILVA: Semion Sevostianov. But everybody calls me Silva.
BUSYGIN: How's that?
SILVA: Buggered if I know. A nickname the lads gave me, and they didn't explain why.
BUSYGIN: I've seen you before. On the main street.
SILVA: Sure! I hold court there from eight to eleven. Every evening.
BUSYGIN: You got a job anywhere?
SILVA: You bet! I'm in trade at the moment. As an agent.
BUSYGIN: What sort of job is it?
SILVA: A perfectly ordinary one. Product control. What about you? One of the toilers?
BUSYGIN: I'm a student.
SILVA: We'll be good friends, you and I. Just wait and see.
BUSYGIN: Wait. Somebody's coming.
SILVA: [*shivering*] Mighty cold tonight, isn't it?
[NEIGHBOUR *returns from walk.*]
BUSYGIN: Good evening!
NEIGHBOUR: Hullo.
SILVA: Could you tell us where the local night club is?
BUSYGIN: [*to* SILVA.] Hold it. [*To* NEIGHBOUR.] Would you mind telling us where the bus stops?
NEIGHBOUR: The bus? . . . Over there, the other side of the railway line.
BUSYGIN: Can we still catch one?
NEIGHBOUR: You might. But I don't think so. [*Makes to go on his way.*]
BUSYGIN: Look, I wonder if you might know where we could spend the night. We've been out visiting, and missed the last train.
NEIGHBOUR: [*looks them up and down with mistrust and suspicion.*] One of those things.
SILVA: Just somewhere to put our heads down till morning, then . . .
NEIGHBOUR: I know, I know.
SILVA: Just a nice cosy corner, nothing much . . .
NEIGHBOUR: Sorry, lads! I can't, lads, I can't!
BUSYGIN: Why not?
NEIGHBOUR: I'd be only too glad, but I don't live alone, you see. There's my wife and mother-in-law . . .

BUSYGIN: I see.
NEIGHBOUR: For myself, I'd be only too glad.
BUSYGIN: That's not much good to us, old fellow . . .
SILVA: Useless old clot!
   [NEIGHBOUR *goes on way in timid silence.*]
   Bloody wind! Where did it come from? Such a fine day — and now this!
BUSYGIN: It's going to rain.
SILVA: That's all we need!
BUSYGIN: Or maybe snow.
SILVA: God! I should have stayed at home. There it's warm at least. And more fun. The old man's a great joker. Never a dull moment when he's around. Always springing something new on you. Like yesterday, for instance. "I'm sick and tired of your pranks," he says. "All this trouble at work because of you. Here's my last twenty rubles," he says. "Go to the boozer, get drunk, and arrange an orgy, a good one, so I won't see you for a year or two after it!" . . . Not bad, eh?
BUSYGIN: Sounds a grand old man.
SILVA: What about you?
BUSYGIN: What about me?
SILVA: You and your old man. Do you have disagreements like that?
BUSYGIN: No disagreements at all.
SILVA: No kidding? How do you manage that?
BUSYGIN: Easy. I haven't got a father.
SILVA: Oh. That's different. Where do you live?
BUSYGIN: In a student hostel. In Krasnoe Vosstanie Street.
SILVA: The medical school hostel?
BUSYGIN: That's the one . . . I don't think much of the climate here.
SILVA: And they call this spring! . . . Brrr . . . And I haven't had a decent night's sleep for a month . . .
BUSYGIN: Right. You go into that building and knock on somebody's door, while I try the private sector. [*Heads towards* MAKARSKAIA's *house.*]
   [SILVA *disappears into apartment building.*]
   [*Knocks on* MAKARSKAIA's *door.*] Hullo there! Anybody in?
   [*Waits, then knocks again.*] Anybody at home?
   [*Window opens.*]

MAKARSKAIA: [*through window.*] Who's there?
BUSYGIN: Good evening, ma'am. I've just missed my train. I'm freezing.
MAKARSKAIA: You can't come in. Don't even ask!
BUSYGIN: Why turn me down flat?
MAKARSKAIA: I live alone.
BUSYGIN: All the better.
MAKARSKAIA: I'm alone, don't you understand?
BUSYGIN: Good! Then you'll have room for me.
MAKARSKAIA: Are you crazy? How can I let you in if I don't know you?
BUSYGIN: No problem. Let me introduce myself: Vladimir Petrovich Busygin, a student.
MAKARSKAIA: So what?
BUSYGIN: So what? Nothing. Now you know me.
MAKARSKAIA: You think that's enough?
BUSYGIN: What else do you want? Oh, yes . . . Without anticipating matters, I can say I like you already.
MAKARSKAIA: What cheek!
BUSYGIN: You might be more polite . . . Why don't you tell me how you feel in your cold . . .
MAKARSKAIA: Go on.
BUSYGIN: . . . empty . . .
MAKARSKAIA: Go on.
BUSYGIN: . . . dark house? Aren't you afraid, being all alone?
MAKARSKAIA: No, I'm not!
BUSYGIN: What if you fall ill at night? You've nobody to get you a glass of water. That's no way to live.
MAKARSKAIA: Don't worry, I won't fall ill! So forget it. We'll have a talk some other time.
BUSYGIN: When? Tomorrow? . . . Can I come and see you tomorrow?
MAKARSKAIA: Just you try!
BUSYGIN: I won't even live till tomorrow. I'm freezing to death.
MAKARSKAIA: Nothing'll happen to you.
BUSYGIN: You know, I still think you'll save us.
MAKARSKAIA: Us? You mean you're not alone?
BUSYGIN: That's the thing. I have a friend with me.
MAKARSKAIA: A friend? . . . What impossible cheek! [*Slams window.*]

BUSYGIN: End of conversation. [*Crosses courtyard, goes out into street, looks around.*]
[*Enter* SILVA.]
How'd it go?
SILVA: A waste of time. I tried three flats.
BUSYGIN: And?
SILVA: Nobody'll open the door. They're afraid.
BUSYGIN: I don't know . . . Begging for charity won't get us anywhere.
SILVA: We've had it. Another half hour and I'll die of cold. I can just see it.
BUSYGIN: What about the hall and stairs?
SILVA: You think it's warm in there? Is it hell! They've turned the heating off. The worst of it is nobody wants to talk. They just ask who's there, and that's it. Not a word more . . . We've had it.
BUSYGIN: Yes . . . And think of all those nice warm flats all around us . . .
SILVA: Never mind the flats! Think of all the booze, all the food . . . Not to mention all the lonely women! Brrr! That's the thing that always gets to me. Come on! We'll knock on every single door.
BUSYGIN: Hold it. What do you intend to say?
SILVA: Say? . . . That we've missed our train . . .
BUSYGIN: They won't believe you.
SILVA: We'll say we're freezing cold.
BUSYGIN: So? Who are you, and why should they care? The winter's over, you'll survive till morning.
SILVA: We'll say the express left without us.
BUSYGIN: Rubbish! They won't swallow that. We have to think of something more . . .
SILVA: We'll say there's a gang of thugs after us.
[BUSYGIN *laughs.*]
Surely they won't turn us away!
BUSYGIN: You don't understand people.
SILVA: Do you?
BUSYGIN: Yes. A bit, at least. And besides, I sometimes attend lectures, and study physiology, psycho-analysis, and useful things like that. And there's one thing I've grasped.

SILVA: What's that?
BUSYGIN: People have thick skin, and it's not that easy to get through it. You have to lie for all your worth, otherwise they don't believe you and don't sympathize. You have to give them a scare, or move them to pity.
SILVA: Brrr . . . You're right there. But first of all we have to wake them up. [*Waves his arms to get warm, then sings, tapping feet in time to song.*]
"When the lanterns of the night are slowly swaying,
And no longer are there people in the street . . ."
BUSYGIN: Cut it out.
SILVA: [*continues*] "Out from the bar I go,
I have nowhere to go,
And no longer can I bear love's deceit."
NEIGHBOUR: [*in gloating voice, from upper storey.*] Hey, you minstrels! Get along, out of here!
SILVA: [*looking up.*] Don't you like it?
NEIGHBOUR: Clear out! We've plenty of our own trouble-makers here without you.
SILVA: Pipe down, Grandpa!
NEIGHBOUR: Layabouts!
[*Window is heard slamming shut.*]
SILVA: Hear that? . . . The same old man. See how he's changed?
BUSYGIN: Yes . . .
SILVA: How can you believe anybody after that? [*Shivers*] Brrr . . .
BUSYGIN: Let's go into the doorway. We can get out of the wind, at least.
[*They head towards the doorway. A light comes on in one of the windows. The two stop and look up.*]
Did you try that door?
SILVA: No. Look, somebody's getting dressed.
BUSYGIN: Looks like two people.
SILVA: Someone's coming down. Let's have a smoke.
[BUSYGIN *and* SILVA *move aside.* SARAFANOV *emerges from the doorway. He looks about him and makes towards* MAKARSKAIA's *door, watched by* SILVA *and* BUSYGIN.]
SARAFANOV: [*knocks on* MAKARSKAIA's *door.*] Natasha! . . . Natashenka! . . . Natashenka! . . .
MAKARSKAIA: [*opening window.*] What a night! Everybody's on the rampage! Who is it this time?

SARAFANOV: Natashenka! I'm so sorry! It's me, Sarafanov.
MAKARSKAIA: Andrei Girgoryevich? . . . I didn't recognize you.
BUSYGIN: [*softly*] Funny . . . She doesn't know us, but she knows him . . .
SARAFANOV: Natasha, forgive me, my dear, for disturbing you so late, but I must see you at once.
MAKARSKAIA: Just a moment. Let me open the door. [*Disappears, then lets* SARAFANOV *in.*]
SILVA: What's going on? She's not a day over twenty-five.
BUSYGIN: And he's not a day under sixty.
SILVA: Not bad going.
BUSYGIN: I wonder who he's left behind at home . . . Can't very well have a wife there . . .
SILVA: I thought I caught a glimpse of a boy.
BUSYGIN: [*thoughtfully*] A boy, you say?
SILVA: A young-looking boy.
BUSYGIN: His son . . .
SILVA: I reckon he's got lots of 'em.
BUSYGIN: [*thinking*] Maybe he has . . . You know what? We'll go and meet him.
SILVA: Meet who?
BUSYGIN: The son.
SILVA: Whose son?
BUSYGIN: Whose son? The son of Andrei Grigoryevich Sarafanov.
SILVA: What for?
BUSYGIN: To get warm . . . Come on! We'll go and get warm, then see where to go from there.
SILVA: I don't understand.
BUSYGIN: Come on!
SILVA: We'll end up at the police station tonight. I can see it coming.
[*They disappear in the doorway.*]

SCENE TWO

The SARAFANOV's *flat. Among the furniture is an old settee and a battered cheval-glass. Door into next room. Curtained window overlooks courtyard. On the table is a packed rucksack.* VASENKA *is sitting at the table, writing a letter.*

VASENKA: [*reading his letter aloud.*] "I love you as nobody else ever will. Some day you'll realize that. For the moment you can rest easy. You've achieved all that you wanted to achieve: I hate you. Goodbye. V.S."
[*Enter* NINA *from next room, wearing slippers and dressing-gown.* VASENKA *hides letter in his pocket.*]
NINA: Written it?
VASENKA: None of your business.
NINA: Then go and lay your epistle in her hands, and come back and go to bed. Where's Dad?
VASENKA: How should I know?
NINA: Where could he have gone running off to at night? . . . [*Takes rucksack from table.*] And what might this be?
[VASENKA *tries to take rucksack from her. They struggle.*]
VASENKA: [*giving in.*] I'll take it when you go to sleep.
NINA: [*shaking out contents onto table.*] What's all this? . . . Where do you think you're going?
VASENKA: Hiking.
NINA: Then what's this? . . . Why do you need your passport?
VASENKA: None of your business.
NINA: What are you thinking of? . . . Don't you know I'm leaving?
VASENKA: So am I.
NINA: What?
VASENKA: I'm leaving too.
NINA: Have you gone right off your head?
VASENKA: I'm leaving.
NINA: [*sitting down.*] Listen, Vaska . . . You're a rat, that's what you are. I ought to just squash you.
VASENKA: I'm not bothering you, so don't you bother me.
NINA: You don't care a damn about me — that's one thing. But you must think about Dad.
VASENKA: You don't think about him, so why should I?
NINA: God almighty! [*Gets up.*] If only you knew how you all make me sick! [*Repacks rucksack and takes it into her room, stopping at door.*] Tell Dad not to wake me in the morning. Let me sleep. [*Exit*]
[VASENKA *takes letter out of pocket, puts it in envelope, writes address. Knock at door.*]
VASENKA: [*mechanically*] Come in.
[*Enter* BUSYGIN *and* SILVA.]

BUSYGIN: Good evening.
VASENKA: Hullo.
BUSYGIN: Could we have a word with Andrei Grigoryevich Sarafanov, please?
VASENKA: [*getting up.*] He's not in.
BUSYGIN: Will he be back soon?
VASENKA: He's only just gone out. I don't know when he'll be back.
SILVA: And where's he gone, if you don't mind my asking?
VASENKA: I don't know. [*Anxiously*] Why?
BUSYGIN: Er . . . How's his health?
VASENKA: Dad's? . . . All right . . . High blood pressure.
BUSYGIN: High blood pressure, eh? Too bad . . . Has he had it long?
VASENKA: Yes.
BUSYGIN: And how is he otherwise? . . . How's life treating him? . . . Cheerful, is he?
SILVA: Yes, how is he? . . . All right?
VASENKA: Why? What's up?
BUSYGIN: Let me introduce myself. I'm Vladimir.
VASENKA: Vasily . . . [*To* SILVA.] I'm Vasily.
SILVA: Semion . . . Everybody calls me Silva.
VASENKA: [*suspiciously*] Silva?
SILVA: Yes. The kids at the . . . er . . . boarding-school called me that because of my love for . . .
BUSYGIN: For music.
SILVA: Exactly.
VASENKA: I see. But why do you want my father?
SILVA: Why? Oh, we've just come to . . . er . . . see him.
VASENKA: Is it long since you last saw him?
BUSYGIN: How shall I put it? The saddest part about it is that we've never seen each other.
VASENKA: [*warily*] I don't follow . . .
SILVA: Nothing to be surprised about . . .
VASENKA: I'm not surprised . . . But how do you know him?
BUSYGIN: That's a secret.
VASENKA: A secret?
SILVA: A terrible secret. But nothing to be surprised at.
BUSYGIN: [*changing tone.*] Okay, that'll do. [*To* VASENKA.] We've come in to get warm. Do you mind if we warm up here for a while?

[VASENKA *says nothing. He is seriously worried.*]
We've missed our train. We read your father's name on the letter box. [*Pause*] Don't you believe me?
VASENKA: [*anxiously*] Why shouldn't I? I believe you, but . . .
BUSYGIN: But what? [*He takes two steps towards* VASENKA, *who backs away. To* SILVA.] He's afraid.
VASENKA: Why did you come here?
BUSYGIN: He doesn't believe us.
VASENKA: If you do anything I'll shout.
BUSYGIN: [*to* SILVA.] What did I tell you? [*He gains time by talking slowly, while warming himself.*] It's always like that at night: if you're alone you must be a burglar; and if there are two of you you must be thugs. [*To* VASENKA.] It's a bad look-out. People ought to trust each other. Didn't you know that? You didn't? . . . Should have done. A gap in your education.
SILVA: Yeah . . .
BUSYGIN: Still, I suppose your father hasn't the time . . .
VASENKA: [*interrupting*] Why do you want my father? What do you want with him?
BUSYGIN: What do we want? A bit of trust. No more than that. All mankind are brothers. I hope you've heard about that. Or is that news to you too? [*To* SILVA.] Just take a look at him. Suffering brethren standing at the door, cold and hungry, and he doesn't even ask them to sit down.
SILVA: [*after listening to* BUSYGIN *in some puzzlement, suddenly comes to life, as if he has understood something.*] Dead right!
VASENKA: Why did you come here?
BUSYGIN: You still don't understand?
VASENKA: Of course not.
SILVA: [*amazed*] Surely you understand!
BUSYGIN: [*to* VASENKA.] Well, you see . . .
SILVA: [*interrupting*] Oh, come on! I'll tell him! I'll tell him straight! He's a man, he'll understand. [*To* VASENKA, *triumphantly.*] Just keep calm, and I'll let you into the secret. The thing is that he [*points to* BUSYGIN.] is your brother!
BUSYGIN: What?
VASENKA: Wh-what?
SILVA: [*insolently*] Well? [*Short pause.*] Yes, Vasily! Andrei Grigoryevich Sarafanov is his father. Surely you've realized that by now!

[BUSYGIN *and* VASENKA *are equally surprised.*]
BUSYGIN: [*To* SILVA.] Now look . . .
SILVA: [*interrupting, to* VASENKA.] Didn't expect it? But there it is. Your dad is his dad, strange to say . . .
BUSYGIN: What's this rubbish you're talking?
SILVA: The meeting of two brothers! What an occasion, eh? What a moment this is!
VASENKA: [*not knowing what to say.*] Yes, I suppose it is . . .
SILVA: What an occasion! Think of it! Come on, boys, we've got to drink to it!
BUSYGIN: [*to* SILVA.] Idiot! [*To* VASENKA.] Don't listen to him.
SILVA: No, no! I reckon it's best to tell the truth right from the start! Straight and honest! [*To* VASENKA] Isn't that right, Vasily? Why beat about the bush when everything's as plain as day? No good beating about the bush. Instead we must drink to your meeting. Got anything to drink?
VASENKA: [*still not knowing what to say.*] Drink? . . . Sure . . . Just a sec . . . [*Looks round at* BUSYGIN, *then goes into kitchen.*]
SILVA: [*delighted*] Brilliant!
BUSYGIN: Have you gone clean off your rocker?
SILVA: I like the way you led up to it!
BUSYGIN: You numbskull! How'd you get that idea into your head?
SILVA: Me? . . . *You* had the idea! You're a genius!
BUSYGIN: Cretin! Do you realize what you've gone and done?
SILVA: "Suffering brethren"! Brilliant! I'd never have thought of it!
BUSYGIN: You muttonhead! . . . Just imagine what'll happen now, if his daddy comes in. Think!
SILVA: Right . . . I've thought. [*Runs to door, but stops and turns back.*] No, we'll be all right. His dad won't be back for an hour, at least. [*Fidgetting in anticipation of a drink.*] Quite a mover, the old man! [*Mimicking*] "I must see you at once!" Old goat! They're all old goats. I bet your old man was another, eh?
BUSYGIN: Mind your own business. [*Goes to door.*]
SILVA: Wait, why shouldn't this one be made to suffer just a little for the sins of the other. Seems perfectly just to me.
BUSYGIN: Let's go.
SILVA: [*stubbornly*] Oh, no! We'll have a drink first, and then we'll go. I don't understand you. Surely you deserve a glass of

vodka for your idea . . . Shh! Here it comes, our little drink. It's on its way. Coming closer. [*Whispers*] Embrace him, stroke his head. Like a long-lost relative.

BUSYGIN: Embrace him, be damned! Why did I have to get mixed up with such an idiot?

[*Enter* VASENKA *with a bottle of vodka and some tumblers, which he stands on the table. He is embarrassed and confused.*]

SILVA: [*filling glasses.*] No need to worry now! If you care to look into it, we've all got far more relations that we ought to have . . . Here's to our meeting!

[*They drain their glasses,* VASENKA *doing so with difficulty.*]

Life's a jungle, Vasia, so don't be surprised at anything. [*Fills the glasses again.*] We've just got off the train. He'd got on my nerves, and worn his own nerves to a frazzle, wondering whether to call on you or not. And he had to, you understand, what with the times we live in . . .

BUSYGIN: [*to* VASENKA.] How old are you?

VASENKA: Me? Sixteen.

SILVA: He's a big lad!

BUSYGIN: [*to* VASENKA.] Well then . . . To your health.

SILVA: Hold it! This won't do. This is no civilized way to drink. Haven't we got anything to eat with it?

VASENKA: Eat? . . . Sure, sure! Let's go into the kitchen.

SILVA: [*holding* VASENKA *back.*] Maybe his father shouldn't see him today, eh? What do you think? You can't do these things in a hurry, with no warning. We'll just stay a little while and . . . come back tomorrow.

VASENKA: [*to* BUSYGIN.] Don't you want to see him?

BUSYGIN: How shall I put it . . . I do, but it's a bit risky. It's his nerves I'm thinking of. He doesn't know anything about me, you see.

VASENKA: Nothing to worry about. Now that you've turned up, you've turned up.

[*All three go into the kitchen. Enter* SARAFANOV. *He crosses to door into next room, opens it, then carefully closes it.* VASENKA *emerges from the kitchen, closing the door behind him.* VASENKA *is visibly drunk, and gripped by a sense of bitter irony.*]

SARAFANOV: [*noticing* VASENKA.] You here? . . . I've just been out for a stroll. It's started raining. I remembered my young days.
VASENKA: [*familiarly*] How very fitting!
SARAFANOV: In my young days I may have done some silly things, but I never went too far.
VASENKA: Listen. I've got something to tell you.
SARAFANOV: [*interrupting*] Vasenka, only weak people behave like that. And besides, you've only a month to go before your exams, don't forget. Whatever you do, you must complete your schooling.
VASENKA: Dad, while you were out strolling in the rain . . .
SARAFANOV: [*interrupting*] And you can't just go off like that, both at once — you and Nina. It's not right . . . No, you're not going anywhere. I won't let you.
VASENKA: Dad, we've got visitors, and they're no ordinary visitors . . . Or one visitor, to be precise, and one other . . .
SARAFANOV: Vasenka, one visitor and one other equals two visitors. Who's come calling? Make yourself clear.
VASENKA: Your son. Your elder son.
SARAFANOV: [*after a pause.*] What did you say? . . . Whose son?
VASENKA: Yours. Now don't get excited . . . I understand all these things, I don't reproach you, and I'm not even surprised. I'm not surprised at anything . . .
SARAFANOV: [*after a pause.*] Is that the sort of joke going the rounds among your friends? Do you think they're funny?
VASENKA: I'm not joking. He's in the kitchen, having supper.
SARAFANOV: [*looking carefully at* VASENKA.] Somebody's having supper in the kitchen. Maybe they are . . . But there's something about this that I don't like, my boy . . . [*Noticing what it is.*] Wait! I do believe you're drunk!
VASENKA: Well, I've had a drink! To the occasion.
SARAFANOV: [*menacingly*] Who gave you permission to have a drink?!
VASENKA: Dad, does it matter? At a time like this! I never knew I had a brother, and suddenly — here he is. Go and have a look at him, and you'll get drunk too, properly.
SARAFANOV: Are you making fun of me, you rascal?
VASENKA: Not at all. I'm serious. He was passing through, he was missing you so much, and he . . .

SARAFANOV: Who are you talking about?
VASENKA: Your son.
SARAFANOV: Then who are you?
VASENKA: Oh, go and talk to him yourself!
SARAFANOV: [*makes towards kitchen, hears voices, stops at the door comes back to* VASENKA.] How many of them are there?
VASENKA: Two. I told you.
SARAFANOV: Who's the second? Does he want me to adopt him too?
VASENKA: Dad, they're grown men. What does a grown man want with parents, do you think?
SARAFANOV: Oh? You think they don't need them?
VASENKA: I'm sorry. What I meant was: a grown man doesn't need anybody else's parents.
[*Silence.*]
SARAFANOV: [*listening*] Very odd. Children running away — that I can understand. But other people's children running to me! Grown-up children at that! How old is he?
VASENKA: About twenty.
SARAFANOV: I'm damned if I can understand it! . . . Twenty, you say? . . . Lot of nonsense! . . . About twenty! . . . [*Becoming thoughtful, despite himself.*] Twenty years . . . Twenty . . . [*Lowers himself onto chair.*]
VASENKA: Don't take it hard, Dad. Life's a jungle . . .
[BUSYGIN *and* SILVA *try to come out of the kitchen, but, seeing* SARAFANOV, *withdraw, leaving door ajar, and listen to his conversation with* VASENKA.]
SARAFANOV: Twenty years . . . The end of the war . . . Twenty years . . . I was thirty-four at the time . . . [*Stands up.*]
[BUSYGIN *pushes door to.*]
VASENKA: I understand, Dad . . .
SARAFANOV: [*with sudden anger.*] What's the point of recalling it? I was a soldier! A soldier, not a vegetarian! [*Paces up and down the room.*]
[*Whenever possible,* BUSYGIN *pulls kitchen door ajar and listens.*]
VASENKA: I understand.
SARAFANOV: What? . . . You seem to understand a little bit too much! I still didn't know your mother then! Don't forget that.
VASENKA: That's what I thought, Dad. But don't upset yourself. If you care to look into it . . .

SARAFANOV: [*interrupting*] No! It's all nonsense . . . Can't make head of tail of it . . .
[*He stands between the kitchen and the door into the hall, thus preventing* SILVA *and* BUSYGIN *from making their escape.*]
VASENKA: You think he's lying? Why should he?
SARAFANOV: He's got something mixed up! You wait and see! And think about it! In the first place, if he were my son, he'd have to look like me!
VASENKA: Dad, he does look like you.
SARAFANOV: What? . . . Tommy-rot! Rot! You must be imagining it . . . Rot! All I have to do is ask him how old he is, and you'll see straight away that all this is pure tommy-rot! Stuff and nonsense! . . . But if it came to the crunch, he'd have to be . . . What would it be? . . .
[BUSYGIN *looks out from kitchen.*]
Twenty . . . Twenty-one! Yes! Twenty-one! There you are! Not twenty, and not twenty-two! . . . [*Turns towards kitchen door.*]
[BUSYGIN *withdraws.*]
VASENKA: What if he is twenty-one?
SARAFANOV: He can't be!
VASENKA: But what if he is?
SARAFANOV: You mean by pure chance, by coincidence, I suppose? . . . Well, that can't be ruled out . . . In that case . . . [*Thinks*] Don't interrupt, don't interrupt . . . His mother's name would be . . . her name would be . . .
[BUSYGIN *looks out of kitchen.*]
Galina!
[BUSYGIN *withdraws.*]
What do you say to that? Galina! Not Tatiana, and not Tamara!
VASENKA: What about her surname? And her patronymic?
[BUSYGIN *looks out.*]
SARAFANOV: And her patronymic . . . [*Uncertainly*] I think it was Alexandrovna . . .
[BUSYGIN *withdraws.*]
VASENKA: All right. And her surname?
SARAFANOV: Her surname . . . Oh, her first name ought to be enough . . . Plenty.

VASENKA: Of course, of course. After all these years . . .
SARAFANOV: That's right! And where's he been till now? So now he's grown up he goes looking for his father. What for? I'll soon winkle it out of him, you'll see . . . What's his name?
VASENKA: Volodia. Chin up, Dad! He loves you.
SARAFANOV: Loves me? . . . But . . . Why?
VASENKA: I don't know, Dad . . . Blood's thicker than water, I suppose.
SARAFANOV: Blood? . . . No, don't make me laugh . . . [*Sits down.*] Just off the train, you say? . . . Did you find them something to eat?
VASENKA: Yes, to eat and to drink.
[BUSYGIN *and* SILVA *try to slip out. They take two or three soft steps towards the front door, but* SARAFANOV *turns in his seat and they immediately return to the kitchen.*]
SARAFANOV: [*getting up.*] Maybe I should have a drink too.
VASENKA: That's the way, Dad.
[BUSYGIN *and* SILVA *reappears.*]
SARAFANOV: Hold on, I'll just . . . button up. [*Turns to* BUSYGIN *and* SILVA.]
[BUSYGIN *and* SILVA *instantly try to look as if they'd only just come out of the kitchen. Silence.*]
BUSYGIN: Good evening!
SARAFANOV: Good evening . . .
[*Silence.*]
VASENKA: There. So now you've met . . . [*To* BUSYGIN.] I've told him everything . . . [*To* SARAFANOV.] Don't worry, Dad . . .
SARAFANOV: Sit down, won't you? . . . Sit down! . . . [*Carefully studying both of them.*]
[BUSYGIN *and* SILVA *sit down.*]
[*Still standing.*] So you . . . you've just come from the station?
BUSYGIN: Yes . . . er, some time ago now. About three hours ago.
[*Silence.*]
SARAFANOV: [*to* SILVA.] I see . . . You're passing through, I hear . . .
BUSYGIN: Yes. I'm on my way home from a competition. I thought I'd look in . . .
SARAFANOV: [*concentrating exclusively on* BUSYGIN.] A sportsman, are you? That's good . . . Fine thing at your age, sport . . . And now you're off to another competition? [*Sits down.*]

BUSYGIN: No. Now I'm going back to the Institute.
SARAFANOV: So you're a student, are you?
SILVA: Yes, we're medical students. Tomorrow's doctors.
SARAFANOV: That's the way! Spare-time sportsmen, and full-time scholars. That's the way! . . . Excuse me, I'll move over. [*Takes a chair closer to* BUSYGIN.] At twenty you have time for everything — both study and sport. Yes, it's a marvellous age . . . [*Summoning up courage.*] You are twenty, aren't you?
BUSYGIN: [*sadly, in a tone of gentle reproach.*] No, you've forgotten. I'm twenty-one.
SARAFANOV: What? . . . Yes, of course! Twenty-one. Of course you are. What did I say? Twenty? Of course you're twenty-one . . .
SILVA: Cheer up though. If you think about it, after all, you ought to be glad, not downhearted. That's what I think.
VASENKA: That's right, Dad.
SARAFANOV: Of course, I'm glad . . . [*Ingratiatingly*] We're all glad, aren't we?
BUSYGIN: Of course we are . . . And most of all me.
SARAFANOV: [*cheering up.*] Vasenka, have we got anything to drink? Get us something to drink!
VASENKA: That's easy. [*Goes out of kitchen.*]
   [*Silence. Then* BUSYGIN *and* SARAFANOV *start talking at once. They apologize at once.*]
BUSYGIN: Go on . . .
SARAFANOV: No, you go on . . . [*Carefully*] Go on . . .
   [VASENKA *comes back, stands a bottle and glasses on the table, then sits down. He rests his hands on the back of a chair and his head drops. He is drunk.* SARAFANOV *hurriedly fills the glasses.*]
BUSYGIN: I was going to say that . . . At last it's come, the moment we . . .
   [*Enter* NINA.]
NINA: [*angrily*] Are you going to let me sleep? . . . What's this? What's going on?
VASENKA: [*raising head.*] Now don't be surprised . . . [*Drops head.*]
   [NINA's *entry makes a deep impression on* BUSYGIN *and* SILVA.]
NINA: What's this gathering in aid of? [*To* SARAFANOV.] Up to now you've always drunk alone at night. What's happened.

SARAFANOV: [*uncertainly*] Nina, this is a happy day for us. Your elder brother's turned up at last.
NINA: What?
SARAFANOV: Your elder brother. Come and meet him.
NINA: What's this? . . . Who's turned up? What brother?
SILVA: [*pushing* BUSYGIN *forward.*] Here he is. This fine fellow here. [*Points*]
NINA: [*to* BUSYGIN.] Are you my brother?
BUSYGIN: Yes . . . Why not?
SILVA: What's so odd about that?
VASENKA: [*without raising his head, in low, drunken voice.*] Yes, what's so odd about that?
SARAFANOV: [*to* NINA.] You didn't know about him. Unfortunately . . . I didn't tell you. [*To* BUSYGIN.] Frankly, I was afraid you might have . . . forgotten all about me.
VASENKA: There. He was afraid.
BUSYGIN: How could I ever have forgotten . . .
SARAFANOV: I'm sorry, it was wrong of me.
NINA: Right. Let's get this straight. You're his father, and he's your son. Is that it?
SARAFANOV: Yes.
NINA: [*after pause.*] Well, I suppose it's perfectly possible.
VASENKA: Perfectly.
NINA: [*to* BUSYGIN.] And where were you all this time?
VASENKA: Yes, where was he all this time?
NINA: [*tapping* VASENKA *lightly on the head.*] Shut up!
SARAFANOV: Nina! You're brother's turned up! Can't you understand that?
NINA: Yes, I understand. But I want to know where he's been all this time.
VASENKA: [*raising head.*] Don't worry. Dad still hadn't set eyes on our mother then. Isn't that right, Dad?
SARAFANOV: Will you shut up?
NINA: Yes. It's been a long time for you. Are you sure he's your son? [*To* BUSYGIN.] How old are you?
[VASENKA *falls asleep.*]
SILVA: Just look at them. Can't you see how alike they are?
NINA: [*after pause.*] No. There's no likeness.
SILVA: [*to* BUSYGIN, *in hurt tone.*] I think they suspect us of something.

NINA: [*to* SARAFANOV, *about* SILVA.] And what about that one? Is he a relation as well?
BUSYGIN: He's my friend. His name's Silva.
NINA: And how old did you say you were?
BUSYGIN: Twenty-one.
NINA: [*to* SARAFANOV.] What do you say to that?
SARAFANOV: Nina! Don't be like that . . . Besides, I've already asked . . .
NINA: All right. [*To* BUSYGIN.] What does your mother look like? What's her name? Where did she meet him? Why didn't she get any maintenance from him? How did you find us? Where've you been? Give us the details.
SILVA: [*uneasily*] Just like the police . . .
NINA: What did you expect? . . . I think you're a couple of crooks.
SARAFANOV: Nina!
BUSYGIN: Why? Do we look like crooks?
NINA: [*after pause.*] Yes. [*To* BUSYGIN.] Tell us. We're waiting.
SILVA: [*to* BUSYGIN, *fearfully.*] If I were you I wouldn't put up with that. I'd walk out. Right away.
BUSYGIN: I only recently found out about my father . . .
NINA: Who from?
BUSYGIN: My mother. Her name is Galina Alexandrovna, and she met my father in 1945 . . .
SARAFANOV: [*stirred*] My son!
BUSYGIN: Dad!

[SARAFANOV *and* BUSYGIN *fall into each other's arms.*]

SILVA: [*to* NINA.] How do you like that? . . . Blood's thicker than water.
SARAFANOV: Nina! There's no doubt about it! He's your brother! Embrace him! Embrace your brother! [*To* BUSYGIN.] Embrace her!
BUSYGIN: I'm glad to meet my little sister . . . [*Suddenly steps up to* NINA *and embraces her, fearfully, but with obvious pleasure.*] Very glad . . .
SILVA: [*enviously*] Who wouldn't be?
SARAFANOV: [*deeply moved.*] Heavens above! Who could have thought . . .
NINA: [*to* BUSYGIN.] Don't you think that'll do? [*Frees herself, greatly embarrassed.*]

SARAFANOV: Who could have thought it? . . . I'm so glad!
BUSYGIN: So am I.
NINA: Yes . . . Very touching . . .
SILVA: Hooray! May I suggest we drink to it?
SARAFANOV: [*to* BUSYGIN.] He suggests we drink to it. What do you say, son?
BUSYGIN: Drink to it? Of course we must.
NINA: Drink? Now I can see the likeness.
[*All laugh.*]
SILVA: [*drinks. To* NINA *and* BUSYGIN.] Stand side by side! . . . That's it! [*Standing them side by side.*] Now hold hands . . . That's the way. [*To* SARAFANOV.] Take a look at them!
[NINA *frees her hand, again with embarrassment, which she cannot completely conceal.*]
Don't they look alike? . . . Don't tell me they don't!
SARAFANOV: Er . . . Yes, of course they do . . .
SILVA: What an occasion, eh? Enough to bring tears to your eyes! . . . Come on, let's have a drink!
SARAFANOV: I'm happy . . . I'm perfectly happy!
SILVA: [*to* SARAFANOV.] Here's to you, and your united family!
BUSYGIN: Here's to you, Dad.
SARAFANOV: [*moved*] Thanks, son.
[*Lights down. Jolly music is heard. Music dies away and lights come on. The same room. Daylight outside the window. Morning.* SARAFANOV *and* BUSYGIN *are sitting at the table. An empty bottle in front of them.* SILVA *is asleep on the settee.*]
SARAFANOV: I was a captain, so they kept me on in the army for a while. Finally got demobbed. I was in the artillery, and that's bad for the hearing, you know. Besides I'd forgotten everything I knew. Clarinets and howitzers don't go very well together. At first I played at dances, then in a restaurant, then I graduated to parks and cinemas. Luckily my deafness passed, and when a symphony orchestra was formed in our town, they took me on . . . You follow?
BUSYGIN: Of course, Dad!
SARAFANOV: That's the story of my life . . . Of course it hasn't all turned out the way I planned when I was young, but still, still. And if you think your father's turned his back on all that he

held dear in his youth, you're wrong. I'll never become flint-hearted, or mouldy, or be turned aside by day-to-day concerns. Never! [*Half-rising, he leans towards* BUSYGIN, *and whispers importantly.*] I'm composing. [*Sits down.*] Every man is born a creator, each in his own field and within the limits of his powers must create. So that the very best that he has in him should remain after him. That's why I compose.

BUSYGIN: [*puzzled*] What do you compose?

SARAFANOV: What do you mean — what? What could I compose if not music?

BUSYGIN: Er . . . Yes, of course.

SARAFANOV: Of course what?

BUSYGIN: Er . . . you compose music.

SARAFANOV: [*mistrustfully, all ready to take offence.*] And you . . . What do you think about that?

BUSYGIN: Me? . . . It's a fine occupation.

SARAFANOV: [*quickly, with some heat.*] I'm not reaching that high, you know. There's just one work I have to finish, just one! I'll only say what matters, what really matters most! I have to do it, it's my duty, because nobody else will do it if I don't. Do you understand?

BUSYGIN: Yes, I do . . . Excuse me, Dad, if you don't mind my asking . . .

SARAFANOV: [*recovering his self-possession.*] What? . . . You can ask me, son?

BUSYGIN: The mother of Nina and Vasenka — where is she?

SARAFANOV: We parted fourteen years ago. She thought I spent too much time playing the clarinet in the evening, and just at that time this engineer came on the scene — a reliable type, and we parted . . . It wasn't at all like with your mother. Your mother was a wonderful woman . . . By heavens! Times were hard then, but how can I ever forget them? Chernigov . . . the river . . . the chestnut-trees . . . You know that seamstress's workshop on the corner? . . .

BUSYGIN: Of course!

SARAFANOV: That's the place! That's where she worked . . .

BUSYGIN: And now she's the manager of a garment factory.

SARAFANOV: I can just imagine it! . . . Is she the same happy soul she used to be?

BUSYGIN: Everybody says she hasn't changed a bit.
SARAFANOV: Is that so? . . . Good for her! And she can't be more than forty-five now!
BUSYGIN: Forty-four.
SARAFANOV: Is that all? . . . And how . . . She's not married?
BUSYGIN: No, no. There's just the two of us.
SARAFANOV: Is that so? . . . But she deserves every possible happiness.
BUSYGIN: My mother doesn't complain about her life. She's a proud woman.
SARAFANOV: Yes . . . Still, it's sad, it really is . . . We were transferred to Gomel, and she stayed behind in Chernigov, all alone in the dusty street . . . Yes, all alone.
BUSYGIN: She wasn't quite alone, as you see.
SARAFANOV: No . . . Of course not . . . But wait . . . Wait! Just wait a minute! Now it's coming back to me! Forgive me for saying so, but she didn't intend to have a child!
BUSYGIN: I was an accident.
SARAFANOV: But why did she keep quiet about it all that time? How could she not let me know?
BUSYGIN: I've told you: she's a proud woman.
SARAFANOV: It's good that it's turned out like this. I'm glad.
BUSYGIN: Who is my father? I kept at her with that question from the moment I learned to talk.
SARAFANOV: You really wanted to find me that badly?
BUSYGIN: When I was still in the Young Pioneers I vowed I'd track you down.
SARAFANOV: [*touched*] Poor boy! After all, when you come to think of it, you should have hated me . . .
BUSYGIN: Hate you? . . . How could I, Dad? Don't exaggerate . . . No, I know how you feel.
SARAFANOV: I see you're a sensible lad. Not like your younger brother. He's too highly strung. Delicate nature, they tell me, but I reckon he's got no backbone.
BUSYGIN: Delicate natures always show themselves in odd ways.
SARAFANOV: Too true! That explains his unhappy love . . . We all lived here as good neighbours, quietly, peacefully, and suddenly — bang! He loses his head, and he's all ready to leave home.

BUSYGIN: Who's the girl?

SARAFANOV: She works in the courtrooms, as a secretary. She's older than him, that's the trouble. She's about thirty, and he hasn't even finished school. Things have got so bad that last night I had to go and see her . . .

BUSYGIN: What for?

SARAFANOV: Late in the evening he showed up and declared that he was leaving. She'd sent him packing — that was obvious from his face. But how could I help him? I thought maybe she was worried about the difference in their ages, or afraid people would reproach her, or even that I would take a dim view . . . And thinking that, I had a talk with her, asked her to change her attitude and not be too . . . hard on him . . . You know what? You could have a word with him. You're his elder brother. You might have some influence.

BUSYGIN: I'll have a go.

SARAFANOV: I'm so pleased to see you, believe me. Having you turn up is a real joy to me.

BUSYGIN: To me too . . . it's a joy.

SARAFANOV: Is that the truth, son?

BUSYGIN: Of course.

SARAFANOV: Let me give you a kiss. [*Gives* BUSYGIN *a fatherly kiss on the forehead, and at once looks embarrassed.*] Forgive me . . . The thing is . . . I was really feeling low.

BUSYGIN: What's the trouble?

SARAFANOV: Well, look for yourself. One of 'em running away from home because of his unhappy love. And the other leaving home because of her happy love . . .

BUSYGIN: [*interrupting*] Who's leaving home?

SARAFANOV: Nina. She's getting married.

BUSYGIN: Getting married?

SARAFANOV: That's the point. In just a few days she's off to Sakhalin. And yesterday her kid brother tells me he's off to a construction site in the *taiga*. Now do you see what happened the moment you knocked at our door?

BUSYGIN: I understood when I knocked . . .

SARAFANOV: [*interrupting*] It's a miracle that's happened! A real miracle! And they keep on saying I'm a failure!

BUSYGIN: So she's getting married . . . Who to?

SARAFANOV: Er . . . Her fiancé's a pilot . . . a dependable fellow. He graduates from flying school in a few days, and he's already been posted to Sakhalin. Incidentally, she wants to introduce him today.
BUSYGIN: I see . . . And how old is Nina?
SARAFANOV: Nineteen.
BUSYGIN: Oh yes?
SARAFANOV: Why? She couldn't be any older. But she's sensible, very sensible. I sometimes think she's too sensible for her own good. Of course, she hasn't had an easy time of it. She's had to keep house, and do her job — she's a seamstress — and study to get into college. She's a good girl.
BUSYGIN: Yes . . . Why doesn't she take you with her?
SARAFANOV: Oh no. Everything I have is here, in this town. I was born here, and . . . No, why should I disturb them? For three months now she's been seeing her fiancé. They're off in a few days, and I've never yet set eyes on him. What do you think of that? But that's enough moaning from me. It's morning already, and you need to catch some sleep. Lie down, son. Will you be all right here for a short while, next to your friend?
BUSYGIN: Fine.
SARAFANOV: And then, when the others get up . . .
BUSYGIN: [*interrupting*] Don't worry about a thing.
SARAFANOV: All right, sleep well. [*Gives* BUSYGIN *another kiss on the forehead.*] Don't be cross, son. I'm so overcome. Sleep.
[SARAFANOV *goes into next room.* BUSYGIN *hurries to* SILVA *and shakes him.* SILVA *moans and resists.*]
BUSYGIN: Get up, Silva! Get up, do you hear?
SILVA: [*waking*] What a life . . .
BUSYGIN: Get up!
SILVA: I haven't had a proper night's sleep for a month. The one day of the week you get a chance is Sunday — and look what happens. But that little sister of yours isn't bad though, eh? I wouldn't put up too much of a fight.
BUSYGIN: Stop talking and get up! BUSYGIN: Throws SILVA *his shirt.*] Get moving! . . .
[SILVA *gets up.*]
While you were snoozing we were getting on each other's nerves, all night long.

SILVA: What? . . . You mean they've tumbled to it already? . . . Have they? [*Dressing hurriedly.*] Even if they haven't, a joke's a joke, but this is serious. Probably punishable by law. [*Pushes feet into shoes.*] Let's get going!
[BUSYGIN *stands still, lost in thought.*]
Well? What's keeping you?
BUSYGIN: That old man's a saint.
SILVA: You sure led him along by the nose. It was a sight to see.
BUSYGIN: No. Spare me ever having to dupe anybody who swallows my every word. Let's go.
[*They make towards the door. As they do so, enter* SARAFANOV *from the other room, carrying a pillow.*]
SARAFANOV: Son!
BUSYGIN: [*turning to* SARAFANOV.] I . . . That is, we . . . We have to be going . . .
SILVA: Yes, we must be off now. The . . . er . . . term starts soon.
BUSYGIN: Yes . . . unfortunately . . .
SARAFANOV: What? You want to go? . . . Today? This minute?
BUSYGIN: Yes, Dad. We've stayed too long as it is. Missed a lot of lectures, and . . .
[SARAFANOV *drops pillow.*]
[*Picking up pillow.*] But don't worry: at the end of term I'll come straight back . . .
SARAFANOV: [*sinking onto chair.*] Of course, I understand . . . Naturally . . . Why should I expect anything else? We've met, had a chat . . . That ought to be enough.
BUSYGIN: I'll come back . . . I'll come in June . . . All right?
[SARAFANOV *says nothing.*]
Don't you believe me?
SARAFANOV: Of course I believe you, but . . . How could you think of leaving without saying goodbye?
BUSYGIN: I . . . er . . . I didn't want to wake you. And to be frank, it's hard for me to say goodbye to you. I wanted to avoid it . . .
SARAFANOV: Is that the truth?
SILVA: Of course it is. He'd been on edge so much . . .
SARAFANOV: [*heartened*] Really? . . . [*Getting up.*] Well, in that case . . . if you have to go you have to go . . . Till the end of June, then?
BUSYGIN: Yes.

SARAFANOV: That's nothing. Only a month and a half . . . And now . . . You have to leave now? This minute?

SILVA: Yes, our train goes at about ten, I think.

SARAFANOV: All right then . . . [*Shakes hands with* SILVA.] Goodbye. Delighted to meet you. Come back together in June.

SILVA: Of course we will.

SARAFANOV: Well, son . . . That's life. Got to take your studies seriously . . . It's a pity of course, but still . . . We've met. That's what counts . . . [*Suddenly*] Hold on. There's one little thing I have to give you.

BUSYGIN: What little thing? What now, Dad? . . .

SARAFANOV: Yes, yes! You must have it! It's only a trifle, but you can't turn it down. Hold on! [*Hurries into next room. From doorway.*] Vasenka! [*Exit*]

[*Short pause.*]

SILVA: What are you waiting for?

BUSYGIN: Go if you want . . . I'll join you later . . .

SILVA: Look! You've led the guy right up the garden path, and that'll do. Let's get out . . .

BUSYGIN: Go on, I'm not keeping you.

SILVA: What on earth do you want? . . . What have you thought up now? Tell me. Maybe I'll take a chance on it too.

BUSYGIN: No, you'd better go.

SILVA: What is it? . . . If it's theft, of course you can count me out. That's not my style.

BUSYGIN: Moron! What if he comes in now and finds us gone? Can you imagine that?

SILVA: Yes. What of it?

BUSYGIN: You can do as you like, but I'm staying for a while. Not for long.

SILVA: What for?

[BUSYGIN *says nothing.*]

Look out, mate, or you'll land right in the stew. I'm warning you, as your friend: let's split while the going's good.

[*Enter* NINA *from next room, wearing dressing-gown, with towel over shoulder.*]

NINA: [*to* SILVA.] Good morning . . . [*To* BUSYGIN.] Hullo, . . . big brother . . .

[BUSYGIN *and* SILVA *greet her.*]

Slept well?
SILVA: Fine, thanks.
NINA: Why are you standing at the door?
SILVA: Us? . . . Oh, just breathing some fresh air . . .
NINA: Open the window then. If you're not afraid of catching cold. [*Exit*]
SILVA: See that, did you? The eyes, the hair? And what legs? She's got everything!
BUSYGIN: Yes, and none of it's for you.
SILVA: Is that what's keeping you, eh? Decided to get to work? . . . Don't forget, you're her brother. It's not allowed. It's all right for me, though.
[*Enter* SARAFANOV, *carrying a snuff-box.*]
SARAFANOV: Here you are, son. It's nothing much, just a silver snuff-box, but in our family it's always belonged to the elder son. My great-grandfather handed it down to my grandfather, and it came to me from your grandfather, that is, my father. Now it's yours.
[*Short pause.*]
BUSYGIN: [*embarrassed, takes the snuff-box and puts it on the table.*] Thank you, Dad . . . You know, I've decided to stay a while. Just a day. And tomorrow I'll take the plane.
SARAFANOV: Can you do that?
BUSYGIN: Why not?
SARAFANOV: That's a wonderful idea! We'll spend the whole day together . . . Is it Sunday today? . . . Oh, what a nuisance! At seven I have to go down to the Philharmonic, but not for long. I'm on in the first half. That'll take an hour, or an hour and a half at most. Yes, aeroplanes are a wonderful invention! What would we do without them? . . . [*To* SILVA.] What about you, Semion? I hope you're staying too — are you?
SILVA: Me? . . . Well, I don't . . .
[*Enter* NINA, *who crosses room and goes into next room.* SILVA *watches her with an unambiguous look.* BUSYGIN *also watches her.*]
Of course I am! Wherever he goes, I go too. We're inseparable.
SARAFANOV: That's fine, then. I see you're really good friends.
[*Enter* VASENKA *from other room. He is frowning, and his hair is tousled.*]

[*Cheerily*] Aha! . . . Sarafanov the younger. In a sorry state.
BUSYGIN: His first hangover.
[SARAFANOV *and* BUSYGIN *laugh.*]
VASENKA: How do you know it's the first? [*Sits down on the settee, hanging his head.*]
SARAFANOV: Drink some water.
SILVA: Or some milk.
BUSYGIN: Or some hot tea.
SARAFANOV: Just as well he doesn't have to go to school today.
VASENKA: I'm not going back there anyway.
SARAFANOV: You still harping on that?
VASENKA: Still? I told you I'm going, and I mean it.
BUSYGIN: If I were you I'd finish school first. You can go off into the *taiga* any time. That's one college that accepts new students all the year round.
SARAFANOV: They need carpenters and lumberjacks there, I believe.
VASENKA: What of it? I'll overcome all difficulties, I'll work hard, and the older hands'll help me.
[*Enter* NINA.]
Besides, we can't all be students. Some of us have to work.
NINA: Where's he off to?
VASENKA: None of your business.
SARAFANOV: Come now, it's as well for you to know your sister's opinion. She's ten times more sensible than you.
VASENKA: I'm a mediocrity, Dad. I've known that for ages. But you've got your daughter, and she's so sensible, so clever, so beautiful . . .
SILVA: You can say that again.
VASENKA: And besides, now that another son's turned up you could all leave me alone and let me be my mediocre self.
SARAFANOV: What's the good of talking to him?
NINA: [*to* BUSYGIN.] My congratulations on entering this madhouse.
BUSYGIN: [*to* VASENKA.] If I were you I really would do what your father says, and your sister. Just this once.
VASENKA: You've come just in time. You can do as they say instead of me.
BUSYGIN: I'm leaving, unfortunately.
NINA: Leaving? . . . When?
BUSYGIN: Tomorrow.

SILVA: We have to get back to our studies, sad to say.
NINA: Oh? . . . But I thought . . .
VASENKA: She thought he was going to stay with Dad. Thought she'd found somebody to shift the load onto.
SARAFANOV: Don't start any scenes, Vasenka . . . And as for Volodia, he'll come and see me in the summer.
NINA: You're just passing through, then . . .
BUSYGIN: And you're about to leave, then?
SILVA: Leave? How's that?
VASENKA: I've got an idea.
SARAFANOV: Ah! My younger son's mind has started ticking over.
VASENKA: Dad must get married.
SARAFANOV: What did you say?
VASENKA: You must get married.
[NINA *laughs.*]
SARAFANOV: [*to* NINA.] Stop it. What's so funny? He's got no manners.
NINA: Who to, Vasenka?
VASENKA: To Volodia's mother. Who else?
SARAFANOV: You've lost all respect, I see.
NINA: [*bantering*] Why not, Dad? Isn't it worth thinking about? [*To* BUSYGIN.] What do you say to that?
BUSYGIN: Me? . . . I don't know what to say.
SARAFANOV: Don't take any notice of them. I've been too soft on them, as you can see.
VASENKA: No need to get angry. I'm not suggesting anything improper. On the contrary . . .
SARAFANOV: Be quiet, you clown! [*To* SILVA.] Semion, what do you think of this family?
SILVA: It's an exceptional family. [*Pointing to* BUSYGIN.] He's very lucky.
SARAFANOV: Nina, Volodia's leaving tomorrow, and I'll be a bit late back from work. [*To* BUSYGIN.] We've got a serious programme today — Glinka and Berlioz. [*To* NINA.] So could you try and get in a little bit earlier? . . .
NINA: All right.
SARAFANOV: And now . . . What's the time? . . . Gone nine? Time we had some breakfast.
NINA: [*going to window, opening it.*] Yes, but first we ought to tidy

up a bit. Everybody into the other room! [*Looking out of window.*] Vasenka, there's Natalia. Dressed to kill. Come and feast your eyes on her.

[SILVA, SARAFANOV *and* BUSYGIN *go to window.*]

SARAFANOV: [*to* BUSYGIN.] That's her.

BUSYGIN: Well, she's a good looker.

SILVA: Who is she?

SARAFANOV: One of our neighbours.

NINA: The local lovely. [*To* VASENKA.] Why are you still sitting there? Go and say goodbye to her. You haven't said goodbye to her yet today.

VASENKA: Leave off!

NINA: Or have you sent her your letter?

VASENKA: Leave off, I said. What do you want with me?

NINA: I don't want you going round the bend. You must think first, and then go round the bend!

BUSYGIN: Really? Better the other way round.

NINA: Is it?

BUSYGIN: That's what I think.

NINA: How silly of you!

SARAFANOV: I think Volodia's right. No harm in thinking, of course, but . . .

NINA: Go on, go on, defend him, stand up for him. If you want him to go quite crazy.

VASENKA: [*getting up, to* NINA.] You can think as much as you like, but I don't want to. I want to go round the bend, do you understand? Go round the bend and not think about anything! Leave me alone! [*Goes into next room.*]

BUSYGIN: [*to* NINA.] Why are you so hard on him?

SARAFANOV: You shouldn't, Nina. Believe me. You're only making things worse.

NINA: What does he think he's up to? Of all the people to grovel in front of!

SARAFANOV: You're wrong there. She's a good girl.

BUSYGIN: It's understandable. She's a good looker . . .

NINA: Oh yes? Do you think so?

BUSYGIN: Sure. Outwardly at least, she's very attractive.

NINA: In that case you've got no taste. Come away from the window everybody. I'm going to start tidying up. Planting herself in that chair! On display . . . Show-time!

SILVA: You know what'd be best of all? Not to think about anything, and not go round the bend. I reckon things'd be quieter that way.
NINA: I said I was going to tidy up. Did you hear?
SARAFANOV: All right, all right. Come along, Volodia.
BUSYGIN: You go. I'll stay here a minute.
SARAFANOV: All right. [*Goes into next room.*]
SILVA: [*at the window.*] You know, Nina, I think you're right. I don't think that Natalia's anything special.
NINA: All right, that'll do. Everybody out! [*Goes into kitchen.*]
SILVA: [*showing his delight, snapping his fingers.*] She's a cracker, your kid sister! Let me help her tidy up.
BUSYGIN: No, I've got to have a chat with her.
SILVA: Now look! You're her brother. What sort of chat can you have together?
BUSYGIN: Family matters. [*Ushering* SILVA *towards the door.*]
SILVA: [*resisting*] What if I've fallen in love?
BUSYGIN: Off you go. And keep Dad out of the way.
SILVA: Who?
BUSYGIN: Her father, who do you think? Don't you understand? . . . Hurry up. [*Having pushed* SILVA *out, closes the door.*] [*Enter* NINA *with brush and cloth.*]
I'll give you a hand . . . if you don't mind.
NINA: Yes, do . . . You can sweep the floor. Know how to? [*Enter* SILVA.]
SILVA: I'll give you a hand.
NINA: Thank you, but I think the two of us can manage.
SILVA: But maybe I could move something, or take something out . . .
BUSYGIN: You'll only be in the way.
SILVA: Just look at you, children! [*Leads* BUSYGIN *and* NINA *to mirror.*] You're so alike! It brings tears to my eyes.
BUSYGIN: Off you go. [*Ushering* SILVA *out.*] Can't I have a word with my sister? [*Closes door behind him.*]
NINA: No, we're not at all alike. Absolutely no resemblance . . .
BUSYGIN: Maybe.
NINA: It's funny . . . Of course, Dad's capable of anything, but I never thought . . . Whoever would have thought I had a brother, an elder brother? And such a good-looking one.

BUSYGIN: And what about me? Do you think I ever imagined I had such a nice little sister?
NINA: Nice?
BUSYGIN: Sure!
NINA: Do you think so?
BUSYGIN: I think you're beautiful.
NINA: Nice? Or beautiful? I don't quite understand.
BUSYGIN: Both, but . . . I must have a talk with you . . .
NINA: Oh?
BUSYGIN: I hear you're leaving home . . .
NINA: Yes, I'm leaving . . . What of it? Father will have told you.
BUSYGIN: Yes . . . And you're going, I gather . . . for good?
NINA: That's right. What's worrying you?
BUSYGIN: Me? . . . The thing is this: Dad's not as young as he used to be, and his health isn't what it was, . . . and you know what he's like . . . Well, being the way he is, and having Vasenka leave home, . . . You see what I mean? . . .
NINA: No.
BUSYGIN: But he'll be left all alone.
NINA: Yes . . . So?
BUSYGIN: But couldn't you . . .
NINA: Take him with me?
BUSYGIN: Well, er . . . Either that or stay here.
NINA: I see . . . Aren't you a dutiful son?
BUSYGIN: But after all he is your father.
NINA: Isn't he yours too? . . . And seeing you're such a dutiful son, why don't you take him home with you?
BUSYGIN: Me?
NINA: Why do you look so surprised? You're the elder son. Come to that, it's your duty . . . Isn't it?
BUSYGIN: Yes, but . . . You see, I . . . I only came along yesterday. And besides, you're forgetting my mother.
NINA: And you're forgetting my fiancé . . . [*Starts tidying.*] It's easy for you to be so dutiful. From the sidelines . . . Nobody's going to abandon him here. He'll come to my wedding, we'll help him, we'll write, and later on . . We're only leaving him here for a while, a year, maybe a year and a half.
BUSYGIN: You mean pilots get a year and a half for their honeymoons?

NINA: Don't you like the fact that he's a pilot?
BUSYGIN: Why shouldn't I? That's fine with me . . . Excellent . . . Splendid. "Fly not from me, my dearest" . . .
NINA: I don't understand your tone . . . I'll introduce you to him today. He's a good boy.
BUSYGIN: I can imagine. I expect he's big, and generous.
NINA: Yes, he is.
BUSYGIN: Ugly, but charming.
NINA: That's right.
BUSYGIN: Cheerful, attentive, talks easily . . .
NINA: Yes, quite right. How do you know all this?
BUSYGIN: Headstrong, purposeful. Put simply, in him you'll have a tower of strength to protect you.
NINA: That's all true. He's headstrong and purposeful. Nothing wrong with that, is there? At least he knows exactly what he wants in life. He won't take on more than he can handle, but he's as good as his word. Not like some, who'll make you a cartload of promises, but can't do more than fool around.
BUSYGIN: I suppose he never ever tells you lies.
NINA: No, he doesn't. Why should he?
BUSYGIN: He doesn't? I want to see him. Show him to me. Let me just get a glimpse of him.
NINA: You'll see him this evening.
BUSYGIN: Can't I see him in daylight? I want to get a good look at him. Never lies, you say. Remarkable.
NINA: Listen! What have you got against him? He's a plain, modest sort of lad. Maybe he won't pluck stars down from the sky, but so what? I actually prefer it that way. I don't want a poet, I want a husband.
BUSYGIN: Oh well, in that case that's fine. Just what you want.
NINA: Wait a minute! You don't even know him!
BUSYGIN: So what? I know you.
NINA: You know me? When did you manage that?
BUSYGIN: Just now.
NINA: Well! Aren't you gifted?! Talks to me for five minutes and knows everything about me!
BUSYGIN: Not everything.
NINA: Then what do you know?
BUSYGIN: I know what you want.

NINA: And what do I want?
BUSYGIN: A husband. You said so yourself.
NINA: [*angrily*] Well! That's a bit much, you know! . . . You . . . Who are you to say things like that to me?
BUSYGIN: Things like what?
NINA: You've never seen him, have you? So why attack him like that? If you want to know, he's no worse than you! Not a bit!
BUSYGIN: I don't doubt it.
NINA: He's a better man than you!
BUSYGIN: I won't deny it. There's no comparison. Of course he's better.
NINA: He's broader in the shoulders, and taller! Half a head taller!
BUSYGIN: [*spreading his arms.*] All the better for you.
NINA: What do you mean — all the better? . . . You're a cheeky upstart! That's what you are!
BUSYGIN: Am I?
NINA: And a crank! Your father's one, and you're another.
BUSYGIN: Thanks.
NINA: Any time!

> [*Pause.* NINA *sweeps floor,* BUSYGIN *wipes furniture. They accidentally bump into each other by the table and stop work.*]

Are you cross?
BUSYGIN: No . . .
NINA: I got steamed up . . . And I might say the same for you.
BUSYGIN: No, you're right. I really shouldn't have gone for him like that.
NINA: Shall we make peace, then? [*Stretches out hands to him.*] You're not angry with me for scolding you?
BUSYGIN: [*draws her to him.*] Of course I'm not.

> [*They stand face to face and seem about to kiss. Short pause. Then they suddenly start back at once.*]

[*Coughing very unnaturally.*] We haven't decided what to do about Father . . .
NINA: [*still thinking about what has just happened.*] You're a bit odd . . .
BUSYGIN: Look, we've got to decide . . .
NINA: Very odd . . .
BUSYGIN: About Dad, I mean . . . What's so odd? It's just that I

didn't sleep all night. Nothing odd about that.
[*Enter* SARAFANOV *and* SILVA. SILVA *strumming on his guitar.*]
Dad! How are you feeling?

SARAFANOV: Fine, son.

SILVA: [*singing*] "Oh, in the station waiting-room
　　　　　　　Two foundlings were discovered.
　　　　　　　The first was eighteen years of age.
　　　　　　　And twenty-three the other!"

ACT TWO
SCENE ONE

The courtyard. MAKARSKAIA's *house, the poplar, the bench, part of the fence. The street cannot be seen.* MAKARSKAIA *is sitting on the bench, looking towards the gate. Enter* VASENKA. *He stops in indecision, then proceeds towards the gate with an exaggeratedly sprightly step.*

MAKARSKAIA: [*noticing him.*] Vasenka!
  [VASENKA *stops dead.*] Come here. I'll give you a spanking. For yesterday's performance.
VASENKA: [*not turning round*] If that's what you want you can find somebody else.
MAKARSKAIA: Come on, don't be afraid.
VASENKA: In a good mood, are you? In the mood to play? . . . I've had enough of playing the mouse.
MAKARSKAIA: Come here, you silly boy.
VASENKA: [*unable to resist, turns and approaches her.*] Here I am . . . You can eat me for breakfast . . . if you want.
MAKARSKAIA: What a funny boy you are . . . Want to go to the pictures with me?
VASENKA: [*after pause.*] Seriously? . . . When?
MAKARSKAIA: What's on? Is there anything worth seeing?
VASENKA: Sure! An Italian film! It's on here, right nearby.
MAKARSKAIA: What's it about?
VASENKA: It's called "Divorce Italian Style".

MAKARSKAIA: About divorce? I'm not going! I'm sick of divorces at work. Two cases out of three are divorces. Hardly a day goes by without one. So it's the same in Italy, is it?
VASENKA: No! It's all different there.
MAKARSKAIA: I've seen enough of them, I tell you! And heard enough! And they've made an impression. I'm not planning to get married.
VASENKA: There's another film on . . . But it's about divorce too. "Day of Happiness".
MAKARSKAIA: Why's it called that?
VASENKA: It's about a woman who leaves a bad husband for a good one.
MAKARSKAIA: She must have got something wrong. Is there anything else on, or is that all?
VASENKA: That's all.
MAKARSKAIA: Let's take the Italian style then.
VASENKA: Shall I go and get the tickets?
MAKARSKAIA: Yes, off you go, Muggins.
VASENKA: Which showing?
MAKARSKAIA: Whichever you like.
VASENKA: Then we'll go to all of them. Non-stop. For the next forty years. [*Exit.*]
MAKARSKAIA: The poor boy's gone quite wild.
[*Enter* SILVA.]
SILVA: Morning, Natasha.
MAKARSKAIA: Good morning.
SILVA: Mind if I sit down?
MAKARSKAIA: I won't object.
SILVA: [*sitting down.*] My name's Silva.
MAKARSKAIA: Good. How come you know my name?
SILVA: Don't be surprised. I've been observing you for a long time.
MAKARSKAIA: Really?
SILVA: Admiring you, I should say.
MAKARSKAIA: And where have you seen me?
SILVA: I'll never tell.
MAKARSKAIA: I see . . . Then I'll tell you.
SILVA: How's that? Have you seen me too?
MAKARSKAIA: Where did you get divorced?
SILVA: Come again?

MAKARSKAIA: Which court did you get divorced in?
SILVA: What's this? I've never done anything like that. I don't like bringing the State into my private affairs. It's got plenty to think about without me.
MAKARSKAIA: I work in court, as a secretary. Isn't that where we met?
SILVA: No. Thank goodness!
MAKARSKAIA: I sometimes think all men have appeared in our court. Just an impression I have.
SILVA: Well, I don't know! A girl like you doing such dirty work . . . Is that your house?
MAKARSKAIA: Yes.
SILVA: And I know you live alone. Why's that, if you don't mind my asking?
MAKARSKAIA: Why do I live alone? I prefer it. Why? Do you object?
SILVA: Not at all! On the contrary. It's romantic. You can invite me to come visiting.
MAKARSKAIA: On what pretext?
SILVA: Don't you like me?
MAKARSKAIA: Like you? You're all right. A likable rogue.
SILVA: Rogue? I don't deny it. But rogues need love too.
MAKARSKAIA: Looks as if the world's split into two camps: serious suitors and rogues. The serious suitors bore you stiff, and the rogues make you cry. What a life!
SILVA: What are you doing this evening?
MAKARSKAIA: I'm going to the pictures. [*Stands up and goes towards house.*]
SILVA: [*following her.*] The pictures . . . That's good . . . But couldn't you postpone it for a while?
MAKARSKAIA: [*on steps.*] Why should I?
SILVA: Can I come and see where you live?
MAKARSKAIA: Come in. I expect you'll break in otherwise.
SILVA: True. [*Follows her into house.*]
[NINA *and* BUSYGIN *emerge from entrance to building.* NINA *in raincoat, with handbag.*]
BUSYGIN: No, go by yourself. I'd better go with Dad. I'll listen to the music. Glinka, Berlioz . . .
NINA: I wouldn't recommend it.

BUSYGIN: Why not?

NINA: You won't hear any Berlioz.

BUSYGIN: How come? Didn't Dad say . . .

NINA: Never mind what he said. It's six months since he last worked for the Philharmonic.

BUSYGIN: No kidding?

NINA: No. And it's best for you to know it.

BUSYGIN: Then where does he work?

NINA: He used to work in a cinema, but not long ago the railwaymen's club took him on. He plays at dances there.

BUSYGIN: Does he?

NINA: But remember: he mustn't know that you know.

BUSYGIN: I see.

NINA: Naturally everybody's known it for ages, but we — that is him, Vasenka, and me — go on pretending he's still in the philharmonic orchestra. It's our family secret.

BUSYGIN: Well, if he prefers it that way . . .

NINA: I don't remember my mother, but a little while back I found her letters. In them she always calls him a simpleton: "My dear simpleton . . ." "You must realize, simpleton though you are" "Think of yourself, simpleton . . ." "You've got a family, simpleton . . ." "Goodbye, simpleton . . ." And she's right . . . He's always getting into trouble at work. He's not a bad musician, but he's never been able to stand up for himself. And to make matters worse, he likes a drink, so last autumn, when they had a cut-back in the orchestra, he was an obvious candidate . . .

BUSYGIN: Just a moment. He said he composed music himself.

NINA: [*ironically*] Sure he does.

BUSYGIN: What sort of music?

NINA: What sort? . . . World-shaking music. Either a cantata or an oratorio. It's called "All Men are Brothers." He's been composing it for as long as I can remember.

BUSYGIN: And how's it going? Is the end in sight?

NINA: Is it hell! He's written one whole page.

BUSYGIN: One?

NINA: One. Just once — last year — he started on Page Two. But now he's back on Page One.

BUSYGIN: I see he's conscientious.

NINA: He's not normal.
BUSYGIN: Maybe that's the way you have to work to compose music.
NINA: That's just the way he argues . . . Still, it's a shame . . .
BUSYGIN: What's a shame?
NINA: It's a shame I have to leave you . . . I can't understand it. I was so anxious to go, and now that I've only a few days left . . . I'm sorry to leave Vaska behind. And you. Even though I didn't know anything about you yesterday . . . Listen! Where were you all that time? Why didn't you come along sooner?
BUSYGIN: But you know why.
NINA: You should have come sooner. You'd have taken me to the cinema, and to dances, protected me, knocked some sense into me. Instead you just turn up, out of the blue — Here I am! On my last day, as if you'd planned it. It really is too low.
BUSYGIN: I can't help that . . . Stay here if you want to. [*Hastily corrects himself.*] Hang on a bit, I mean.
NINA: What for?
BUSYGIN: What for? . . . We'll go to the cinema, to dances . . .
NINA: But you're leaving tomorrow.
BUSYGIN: But . . . I'll come back.
NINA: No, everything's arranged now.
BUSYGIN: Where are you meeting him?
NINA: In town, as usual.
BUSYGIN: When'll you be back?
NINA: We're going to the pictures. We'll get here about eight . . . Come with us if you like.
BUSYGIN: What'd I do there? . . . No. I'll meet your pilot this evening.
NINA: I hope you'll like him. He's nice, he treats me well . . . And don't get the idea he's the first to fancy me. I had plenty to choose from.
BUSYGIN: Why choose him? Is he better than all the rest?
NINA: He loves me . . . You know, it's all very well having wild, romantic flings, but you need to have something fixed and permanent in life.
BUSYGIN: I see.
NINA: What do you see this time?

[*Sound of* MAKARSKAIA's *laughter from her house.*]

BUSYGIN: She's a happy soul.
NINA: That's putting it mildly. She's made another pick-up . . .
BUSYGIN: You're too hard on her. She's a nice woman.
NINA: How do you know what she's like?
BUSYGIN: I know her.
NINA: Do you?
BUSYGIN: Last night when we were looking for your flat I spoke to her . . .
NINA: Did you?
BUSYGIN: I liked her.
NINA: You liked her, did you?
BUSYGIN: Why shouldn't I?
NINA: Her?
BUSYGIN: And why not? She's likable . . .
NINA: She's old.
BUSYGIN: She's blonde. I like blondes.
NINA: Her hair's dyed.
  [MAKARSKAIA's *laughter is heard again.*]
BUSYGIN: Plenty of *joie de vivre*. I like women like that.
NINA: I can't bear her!
BUSYGIN: She's lonely. I always feel sorry for lonely people.
NINA: I loathe her!
BUSYGIN: [*flirtatiously*] I think I might give her a try.
NINA: No! Don't you dare go near her!
BUSYGIN: Hey! . . . That sounds like jealousy speaking.
NINA: [*surprised*] What?
BUSYGIN: Not jealous, are you?
NINA: [*scared*] Jealous? . . . [*Confused*] Yes . . . Of course I'm jealous. Can't a sister be jealous?
BUSYGIN: [*forgetting his role.*] Sister? Some sister! . . . [*Remembering his role.*] Oh yes, a sister can be jealous! Of course she can. If she likes . . . If she gets on well with him . . .
NINA: [*uncertainly*] Of course . . .
BUSYGIN: That's quite normal. In the Caucasus they even cut each other's throats for less . . . But you've got to hurry, or you'll be late.
NINA: [*collecting thoughts.*] Oh yes! It's late . . . I'm off . . . [*Starts to leave, but turns back.*] In the Caucasus doesn't it sometimes happen that a sister falls in love with her brother?

BUSYGIN: Falls in love? . . . No, that never happens.
NINA: Is that so? [*Laughs*] I thought it did . . .
BUSYGIN: [*also laughing.*] I don't think it's possible.
NINA: [*laughing*] Not possible?
BUSYGIN: I don't think so.
NINA: [*laughs*] What a pity . . . [*Stops laughing.*] There's never a dull moment when you're around, you know?
BUSYGIN: With me? No, never!
NINA: Right, I'll be going . . . Wake Dad at about two. The food's on the stove. Just heat it up. And keep an eye on our little brother. See he doesn't run away.
BUSYGIN: He won't. We've got an agreement.
NINA: Watch him, Dad's counting on you . . . See you! [*Comes close to him.*] And don't get mixed up with her. [*Gestures towards* MAKARSKAIA*'s house.*] Okay?
BUSYGIN: Okay . . . See you.
NINA: 'Bye, brother. [*Exit.*]
BUSYGIN: [*waving, in soft voice*] Goodbye, sister.
  [SILVA *and* MAKARSKAIA *emerge onto the steps.* MAKARSKAIA *is laughing.* BUSYGIN *stands by the gate, out of sight to them.*]
SILVA: So when the evening sun gilds the treetops we'll . . .
MAKARSKAIA: [*in doorway, laughing.*] All right, all right . . . See you later!
SILVA: [*in businesslike tone.*] At ten, then.
MAKARSKAIA: Yes, at ten . . . [*Vanishes, closing door.*]
  [SILVA *comes down steps. Notices* BUSYGIN.]
SILVA: Ah, Monsieur Sarafanov! [*Coming closer.*] Life surges on. [*Gestures towards* MAKARSKAIA*'s house.*] Did you hear?
BUSYGIN: Yes.
SILVA: What are you so glum about? What's up? Are you the son of the family, or a poor relation?
BUSYGIN: Don't you think we've outstayed our welcome?
SILVA: Not at all. Everything's as it should be. I'm getting to like it here. It's not bad for you either. You're making headway.
BUSYGIN: Headway with what?
SILVA: I mean affairs of the heart.
BUSYGIN: There's nothing like that . . .
SILVA: Pull the other leg! Think I can't see? You're onto a good deal. And it's mutual. I can hardly bear to look at the two of you — it brings tears to the eyes.

BUSYGIN: Cut it out. She's getting married.
SILVA: So I've heard, but . . .
BUSYGIN: [*interrupting*] And she's leaving in a few days. So much for the good deal . . . We've had a good time, enjoyed our stay, and now it's time we were on our way. Get ready to go.
SILVA: Go where?
BUSYGIN: Home.
SILVA: Hold it . . . Why? I've got a date at ten.
BUSYGIN: It's off. Why the hell do you have to push in where you're not wanted? Can't you see what a state the kid's in because of that woman?
SILVA: Is that my fault?
BUSYGIN: Stop playing the fool. And no dates. We're going home.
SILVA: Not on your life! I can't let the lady down.
BUSYGIN: Oh yes, you can. Go and say goodbye to her. Tell her that when the evening sun gilds the treetops you'll be far away.
SILVA: What have you thought up this time? . . . We'll come back here tonight, eh?
BUSYGIN: What for?
SILVA: We won't? Then you go, and I'll . . .
BUSYGIN: We'll go together.
SILVA: Why? . . . Look, I realize you've got some plans of your own. But I don't know what they are, so why should I have to suffer? If you'd tell me, that'd be different. But you're keeping me completely in the dark. That's not right. No way for a friend to behave.
BUSYGIN: All right. Since we're friends, I'm asking you as a friend to go with me. You said yourself that you're my friend.
SILVA: That's true, I am. But that doesn't mean you can walk all over me. I can't touch your sister, and now I can't touch the other one either. What sort of life is that?
BUSYGIN: To put it plainly: if you so much as tap on that door ever again [*Indicates* MAKARSKAIA's *door.*] it'll end badly for you. Clear? . . . Well? Are you staying?
SILVA: To hell with her! Why should we fall out because of a woman? Let's go . . . I'm only making this stupid gesture because you're my friend. In the name of male friendship.
BUSYGIN: All right, all right . . .
SILVA: Wait for me here. I'll get my guitar.

BUSYGIN: I'll go in as well.
SILVA: I wouldn't do that if I were you. The old man's there. He'll keep you talking for another two hours.
BUSYGIN: He's asleep. I'll leave him a note.
[*Enter* VASENKA *suddenly.*]
SILVA: Ah! Our little pigeon's come flying home!
VASENKA: Crawled out to warm yourselves, have you?
BUSYGIN: Where've you been, lad?
VASENKA: None of your business, you vultures!
SILVA: You're in a good mood. Just won a game of hop-scotch?
VASENKA: Dad in?
BUSYGIN: He's asleep.
VASENKA: What are you up to?
SILVA: Us? Your brother's up to his knightly deeds, and me . . . I wouldn't mind a drink.
VASENKA: Go in, then. We've got some in the kitchen, behind the radiator. That's where Dad keep his emergency stocks.
SILVA: Emergency? What is it exactly?
VASENKA: I don't know. Some herbal spirit, I think. That do?
SILVA: Herbal? Well, there are better things to drink . . . Still, it'll do.
BUSYGIN: [*to* SILVA.] Go on, I'll follow.
[SILVA *disappears in doorway.*]
Well then, are we agreed?
VASENKA: Everything's fine.
BUSYGIN: As for me, I've got to go . . . Maybe even today. And I hope you won't let me down.
VASENKA: I'm staying. Nothing'll alter that now.
BUSYGIN: I know. You're a strong-minded lad.
VASENKA: All right then. Off you go.
BUSYGIN: Yes, sir! [*Disappears in doorway.*]
[VASENKA *knocks on* MAKARSKAIA's *door.* MAKARSKAIA *comes out.*]
MAKARSKAIA: Got the tickets?
VASENKA: Yeah! You should have seen the scramble for them!
MAKARSKAIA: I can imagine. Where are your buttons?
VASENKA: Scattered all over the place!
MAKARSKAIA: Give me that one, at least. Wait here. [*Goes into house.*]

[VASENKA *takes sealed envelope and matches from pocket, and lights envelope by steps of her house.*]
[*Reappearing*] What are you doing?
VASENKA: [*brightly*] Just burning a letter.
MAKARSKAIA: Give me your jacket.
[*They sit for a while in silence, side by side on the steps.* VASENKA *suddenly buries his head in her shoulder.*]
What's the matter?
VASENKA: I don't know.
MAKARSKAIA: Steady, steady! . . . [*Raising his head with a condescending gesture.*] Gone all soppy, the silly boy!
VASENKA: Sorry. It . . . It'll pass . . .
MAKARSKAIA: [*hands back his jacket.*] There you are. When that button falls off you'll forget me. It'll be a sign . . . Hold on. Which showing did you get tickets for?
VASENKA: The last. At ten o'clock . . . Why?
MAKARSKAIA: Ten o'clock? Are you mad?
VASENKA: But you said — any one you like.
MAKARSKAIA: Any one except that one!
VASENKA: You said . . .
MAKARSKAIA: Vasenka, my dear boy, I can't come at ten.
VASENKA: Any one you like — you said.
MAKARSKAIA: Vasenka! I can't possibly come at ten!
VASENKA: Why not?
MAKARSKAIA: I just can't.
VASENKA: Why can't you?
MAKARSKAIA: If I say I can't, I can't! Go and get some other tickets if you still want to take me to the pictures.
VASENKA: But why? I have to know.
MAKARSKAIA: Have to know? What makes you think that? Why should you have to know everything? . . . And don't look at me like that.
VASENKA: What's happened? You've got a date.
MAKARSKAIA: Since when were you the public prosecutor? [*Screams*] Don't look at me like that, I tell you! Who gave you the right to look at me like that?
VASENKA: Have you got a date?
MAKARSKAIA: Yes, you've guessed it! I have! What about it?
VASENKA: Why did you do that?

MAKARSKAIA: It just happened that after you'd gone for the tickets the situation changed.
VASENKA: What changed?
MAKARSKAIA: Will you stop interrogating me?
VASENKA: What changed?!
MAKARSKAIA: I took a liking to a boy, that's what! You asked for it. There you are!
VASENKA: And where did this boy suddenly spring from, eh?
MAKARSKAIA: My God! You make me tired! . . .
VASENKA: Why did you send me off to get these tickets, you sadist?
MAKARSKAIA: Because I felt sorry for you! Sorry for your father.
VASENKA: W-what? . . . How does my father come into it?
MAKARSKAIA: He was here last night, matchmaking.
VASENKA: I don't believe you!
MAKARSKAIA: What sort of family do you come from? For goodness sake! Trying to pair me off with a little idiot! What an idea!
VASENKA: [*grabbing her by the arm.*] I'll . . . I'll kill you!
MAKARSKAIA: You? Ha-ha! Don't make me laugh. You wouldn't hurt a fly. You couldn't. [*Jerks her hand free.*] Listen, child, that'll do. The show's over. Off you go and don't get into mischief. Before you get a whipping. [*Exit, slamming door.*] [BUSYGIN *and* SILVA, *with guitar, emerge from doorway. They see* VASENKA *suddenly tearing off the button sewn on by* MAKARSKAIA, *and flinging it onto the ground.*]
BUSYGIN: What's the trouble, little brother? . . . What's happened?
[VASENKA *stands speechless.*]
Somebody hurt your feelings? . . . Not her?
SILVA: [*to* VASENKA.] Know what my advice to you is, old fellow? Forget it. For the time being. You love a girl, and she's giving you the run-around. That's normal. But you just wait and see what she does when you stop loving her.
BUSYGIN: Cut that rubbish out!
[VASENKA *runs into doorway. Exit.*]
You blockhead. See what you've done?
SILVA: Why do you take it so much to heart, eh? You feeling all right? Do you think he really is your brother, or something?
BUSYGIN: Damnation . . . What do we do now?
SILVA: What do we do? Clear out, now that we're all ready.

[*Enter* SARAFANOV.]
[*softly*] Too late. He's woken up.
SARAFANOV: Volodia!
BUSYGIN: What is it?
SARAFANOV: [*despairingly*] He's packing his rucksack! [*Disappears in entrance.*]
SILVA: That'll do. Let's get going.
BUSYGIN: [*annoyed*] I'm staying.
SILVA: Well! That's news! [*Runs his thumb over the strings of his guitar.*] Here we go again, eh? . . . You know, I've had enough of this game.

SCENE TWO

The SARAFANOVS' *flat. After eight in the evening.* BUSYGIN *is standing by the door into next room.* SILVA *is lying on settee, playing his guitar.*

SILVA: [*singing*] "Ah, children, children, dearest children,
             My heart would break to see you so.
             It cannot be, the laws forbid it,
             That a boy should love his sister so . . ."
BUSYGIN: Be quiet.
SILVA: I reckon he's been asleep a long time.
BUSYGIN: He's not asleep, that's the point. He's been staring at the ceiling [*Glances at his watch.*] for over five hours.
SILVA: Maybe he's dead.
BUSYGIN: [*opens door slightly.*] Listen, lad, what are you staring at? Learned something interesting? About the life-cycle of the cockroach? . . . [*Pauses, then closes door.*] It's no use.
SILVA: Why do you have to stand guard over the boy just because you fancy the girl? I don't follow. Hey! What relation will that guy be to you if she marries . . . Your brother-in-law?
BUSYGIN: I suppose so.
SILVA: So he will. Your brother-in-law. [*Laughs*] I envy you already. What does he do?

BUSYGIN: He's an air force cadet. Top of the class in political and combat training.
SILVA: I can just see what's going to happen here. Maybe you'd better make yourself scarce . . . I know: you want to see your little sister again.
BUSYGIN: Maybe I do.
SILVA: I know. You want to have a heart-to-heart talk with her. Right?
BUSYGIN: Mind your own business.
SILVA: And what about the cadet? And then the old man'll roll up. You'll have a great time. And what do I do? [*Lays guitar aside. Picks up the* SARAFANOV *family album and starts leafing through it.*]
BUSYGIN: You can go to the cinema. Here are some tickets. He threw them away.
SILVA: Did he now? They lay on everything in this house. [*Takes tickets.*] I'll think about it. [*Turns pages of album.*]
BUSYGIN: Have you spoken to that girl?
SILVA: What about? [*Shows album to* BUSYGIN.] Look at this. Looks like the old man was young once.
BUSYGIN: Have you told her it's all over between you?
SILVA: No, I haven't seen her again.
BUSYGIN: You might let her know.
SILVA: She'll be all right. She's a big girl. I've forgotten I ever knew her — that's what you wanted . . . Not bad, though, is she? . . . What do you reckon?
BUSYGIN: Don't you dare take her to the pictures.
SILVA: Come on! What do you take me for? . . . With women the main thing is never to forget that there are plenty of other women in the world . . . I'm giving up this one. In the name of male friendship. Although there is something rather satisfying about it — a sacrifice for the sake of your friend. It's even good for my self-respect. Yes, here I lie, respecting myself. [*Turns pages, shows* BUSYGIN.] Here's your sister in her early youth. In classical pose. Take a look. Feast your eyes.
BUSYGIN: I've seen it.
SILVA: [*turning pages again.*] What about this? After the school-leavers' ball. Strolling in the street. What a beauty! . . . Wow! She's the nicest of the lot. [*Turns pages again, groans.*] Mmm

... The beach! This is the best one ... [*Shows* BUSYGIN.] Seen this?

BUSYGIN: Yes, unfortunately. Best if I don't look at that one.

SILVA: Know what happened to me at the beach once? This girl was drowning, and I pulled her out.

BUSYGIN: [*absent-mindedly*] And?

SILVA: And nothing. As long as I was dragging her I couldn't see anything, but when I'd fished her out I looked — and she was ugly. Real tough luck. [*Flicks the photograph.*] If only I could save one like that! Her drowning, and me saving her! That wouldn't be a bad start, eh?

BUSYGIN: Why don't you go to the cinema?

[*Knock at door is heard.*]

Come in, the door's open.

[*Enter* KUDIMOV, *a flying-school cadet, with a bouquet and two bottles of champagne in his hands.*]

KUDIMOV: Good evening.

BUSYGIN: Good evening.

KUDIMOV: Is this the Sarafanovs' flat?

BUSYGIN: Yes.

KUDIMOV: Isn't Nina back yet?

BUSYGIN: Not yet.

KUDIMOV: [*approaching table.*] What a damned nuisance! I haven't got that long.

[*Stands bottles on table.*] We lost each other in the grocer's shop. [*Takes a glass from the table. His movements are energetic.*]

BUSYGIN: [*politely*] I gather you haven't been here before?

KUDIMOV: [*pushing bouquet into glass.*] That's right, I haven't. [*Smiles. Now, as later, he smiles a lot. Seems good-natured.*]

BUSYGIN: But you've ... er ... got your bearings all right?

KUDIMOV: Sure! [*Winks*] I know my way around. [*Stands glass with flowers on table.*] Well then, fellers, let's get to know each other.

BUSYGIN: All right. [*They shake hands.*]

KUDIMOV: Mikhail's the name.

BUSYGIN: Vladimir.

KUDIMOV: So you're the one? ... I've heard all about it ... My sympathies ... Pleased to meet you.

BUSYGIN: Thank you for your sympathy.
KUDIMOV: [*to* SILVA.] Mikhail.
SILVA: [*with dignity.*] Semion Paramonovich Sevostianov.
KUDIMOV: Paramonovich? Not the comedian, are you?
SILVA: Comedian? I beg your pardon. Whom do you have in mind?
KUDIMOV: You know. The actor, Paramonovich. [*Claps* SILVA *on the shoulder.*]
SILVA: [*coldly*] Don't you think you're being a little bit too free and easy?
KUDIMOV: Okay, okay, take it easy! . . . [*Looks at watch.*] Blast! I have to be back at barracks by half past ten. Well, shall we have a drink now, or wait for Nina?
SILVA: [*coldly*] We'll have one now.
KUDIMOV: Where's the old man?
BUSYGIN: Whom are you referring to as "the old man"?
KUDIMOV: Who do you think? . . . Nina's dad, your dad!
BUSYGIN: You don't even know him, and you're already calling him "the old man" . . . Anyway, he's at work.
SILVA: Do take a seat.
KUDIMOV: Bugger this! Why are you being so polite?
SILVA: And why are you being so familiar? We find it quite shocking.
KUDIMOV: [*heartily*] Come on, fellers! Let's have a bit less of this formality. I've had seniority and juniority up to here. [*Points*] Let's do without any of that! . . . And drink to it!
[KUDIMOV *and* SILVA *drink.*]
SILVA: [*to* BUSYGIN.] These airmen are always the same. You can't change them. [*Sits down on settee. To* KUDIMOV.] Pray be seated.
KUDIMOV: Oh, come on! Is this some sort of parliament, or something?
SILVA: Something like that. [*Strums on guitar.*] Do your superiors allow you to get married, I wonder?
BUSYGIN: [*to* SILVA.] Be quiet.
KUDIMOV: Why shouldn't they? I'm finishing flying school.
SILVA: But I wonder . . .
BUSYGIN: I said shut up.
KUDIMOV: It's all right. Let him have his little joke. I don't mind.
[*Enter* NINA.]

NINA: [*to* KUDIMOV.] Ah, here already. [*To the others.*] Hullo. [*Comes into room.*] Introduced yourselves, have you?
SILVA: That we have.
KUDIMOV: Pair of merry lads, these. That's what I like . . . Well, let's have a drink, shall we? Mustn't waste time.
SILVA: Quite right.
NINA: There's no hurry. Let's wait for Dad.
KUDIMOV: All right, we'll wait. But I have to go in half an hour.
SILVA: What a life! Rules and regulations. The slightest offence, like being late, and it's off to the glasshouse you go. Tough, isn't it?
KUDIMOV: I'm not complaining.
BUSYGIN: What's the penalty for being late?
KUDIMOV: I'm never late.
BUSYGIN: I thought as much.
NINA: Come to think of it, it wouldn't be such a disaster if you were late today. Just for once.
KUDIMOV: Why should I be late?
BUSYGIN: Yes, why should he be late?
NINA: [*to* KUDIMOV.] Today you'll be a little late.
KUDIMOV: Why?
NINA: Because I say so. You just will.
KUDIMOV: If it's really necessary, I don't mind. But I don't see any point in being late for no reason. I'm sorry.
BUSYGIN: That's the way, cadet. Don't give in. Discipline must come first.
KUDIMOV: That's not the point. I've promised myself never to be late. And I always keep my promises.
NINA: But you'll be late today. I want you to.
BUSYGIN: Don't listen to her, cadet. Stick to your principles.
[*Enter* SARAFANOV, *looking exhausted, but in lyrical mood.*]
SARAFANOV: Evening, you ruffians! [*Sees* KUDIMOV.] So sorry.
NINA: Dad, come and meet Mikhail . . .
KUDIMOV: Kudimov's the name, Mikhail.
SARAFANOV: [*ceremoniously, with exaggerated dignity, and something of the air of a touring conductor, the darling of the audience.*] Sarafanov . . . Delighted to make your acquaintance . . . At last we meet in the flesh, so to speak. Delighted. Do sit down. [*To* BUSYGIN.] Is Vasenka in?

BUSYGIN: Yes. But he's in a bad mood.

[SARAFANOV *takes off his hat and puts it on the table. Sits down, still wearing his coat.* NINA *takes his hat out into the hall.*]

SARAFANOV: [*to* KUDIMOV.] This is my elder son. Have you met?

KUDIMOV: Yes, we have.

[NINA *returns.*]

SARAFANOV: Thank you . . . [*To* NINA *and* KUDIMOV.] Well then, you young people . . . You've already thought it over, and made up your minds, and as for us . . . We parents have to accept things as they are. That's our lot in life.

KUDIMOV: [*pouring champagne for all.*] With your permission — here's to your health, and our meeting.

[*All rise.*]

SARAFANOV: Well, I'm very glad. We're all glad, aren't we, Volodia?

NINA: [*to* BUSYGIN.] Are you glad or aren't you?

BUSYGIN: Your health, Dad.

KUDIMOV: Your health.

SILVA: Your health.

SARAFANOV: Thank you, thank you. But I have another toast to propose, my friends . . . I'll sit down, if you'll excuse me. [*Sits down.*] I'm tired . . . I'm tired today. I feel as if I'd walked from one end of town to the other . . . [*Seems embarrassed for a moment, then continues, posing slightly as before.*] Glinka, as you may know, was very fond of the clarinet, and in his compositions he always gave it plenty to do . . .

[*While* SARAFANOV *is speaking,* KUDIMOV *studies his face intently.*]

Yes . . . So here we are. Just now, on my way home, I was thinking about life. Whatever anybody says, life is always too clever for all of us who live and philosophize about life. Yes, life is just and merciful. It makes the heroes have doubts, and always consoles those who have accomplished little, even those who've accomplished nothing, but have lived their lives in purity of heart. Today I would like to drink to my children . . . [*Noticing* KUDIMOV'*s intent stare.*] Excuse me, but why are you looking at me like that?

KUDIMOV: I'm sorry, but I think I've seen you somewhere. I can't quite recall where or when, but I've seen you somewhere.

SARAFANOV: [*uneasily*] Perhaps so . . . I would like to drink to my children: to you, Volodia . . . [*to* NINA.] to you, and to Vasenka. [*To* KUDIMOV.] That's my youngest boy. He's having a rest at the moment. Here's to you, children. Your health, and happiness . . .
[*All drink, except* BUSYGIN.]
BUSYGIN: Your health, Dad. [*Drinks.*]
KUDIMOV: [*looking at* SARAFANOV.] I can't think where, but I've seen you. That's for sure.
NINA: Suppose you have, so what?
KUDIMOV: But where?
NINA: Does it matter?
KUDIMOV: I won't rest until I remember. It's always like that with me. Where was it? Where?
SARAFANOV: [*more uneasily, but not without optimism.*] I'm a musician. You might have seen me on the stand.
NINA: Dad's a musician. You know that perfectly well.
SARAFANOV: [*more uneasily, but still with some hope.*] At the Philharmonic, perhaps?
KUDIMOV: No, no . . .
SARAFANOV: [*hastily and categorically.*] Then it must have been at the theatre.
KUDIMOV: No, not the theatre . . .
NINA: Heavens! As if it mattered!
KUDIMOV: Just a minute, just a minute . . .
BUSYGIN: [*to* KUDIMOV.] Won't you be late? You've got eighteen minutes left.
KUDIMOV: Thanks, I'm keeping an eye on the clock . . . But I must remember where it was . . .
NINA: Oh, that's enough now! At this rate you'll be at it till your dying day.
KUDIMOV: That's it!
SILVA: At last.
KUDIMOV: I saw you in the street!
NINA: Thank heavens for that! I hope you feel better now.
KUDIMOV: Of course! You said "till your dying day", and it came to me at once.
[*To* SARAFANOV.] I saw you at a funeral.
[*Short pause.*]

NINA: What funeral?
KUDIMOV: Blast it! How could I forget? It was only last week, and you had that clarinet in your hands!
NINA: No, you're mistaken.
KUDIMOV: Never! It was some driver's funeral. You were going along Komintern Street at four o'clock.
NINA: You're mistaken, I tell you.
KUDIMOV: I'm not, Nina! I may have only caught a glimpse, but I have a good visual memory.
BUSYGIN: It's playing tricks on you this time. You've got him mixed up with somebody else.
KUDIMOV: Not at all. [*To* SARAFANOV.] Were you wearing a raincoat, and that hat? Tell me.
SARAFANOV: Er . . .
BUSYGIN: [*interrupting*] That's what you thought.
KUDIMOV: I'm certain!
BUSYGIN: You've made a mistake.
KUDIMOV: [*to* SARAFANOV.] Why don't you tell them?
BUSYGIN: Keep quiet, Dad. [*To* KUDIMOV.] You've made a mistake. Can't you understand that?
KUDIMOV: I swear I'm right!
BUSYGIN: Look! You're wrong, that's clear to everybody, including you.
KUDIMOV: No, just a moment!
BUSYGIN: You know you're wrong, yet you go on insisting you're right. I don't like that. It looks as if you're lying.
KUDIMOV: [*jumping up.*] What? Don't talk to me like that or I'll . . .
SILVA: [*surreptitiously tugging at* KUDIMOV's *belt to pull him back into his seat.*] Sit down and keep quiet.
BUSYGIN: [*getting up.*] Besides, it's time you were back at barracks. You've only got thirteen minutes left.
NINA: Stop this at once!
SARAFANOV: Yes, come on, boys. No need to argue . . .
KUDIMOV: I'm talking normally and telling the truth, and if anybody doesn't like it [*Turns to* BUSYGIN.] he can go to hell.
SARAFANOV: What do you mean by "anybody"? You're talking to my son and my daughter's brother, and you ought to be polite.
KUDIMOV: But what about you? Why don't you say something? I know it was you at the funeral. Why don't you say so?

SARAFANOV: Yes, I must admit . . . Mikhail is right. I play at funerals. And at dances . . .
KUDIMOV: There! What did I tell you?
SARAFANOV: [*to* BUSYGIN *and* NINA.] I understand your attitude . . . Thank you . . . But I don't see anything shameful about playing at funerals.
KUDIMOV: Who says it's shameful?
SARAFANOV: Any job's fine, if it has to be done . . .
KUDIMOV: Oh, don't imagine I brought it up because I don't like your job. It doesn't matter one bit to me where you work.
BUSYGIN: To you.
SARAFANOV: Thanks, son . . . I must confess all to you. It's six months since I last played in the orchestra.
NINA: Never mind, Dad . . .
KUDIMOV: [*to* NINA *and* BUSYGIN.] Didn't you know?
SARAFANOV: No. I kept it from them . . . Quite wrongly . . .
KUDIMOV: I see . . .
SARAFANOV: Yes . . . I hadn't the makings of a serious musician. I have to admit it . . .
KUDIMOV: Well, better the bitter truth than any of this . . .
BUSYGIN: [*showing* KUDIMOV *his watch.*] Ten minutes. [*To* SARAFANOV.] What are you looking so sad about, Dad? People need music when they're happy and when they're sad. Where's a musician's place, if not at dances and funerals? I reckon you're doing the right thing.
SARAFANOV: Thanks, son . . . [*To* KUDIMOV.] You see? Where would I be if I didn't have children? No, you can't call me a failure. I've got wonderful children . . .
[VASENKA *emerges from next room, wearing raincoat, with rucksack on back.*]
VASENKA: Great excitement, I see, in our family life . . . Well, keep it up. I wish you all the best.
SARAFANOV: Vasenka, . . . This really isn't the moment . . .
VASENKA: No, Dad! You can't stop me this time.
BUSYGIN: [*going up to* VASENKA *as if to take off his rucksack.*] Listen, lad. Take that thing off. There's no hurry.
NINA: [*going up to* VASENKA.] Take your coat off. [*Tries to pull his coat off.*]
VASENKA: [*to* NINA.] Leave me be! [*Tears free.*] What do you want? Whatever you want, you can count on Dad. He'll fix you up.

SARAFANOV: Vasenka!
VASENKA: Why did you go and see her last night? Who asked you to do that?
SARAFANOV: Vasenka! I wanted to help you.
VASENKA: You're crazy! Things were better when you didn't bother about me!
NINA: [*screams*] Be quiet, the lot of you!
SILVA: [*glances at watch, and gets up.*] This is a bit awkward . . . I think I'd better go. I've got a ticket for the pictures. I hope nobody'll mind . . . [*Exit.*]
NINA: Don't you think that'll be enough? Or have you decided to give us the whole routine today, from beginning to end?
VASENKA: Goodbye! [*Goes to door.*]
SARAFANOV: Wait!
[BUSYGIN *restrains* VASENKA.]
Wait. I'm prepared to ask your forgiveness, but I forbid you to go.
BUSYGIN: [*to* VASENKA.] What about our agreement, old fellow?
VASENKA: [*trying to break free.*] Let go! You stay with him, if you want to! I'm sick to death of all of you! [*To* BUSYGIN.] Of you too! Let go! Do you hear? I can't bear the sight of any of you!
SARAFANOV: [*losing his temper.*] Let him go . . . If that's how he feels let him get out! We won't keep him here by force.
[BUSYGIN *releases* VASENKA, *who goes out at once.*]
Never mind, never mind. Let him go and wander by himself for a while . . .
NINA: You really have shown us your paces . . . Marvellous! A whole concerto for clarinet and orchestra!
SARAFANOV: [*running about the room.*] Now it's your turn. Well, come on! Let's get it over with! Tell your father where he can go! I know you won't stand on ceremony!
NINA: Here we go. [*To* KUDIMOV.] You're about to witness the whole bag of tricks.
KUDIMOV: Don't mind me . . . I won't take any notice.
SARAFANOV: That's the way! Take no notice! Wash your hands of us! Do as you please! [*Runs into bedroom.*]
BUSYGIN: [*to* KUDIMOV, *in a whisper.*] Time to go home, cadet.
NINA: [*to* BUSYGIN, *screaming.*] Stop it! Why can't you keep out of anything?

KUDIMOV: He's quite right. It's time I was off.
NINA: No. Stay here. We need at least one person who's capable of thinking rationally.
SARAFANOV: [*shouts from bedroom.*] You don't need me here! I can see that!
NINA: Dad, you'd better be quiet for a bit . . .
KUDIMOV: I'm sorry, but I really must go.
NINA: No, you're staying.
KUDIMOV: Get this clear. To you it's a whim, but I've made myself a promise . . .
NINA: [*unexpectedly drily.*] All right. Off you go. You never know, you really might be late.
KUDIMOV: Right. See you tomorrow. [*Exit.*]
[NINA *goes out after him.*]
SARAFANOV: [*emerging*] Where's he gone? Why? I'm not wanted here. I'm like that old couch she's been planning to throw out for years . . . That's my children for you! I'd just been praising them, and what do I get? . . . And all in return for my tender feelings!
[*Enter* NINA, *pausing at the door.*]
Yes, I've raised a pair of cruel egoists, hard-hearted, calculating, ungrateful . . .
BUSYGIN: Calm down, Dad. You're being unfair.
SARAFANOV: I've done what I had to do, I've reared them to adulthood . . . [*Bitterly*] And now I'm free to enjoy the solitude of my old age . . .
BUSYGIN: You won't be alone . . . If you've no objection, I'll stay with you.
[*Short pause.* NINA *raises her head.*]
SARAFANOV: Did you say . . .
BUSYGIN: Yes. If you're left here by yourself, I'll move in with you. If you want me to . . . There's a medical school in this town too.
SARAFANOV: [*touched*] My son . . . You're all I've got . . . My only son. What would I do without you?
BUSYGIN: Steady now . . . I think you ought to lie down. You've had too much excitement. Come on. You'll have a rest and calm down . . . [*Leads* SARAFANOV *into the next room, then returns.*]

NINA: Do you really intend to stay here?

BUSYGIN: Yes . . . What else can we do? You don't think he can be left alone, do you? [*Goes up to her.*] Are you very upset about your cadet?

NINA: Forget it. You all treated him to the whole performance, . . . showed him everything you know.

BUSYGIN: Nobody wanted to upset you.

NINA: But why do you have to interfere? What for? Why did you make him look an idiot?

BUSYGIN: I don't like him.

NINA: So what? You're not planning to marry him! . . . What do you want? . . . [*Pause*] So maybe he isn't the cleverest, the handsomest — but what's that to you?

BUSYGIN: Oh, he's not a bad fellow . . . That's not the point . . .

NINA: Then what is the point? Tell me!

BUSYGIN: I don't like him because I like you.

NINA: What? . . . Is that why you staged that little scene?

BUSYGIN: Maybe it is.

NINA: You're mad! Come home to punish me, have you? . . . Big brother! . . . What a family! You were the last straw . . . I know one thing this family has in common: congenital schizophrenia!

BUSYGIN: Take it easy! [*Sits down beside her, puts his arm round her, comforts her.*] He's not a bad fellow, but take it easy.

NINA: But what if I love him? What then?

BUSYGIN: Then there's nothing to worry about. He'll be waiting for you tomorrow.

NINA: Yes, he will.

BUSYGIN: So there you are. And you'll get married, and go off to Sakhalin.

NINA: [*calmly, after pause.*] I'm not going anywhere.

BUSYGIN: How come?

NINA: You're right. Dad mustn't be left alone. I realized that today. And I also realized that I take after Dad. We all do. We all have the same nature . . . To hell with Sakhalin!

BUSYGIN: All right . . . But what about your pilot? Will he agree to stay?

NINA: I don't know. I've no idea . . . Perhaps he will, or perhaps he'll go. When I see him we'll talk it over. At the moment I don't care very much.

BUSYGIN: Best not to upset yourself. If there's one person who only has to whistle for the boys to come running it's you. You'll have to stack them like logs.
NINA: [*laughing*] That's no problem. You can help me.
BUSYGIN: No. I shan't be doing any more . . . If you stay I go.
NINA: What? Why on earth should you do that?
BUSYGIN: Why? . . . Because . . . Because I'm an idiot and I can't think of any other solution!
NINA: Solution? To what? . . . Oh yes, you're abnormal. There's no escaping the fact. Have you always been like that, or did it just start recently?
BUSYGIN: Just recently.
NINA: What happened?
BUSYGIN: I fell in love.
NINA: Who with?
BUSYGIN: How shall I put it? . . . She belongs to another.
NINA: Win her over. You shouldn't have any trouble.
BUSYGIN: Easier said than done.
NINA: What's to stop you? . . . Well? Why don't you say something? . . . I don't know who she is but [*With surprise in her voice.*] I envy her. Sometimes I even feel sorry that you're my brother.
BUSYGIN: I'm not . . .
NINA: What?
BUSYGIN: I'm not your brother . . . and never was.
NINA: [*gets up.*] It's not true . . .
BUSYGIN: [*gets up.*] I'm not joking. I haven't got a sister, and I've never had one.
NINA: It's not true . . . [*Backs away.*] I don't believe you.
BUSYGIN: It's the truth. I never knew my father, but my mother lives in Cheliabinsk. Your father's never been there. I deceived him.
NINA: Why?
BUSYGIN: It fell out that way quite by accident.
NINA: You . . . Why did you keep quiet for so long?
BUSYGIN: You father took me for his son. And it started from there. First him, then you. I got into a complete tangle . . .
NINA: You're . . . You're mad . . .
BUSYGIN: Maybe I am, but I don't want to be your brother any longer.

NINA: You're . . . you're an unprincipled opportunist. We ought to turn you over to the police!
BUSYGIN: So turn me in. I'd rather sit in the cells than be your brother.
NINA: We ought to kick you out of the house . . . throw you down the stairs!
BUSYGIN: Ought you? . . . When I was your brother you liked me. A bit anyway.
NINA: Be quiet, you unscrupulous trickster! . . . When did anyone ever see the like of this?
[*Enter* SARAFANOV.]
SARAFANOV: Volodia! It's all clear to me now. I have to leave this house. Leave it before they have to carry me out! [*Enthusiastically*] I've thought it over, son! We're going to Chernigov! [BUSYGIN *looks bewildered.*]
We're going together! Today! Now! Let's go! Let's go!
NINA: [*bursting out laughing.*] You're off to get married, I suppose?
SARAFANOV: [*shouting*] You never know! And I don't see anything funny about that! [*To* BUSYGIN.] I was thinking about that, actually. If your mother . . . But I want to see her anyway . . . [*To* NINA.] Stop that! [*To* BUSYGIN.] Just look at her! She holds nothing sacred. You can see why I can't stay here. I'll get my things together now, right away, in one minute. [*Goes into next room, but in doorway turns to* NINA.] I'll take my clarinet and my music, and nothing else . . . What time does the train leave? . . .
BUSYGIN: I . . . I don't know . . .
SARAFANOV: It doesn't matter! I'll get my things together. Right away! [*Exit.*]
[*Silence.*]
NINA: Well? . . . What do you propose to do?
BUSYGIN: [*absently*] I don't know . . .
NINA: Now do you realize what you've gone and done? Do you see? You're his favourite all of a sudden, and he's disowned his own children. He worships you. Can you imagine what'll become of him when he learns the truth?
BUSYGIN: [*anxiously*] What can I do? Say nothing? [*Short pause. They look at each other.*] No! That won't do! I must tell him, explain everything . . . He isn't my father, but all the same

he's ... and I ... Anyhow if ... [*Lowers voice.*] if you leave I really will move in with him. If he understands, of course. But how can I explain everything to him?

NINA: I don't know. You're all mad. It's up to you. I don't know.

[*Enter* SARAFANOV, *carrying suitcase and clarinet.*]

SARAFANOV: I'm ready.

[BUSYGIN *and* NINA *look at him in silence.*]

NINA: Ready? Got everything you need? [*Laughs.*]

SARAFANOV: Look at her! Can she really be my daughter? Gets rid of her father and doesn't trouble to hide her joy. [*To* NINA.] Don't you worry. You'll remember me yet! Lord, how ridiculous this is! Just think! I might have stayed with these two. For the rest of my life! And they don't need me! No! Not me! They need somebody else, always have done, right from the start! Do you understand? For the last twenty years I've been living somebody else's life! I left my own happiness behind in Chernigov. Heavens! Why didn't I look for her before? How could I? I don't understand! But all that's over now. It's over. I'm going back to her! [*To* BUSYGIN.] Your mother will be happy, you'll see ... [*more rationally.*] if she wants ... What's wrong? ... Don't you believe me? ...

BUSYGIN: Yes, I believe you, but ... What's all the hurry?

SARAFANOV: No! We must go at once! End all this at one stroke! Once and for all! Let's go to the station! To the station! ... What is it, son? Let's go!

NINA: [*with unexpected gentleness.*] Don't go, Dad. Calm down. There's no need to get so excited ... [*Sits him down on chair.*] Sit down, and calm yourself.

[*Short pause.*]

SARAFANOV: [*sits down, puzzled.*] What's going on? ... What's happened? ... Volodia? ... Are you keeping something from me?

NINA: Dad, I'm not going anywhere. I'm staying.

[VASENKA *appears in doorway, with a frightened, but triumphant expression. All turn to him. Silence.*]

[*to* VASENKA.] What's happened? ... What is it?

[*Short pause.*]

VASENKA: It's all over. I've set them on fire.

BUSYGIN: Set them on fire? ... Who?

VASENKA: Her and her lover.
SARAFANOV: God in Heaven!
   [*All except* VASENKA *rush to window.* SILVA *appears in doorway, his face black with soot. His clothes are charred, particularly his trousers, and still smoking slightly. Silence.*]
SILVA: I've had a nasty accident. I need some trousers.
   [*Enter* MAKARSKAIA.]
SARAFANOV: [*to* MAKARSKAIA.] What's happened?
MAKARSKAIA: Can't you see? This afternoon he threatened to kill me, and now he's doing his best!
NINA: Vasenka trying to kill you?
SARAFANOV: He can't be!
MAKARSKAIA: Can't be but he is! That's what I thought, but it's him all right! He's gone raving mad!
SARAFANOV: [*to* VASENKA.] How could you do it? . . . How could you?
MAKARSKAIA: Easy as wink. The window was open. He set the curtain alight, just above the carpet, and the whole room went up. He wanted to burn me to death.
SILVA: [*to* SARAFANOV.] Lend me some trousers.
BUSYGIN: [*going up to* SILVA.] What have you got to say, lover-boy?
SILVA: Some love! I was too busy fighting the flames. I don't want anything to do with that sort of love.
MAKARSKAIA: What? . . . So that's the way you talk about it now.
SILVA: What do you expect? If it's you he's after you can burn, but why should I have to suffer?
BUSYGIN: What a pity your hide didn't get properly roasted!
SILVA: Why? What do you mean?
BUSYGIN: Didn't I warn you?
SILVA: So that's it. Still playing the son and brother, are you?
BUSYGIN: Look, get out of here before you get hurt.
SILVA: Looking like this? Where do I go?
MAKARSKAIA: [*to* VASENKA.] Did you really want to burn me alive?
VASENKA: [*with unexpected calm.*] As you see, it didn't work.
MAKARSKAIA: [*with surprise, and a hint of respect.*] You little thug! In one day you've turned into a thug.
SILVA: It wasn't him. How could he do it? [*To* BUSYGIN.] Give us some trousers, quick! A joke's a joke, but I could sue you for

this. Arson's no joke. [*Indicates* MAKARSKAIA.] She'll back me up.

MAKARSKAIA: [*to* SILVA.] Don't count on me.

SILVA: Oh? Then perhaps you'll thank him for setting fire to you, eh?

MAKARSKAIA: Perhaps I will. [*To* VASENKA.] No, I won't thank you, but I will say I never expected anything like that from you.

SILVA: You think it was him? You're wrong.

MAKARSKAIA: [*to* SILVA.] I never want to see you again.

SILVA: The feeling's mutual. [*Takes guitar.*] I'm leaving . . . But lend me some trousers! Just till tomorrow.

BUSYGIN: You'll manage without. It suits you, actually. Off you go . . . Or would you like me to see you on your way?

[*Enter* SARAFANOV, *with trousers in hand.*]

SILVA: [*in doorway.*] Thanks, old fellow. Thanks for everything. You're a real friend . . . I'm leaving. But first I must reveal something to the assembled company. The one who set the house alight was him, [*Points to* BUSYGIN.] and him alone. And he's the one who's been stirring up all the trouble here. He's a confirmed trouble-maker. Haven't you noticed? . . . Well, watch out, or he'll be at it again. And by the way, [*To* NINA.] if he's your brother, then I'm his niece! Take note, before it's too late. [*To* SARAFANOV.] As for you, Grandpa, if you think he's your son you're making a big mistake. My apologies.

SARAFANOV: Get out of here! Out!

[*Exit* SILVA.]

What a scoundrel!

[*Short pause.*]

BUSYGIN: But he's right.

SARAFANOV: Who's right?

BUSYGIN: I'm not your son.

SARAFANOV: What's this? . . . What do you mean?

BUSYGIN: I'm not your son. I deceived you yesterday.

SARAFANOV: Volodia! What are you saying? . . .

BUSYGIN: Believe me, I didn't mean to! It just accidentally turned out that way. Yesterday, when you knocked on her door, [*Indicating* MAKARSKAIA.], I found out your name and noticed your flat. That's how it all started. We just wanted to get warm, then go on our way . . .

MAKARSKAIA: Wait a moment! Was that you looking for a place to sleep last night?

BUSYGIN: Yes. It just turned out that way. And in the morning, instead of leaving . . .

SARAFANOV: Impossible! . . . I don't believe it. It can't be true!

BUSYGIN: I hope you'll be able to forgive me, because I . . . Well, . . . I'm glad I chanced on you . . .

SARAFANOV: You mean you're not my . . . And I'm not your . . . How's it possible? No, I don't believe it! Tell me you're my son! . . . Well? You are my son, aren't you? Are you?

BUSYGIN: No . . .

SARAFANOV: Then who are you? Who?

NINA: He's a nut. He's a real nut, and we're just novices. Even you, Dad. You could learn a lot from him about being nutty. He's a *real* lunatic.

VASENKA: What a mix-up . . .

MAKARSKAIA: Yes, quite a to-do . . .

SARAFANOV: But I don't believe it! I won't believe it!

BUSYGIN: To be quite frank, I can hardly believe it myself . . . that I'm not your son. [*Glances at* NINA.] But that's the truth of the matter.

SARAFANOV: I don't believe it! I don't understand! I won't hear of it! You're a true Sarafanov! You're my son! And my favourite son, what's more!

NINA: [*to* BUSYGIN.] I told you so . . . [*Brightly, to* SARAFANOV.] And what about me? And Vasenka? Do you still regard us as your children?

SARAFANOV: Nina! You're all my children, but he's . . . He's still the eldest.

[*All laugh.*]

MAKARSKAIA: You're an odd crowd, you lot.

NINA: [*laughing*] Odd? And nearly burned your house down.

[MAKARSKAIA *dismisses the matter with flap of hand.*]

SARAFANOV: None of this changes anything. Volodia, come here . . .

[BUSYGIN *approaches. He,* NINA, SARAFANOV, *and* VASENKA *stand side by side.* MAKARSKAIA *stands aside.*]

Whatever might have happened, I consider you my son. [*To all three.*] You're my children, because I love you. However good or bad I may be, I love you, and that's the main thing.

MAKARSKAIA: [*to* BUSYGIN.] Excuse me, but I'd like to know . . . Are your parents alive?
BUSYGIN: I have my mother in Cheliabinsk.
NINA: Is she alone? [*Laughing*] Dad, aren't you interested?
BUSYGIN: She lives with my elder brother.
NINA: What about you? How do you come to be here?
BUSYGIN: I'm studying here.
SARAFANOV: Where are you living?
BUSYGIN: In a student hostel.
SARAFANOV: Student hostel. But that's a long way . . . And not very comfortable. I can't stand hostels . . . What I mean is . . . If you're agreeable . . . Well, er . . . Come and live with us.
BUSYGIN: Oh, why should you . . .
SARAFANOV: I mean it with all my heart . . . Nina! Why don't you say something? Invite him, persuade him.
NINA: [*capriciously*] Whatever for? Why should he come and live with us? I don't want him to.
BUSYGIN: I'll come and visit you. I'll come every day. You'll have plenty of time to get tired of me.
SARAFANOV: Volodia! I want you to come and live with us. And don't argue.
BUSYGIN: I'll come tomorrow.
NINA: At what time?
BUSYGIN: At seven . . . At six . . . By the way, what's the time now?
NINA: Half past eleven.
BUSYGIN: You can all congratulate me. I've missed the last train.

Duck-Shooting
A play in three acts

translated by Kevin Windle

CHARACTERS

VIKTOR ALEXANDROVICH ZILOV, (Vitia)
BOY; Vitia
TOLIA SAIAPIN
NIKOLAI KUZAKOV, (Kolia, Kuzia)
VALERIA SAIAPINA
VERA
VADIM ANDREEVICH KUSHAK
GALINA ZILOVA, (Galia)
IRINA NIKOLAEVNA ROZHKOVA, (Ira)
WAITER; Dima

ACT ONE
SCENE ONE

A flat in a standard-type modern building. Front door, door into kitchen, door into other room. One window. Ordinary furniture. On the window-sill is a large toy cat with a ribbon round its neck. The flat is in disorder.

In the foreground is a couch, on which ZILOV *is asleep. A small table with a telephone on it stands by the head of the couch.*

Through the window the top floor and roof of the standard-type building opposite is seen. Above this a narrow strip of grey sky. A rainy day. The telephone rings. ZILOV *wakes gradually and with a great effort. Once awake he lets the phone ring two or three times more, then frees his hand from under the blanket and reluctantly picks up the receiver.*

ZILOV: Hullo? . . .
[*Short pause. A puzzled frown appears on his face. It is clear that the person on the other end has hung up.*]
Funny . . . [*Hangs up and turns onto his other side, but immediately turns over onto his back, then, a moment later, throws off the blanket. With some surprise he discovers that he has slept in his socks. He sits up on the bed and puts his hand to his brow. Gingerly touches his jaw, wincing slightly as he does so. He sits for a while staring at one spot as he remembers something. He turns, goes quickly to the window,*

opens it. Flaps his hand in irritation. He is clearly very annoyed to find that it is raining.
ZILOV *is about thirty, fairly tall, of sturdy build. His gestures, gait and manner of speaking are extremely casual, a result of his complete confidence in his physical self. But at the same time his gestures, gait and conversation sometimes betray a don't-care attitude and boredom, whose cause cannot immediately be established. He goes into the kitchen and returns with a bottle and a glass. Drinks beer, standing by window. With bottle in hand he starts doing some exercises, but, feeling in no state for them, soon stops.*
Phone rings. He goes to phone and takes receiver.]
Yes? . . . Are you going to say something? . . .
[*As before, other end hangs up.*]
Fun and games . . . [*Hangs up. Finishes his beer. Takes receiver, dials number, listens.*] Idiots . . . [*Presses on cradle, dials again. Speaks in a monotonous voice, imitating a weather forecaster.*] During the coming twenty-four hours variable cloud is expected, with light to moderate winds and a temperature of sixteen degrees. [*In his normal voice.*] Hear that? This is what they call variable cloud — it's coming down in buckets . . . Hullo, Dima . . . Congratulations, you were right . . . About this blasted rain of course. You wait and wait all year long, and what happens? . . . [*Puzzled*] Who is it? . . . Me, Zilov . . . Of course it is. What's up? Can't you tell by my voice? . . . Died? . . . Who's died? . . . Me? . . . I don't think so . . . I seem to be alive . . . That so? . . . [*Laughs*] No, no, I'm still alive. That'd be the last straw — if I died just before the season started! . . . What?! Me? Not going?! What gave you that idea? . . . Think I've gone crazy? Or don't you want to go shooting with me? . . . Then what's the matter? . . . Of all the things to joke about . . . My head? Yes, [*Holds his head.*] it does a bit, of course . . . But it's still in one piece, thank goodness . . . Yesterday? [*With a sigh.*] I'm trying to remember . . . No, I can't remember everything, but . . . [*Sighs*] A row — yes, I remember that . . . Why did I start it? I'm wondering about that too. Damned if I know why . . . [*Listens, annoyed*] I remember that part . . . yes, and that . . . No I don't remember the end of it. Why, Dima? Did anything

happen? . . . I tell you I really can't remember . . . The police didn't come, did they? . . . No outsiders? Thank goodness for that . . . Offended? . . . Are they? . . . Can't they take a joke? . . . To hell with them, then. They'll get over it, won't they? . . . That's what I reckon . . . All right. Where does that leave us now? When do we leave? . . . We wait? When did it start? . . . Yesterday? Did it really? . . . I don't remember. No, I don't! . . . [*Feels his jaw.*] Listen, was there a fight last night? . . . There wasn't? . . . Funny . . . Yes, somebody gave me one . . . Yes, in the face . . . With his fist, I'd say . . . Didn't see who, did you? . . . Oh well, it doesn't matter . . . Nothing serious, no. Perfectly clean punch . . .
[*Knock at door.*]
Hey, Dima! What if this rain's set in for a week? . . . No, I'm not worried . . . Of course . . . I'll stay in. All ready to go. I'll be waiting for you to call . . . Right . . . [*hangs up.*]
[*Knock at door.*]
Come in.
[*A wreath appears in the doorway. It is large and cheap, made of pine needles, with big paper flowers and a long black ribbon. Behind it comes a boy of about twelve, carrying it. He is wholly preoccupied with the serious mission he has been entrusted with.*]
[*Cheerily*] Hullo, there!
BOY: Good morning. Are you Mister Zilov?
ZILOV: Yes.
BOY: [*leaning wreath against wall.*] This is for you.
ZILOV: For me? . . . What for?
[BOY *says nothing.*]
Look here, boy. You've got something mixed up . . .
BOY: You are Mister Zilov?
ZILOV: What if I am?
BOY: Then this is for you.
ZILOV: [*after pause.*] Who sent you? . . . Come and sit down, will you?
BOY: I've got to be going.
ZILOV: Sit down.
[BOY *sits down.* ZILOV *examines wreath, picks it up, straightens black ribbon, and reads inscription aloud.*]

"In memory of the unforgettable Viktor Alexandrovich Zilov, whose untimely death from overwork fills his friends with grief." . . . [*Pauses, then laughs, but only briefly and without mirth.*] Do you understand this? . . . Viktor Alexandrovich Zilov, that's me. And I'm alive and well. See? . . . What do you think of that?

[BOY *says nothing.*]

Where are they? Downstairs?

BOY: No, they've gone.

ZILOV: [*after pause.*] Had their little joke and left . . .

BOY: I'll be going.

ZILOV: On your way. No, wait. Tell me: do you like this sort of joke? . . .Do you think it's funny?

[BOY *says nothing.*]

Come on, tell me: don't you think it's a low-down trick to send your mate one of these things the morning after, and in weather like this? . . . Is it a friendly thing to do? What do you think?

BOY: I don't know. They asked me to deliver it, and I did . . .

[*Short pause.*]

ZILOV: A fine one you are. Delivering wreaths to the living. And I bet you're in the Young Pioneers too. At your age I'd never have agreed to anything like that.

BOY: I didn't know you were alive.

ZILOV: And if you'd known, would you have delivered it?

BOY: No.

ZILOV: Let's be thankful for small mercies.

[*Short pause.*]

BOY: I'll be going.

ZILOV: Wait. What did they say to you?

BOY: They said, fifth floor, flat twenty . . . They said to knock, ask for Mister Zilov, and hand this over. That's all.

ZILOV: All so easy! And what a laugh! . . . [*Puts head through wreath.*] Isn't it funny? [*Goes up to mirror, with a show of combing his hair.*] Isn't it? . . . Why aren't you laughing ? . . . You can't have much of a sense of humour. [*Turns to boy and raises right hand in victorious sportsman's salute.*] Vitia Zilov! U.S.S.R.! First place . . . What for? . . . [*Lowers hand.*] Isn't that funny? . . . Not terribly, is it? [*Tosses wreath*

aside, sits down on bed, with face towards window.] Or could it be that you and I really can't take jokes any longer? [*Pause*] Have you got to go?
BOY: Yes . . . I've got to do my homework . . .
ZILOV: Yes . . . Homework's very important . . . What's your name?
BOY: [*after pause.*] Vitia.
ZILOV: Really? So you're Vitia too . . . Don't you think that's funny?
BOY: I don't know.
[*Short pause.*]
ZILOV: All right then, Vitia. Off you go. Do your homework. Call in sometime . . . Will you?
BOY: All right.
ZILOV: Off you go.
[*Exit* BOY. *Short pause.*]
So they had their bit of fun, and went home . . .
[ZILOV *sits on his couch, gazing into the middle of the room. A funeral march is heard, its strains gradually swelling. The light slowly fades and two spotlights come on equally slowly. One of them, at half strength, picks out the figure of* ZILOV *sitting on his couch. The other, brighter, lights up a circle in the middle of the stage. The rest of* ZILOV's *flat is in darkness. In the area lit by the brighter spotlight people appear and conversations are heard — the product of* ZILOV's *imagination. By this time the funeral march has in some strange way been transformed into gay, light music. It is the same tune, but played with a different rhythm and tempo. It continues to play softly throughout this scene. The characters appearing in this scene must convey an air of parody, of farce, in their behaviour and speech, but not without a measure of grim irony. Enter* SAIAPIN *and* KUZAKOV.]
SAIAPIN: He isn't. I don't believe you. He couldn't have done.
KUZAKOV: It's a fact.
SAIAPIN: Must have been another of his little jokes. You know what he's like, don't you?
KUZAKOV: Not this time, unfortunately. This time there's no joking.
SAIAPIN: I bet it's just a rumour he's put about, and he's sitting quietly in the "Forget-me-not".

[KUZAKOV *and* SAIAPIN *vanish. Enter* VERA *and* VALERIA, *then* KUSHAK.]

VALERIA: Just imagine! Yesterday he was getting ready to go out shooting, cracking jokes ... Only yesterday! And now this ...

VERA: I'd never had thought it of him. He was the dearest Oleg of them all.

KUSHAK: What a shame! I'd never have believed it, but you know, lately he'd been acting ... I'm no prude, but I must say he'd been acting most ... er ... reprehensibly. That sort of behaviour never does anybody any good.

[VERA, VALERIA, *and* KUSHAK *vanish. Enter* GALINA, *followed by* IRINA.]

GALINA: I can't believe it, I can't, I can't! ... Why did he do it?

IRINA: Why?

GALINA: [*to* IRINA.] Did he love you?

IRINA: I don't know.

GALINA: We lived together for six years, but I could never work him out. [*To* IRINA.] You and I are going to be friends, I hope.

IRINA: Yes ...

[*They embrace and weep.*]

GALINA: I'm leaving ... For good ... Will you write to me?

IRINA: [*through tears.*] Yes ...

[GALINA *vanishes. Enter* KUSHAK *and* WAITER.]

KUSHAK: [*to* IRINA.] How nice to see you ...

WAITER: You shouldn't be alone in your state, love.

KUSHAK: No, but ... Of course she shouldn't ... All the same ...

WAITER: We'll expect you at six in the "Forget-me-not". All right?

IRINA: [*through tears.*] Yes ...

[IRINA, KUSHAK, *and the* WAITER *vanish. Enter* KUZAKOV.]

KUZAKOV: Who's to tell? ... When you come to think about it, life's over and done anyway ... [*Vanishes*]

[*Enter* WAITER *with tray.*]

WAITER: All right, folks! Let's have a whip-round. [*Smirks*] No, not for a bottle. For a wreath.

[GALINA, KUZAKOV, SAIAPIN, VALERIA, VERA, KUSHAK, *and* IRINA *walk past one by one, tossing coins onto tray. The light music abruptly reverts to the funeral march. Spotlights fade. Music stops. The tinkle of coins is heard in the darkness.*]

[*The whole stage is lit up.* ZILOV *is sitting on his couch, gazing into the middle of the room as before.*
He gets up, goes into the kitchen, and returns with a bottle. He stands for a time at the window, whistling the tune of the funeral march which he heard in his reverie.
He seats himself on the windowsill, placing bottle and glass beside him. Takes toy cat and turns it over in his hands, studying it long and intently, as if seeing it for the first time.
Gets up, goes to phone, dials number.]

ZILOV: Is that the shop? . . . Can I speak to Vera? . . . Who? Say it's Zilov . . . [*Waits*] She's busy? . . . Right. [*Hangs up, returns to windowsill, drinks beer, lost in thought.*]

[*Lights fade, stage is rotated, and lights come on again, revealing new set.*
First memory begins.
A corner of the Café Forget-me-not. One small window. Two or three tables. Door into street. ZILOV *and* SAIAPIN *take seats at one of the tables.*
SAIAPIN *is about* ZILOV's *age, but already plump and balding. He has an ingenuous air, and enjoys a laugh. Often laughs at the wrong moments. Sometimes is unable to hold back laughter, even at own expense.*]

SAIAPIN: [*loudly*] Hullo there, Dima! . . . Come over here.

[*Enter* WAITER. *He is the same age as* ZILOV *and* SAIAPIN, *tall, with the build of a sportsman. He is unfailingly cheerful, efficient, and self-assured. His bearing betrays an exaggerated sense of his own worth, which makes him look mildly comical when he is at work.*]

WAITER: [*approaching*] Hullo, fellers.
SAIAPIN: Hi, Dima.
ZILOV: How are you, mate?
WAITER: Not too bad. And yourself?
ZILOV: Not bad.
WAITER: Already getting your gear together, eh?
ZILOV: I'm ready to go now.
WAITER: [*with slightly mocking laugh.*] Already? . . . Good for you.
ZILOV: [*miserably.*] Another month and a half to go! I can't bear to think . . .
WAITER: [*smirking*] Will you last that long?

ZILOV: I don't know, Dima. I don't know how I'll manage it.
WAITER: Just wait calmly. If you want to be a good hunter you can't afford to lose your patience. Patience is vital.
SAIAPIN: Look here, you've got a month and a half till the shooting season starts, and thirty-five minutes till the end of the lunch break. [*To* ZILOV.] Have you forgotten why we came here?
ZILOV: Yes, Dima. We've only got half an hour for a drink and a bite to eat. Can we fit it in?
DIMA: We'll have a go.
ZILOV: Then I think we'll make it three salads, three kebabs, and some booze. [*To* SAIAPIN.] What does he drink?
SAIAPIN: In public I don't think he drinks at all.
ZILOV: What about some wine?
SAIAPIN: During the lunch hour? You know what he's like about that . . .
ZILOV: [*to* WAITER.] We're waiting for the boss.
WAITER: I see.
ZILOV: I think he tucks into the vodka. At night.
SAIAPIN: And so he should. That's the way to drink. He knows how to. He can do anything.
WAITER: We've got some cold beer.
ZILOV: We don't want that. Get us a bottle of wine. Make it two. I'm celebrating.
SAIAPIN: [*to* WAITER.] You can congratulate him. He's got a flat at last.
WAITER: No kidding?
ZILOV: I can't believe it myself.
WAITER: Where?
ZILOV: By the bridge.
WAITER: That so? You'll be my neighbour, then.
ZILOV: Flat twenty, thirty-seven Maiakovsky Street.
WAITER: That's great. Good for you, old feller.
ZILOV: The house-warming's at eight. Tonight. You're expected.
WAITER: Thanks, Vitia, but I can't. I'm working till eleven.
ZILOV: Swap shifts with somebody.
WAITER: Not a hope. Everybody's on holiday.
ZILOV: Then fall ill suddenly.
WAITER: No, I don't go in for that sort of thing. Sorry.
ZILOV: Pity . . .

WAITER: I'm sorry, but there's no way I can make it tonight. I can't do anything about it . . . [*Writes*] Two bottles of wine, three salads, three kebabs . . . [*to* ZILOV.] Don't forget, you owe me half a litre.

ZILOV: You needn't worry.

[*Exit* WAITER.]

SAIAPIN: [*about* WAITER.] Just look how he's turned out. And he was such a shy little kid at school. Who'd have thought he'd make a waiter.

ZILOV: You want to see him with a shotgun. He's a tiger.

SAIAPIN: Is he?

ZILOV: A killer. Knocks 'em out of the sky at fifty metres. Wish I could!

SAIAPIN: Listen, will the boss be at this house-warming?

ZILOV: Yes. He'll pick you up.

SAIAPIN: Why'd he take it into his head to have lunch with us?

ZILOV: Where else could he have lunch?

SAIAPIN: He lives right next door. And you know he doesn't go anywhere without his wife's say-so.

ZILOV: He packed her off to the south yesterday.

SAIAPIN: So that's it. So he's making the most of it . . . Still, whatever you say, he's got his head screwed on right . . . Like with the flats. Promised he'd fix it, and he did. Got you one, and he's getting one for me. I hear he's got pull up there [*Points upward.*] That right?

ZILOV: [*seeing somebody.*] Stop! Move over . . . [*Hides*] That's it! Move this way! . . . This way! [*Moves* SAIAPIN.]

SAIAPIN: [*looking round.*] What's wrong? . . . That's Verochka. Your true love, if I'm not mistaken. "The course of true love never did run smooth . . ."

ZILOV: Sit still. [*Hiding*] It's best if we don't meet today. Anyway I'm sick of her.

SAIAPIN: It's no good, Vitia. She's seen you.

ZILOV: [*returning to his chair.*] Damnation! Some discipline they have in these shops! She's forever wandering around in working hours . . . [*Waves*] Hullo.

[*Enter* VERA. *She is about twenty-five, attractive, if a little common, lively, always in form. Now she is wearing a shop-assistant's smock. She usually dresses attractively and always has a splendid hair-do.*]

VERA: Hullo, my Olegs! Haven't seen you for ages. [*Sits down.*]
[WAITER *brings wine and salads.*]
So you were waiting for me, were you? . . . How lovely.
WAITER: [*to* VERA.] Hi there, darling.
VERA: Hullo, Oleg.
WAITER: [*to* ZILOV.] Will that be another kebab?
ZILOV: Yes, be a pal.
[*Exit* WAITER.]
VERA: [*to* ZILOV.] Living it up? Got your flat, have you?
ZILOV: Yes.
VERA: I'm so glad. Where've you been?
ZILOV: At home, Verochka. At home and at work.
VERA: Didn't you think I might be missing you? You can't just disappear for weeks on end.
ZILOV: I've had urgent business, keeping me busy day and night.
SAIAPIN: Everybody's on holiday in our office. There's only the two of us left, working flat out.
ZILOV: Yes. Afire with the flames of lovely labour.
VERA: Be careful, Oleg, or I'll find somebody else.
ZILOV: By yourself, or should I help you?
VERA: No thanks. I'm a big girl now.
SAIAPIN: Listen, why do you call everybody that?
VERA: What, Oleg?
SAIAPIN: Yes, Oleg. We're all Olegs to you. What does it mean? Alcoholegs, maybe?
ZILOV: She doesn't know herself.
SAIAPIN: Or was your first love called Oleg?
VERA: That's right. My first love was an Oleg, and my second, and my third. They're all Olegs.
ZILOV: [*to* SAIAPIN.] Make any sense to you?
SAIAPIN: [*seeing somebody.*] Here he comes. [*To* VERA.] Our boss. I wouldn't make a show of your relationship if I were you. He has strict views. [*Gets up.*]
ZILOV: [*grasping at this idea.*] Yes, go easy when he's around.
VERA: Okay, okay. I get the point.
SAIAPIN: You're good friends, and that's all. Right?
VERA: Sure, Oleg. We went to school together.
[*Exit* SAIAPIN.]
Shall I see you tonight?

ZILOV: Tonight? No, Verochka. I can't make it tonight.
VERA: Why not? . . . Give it to me straight.
ZILOV: Sure. It's our house-warming tonight.
VERA: House-warming . . . Why shouldn't you invite me?
ZILOV: You? . . . I'd love to, but I don't think my wife would like it.
VERA: Why not? You meet an old schoolfriend and invite her along — is that so strange?
ZILOV: Do you think my wife's that stupid?
VERA: You mean she's clever? . . . Introduce me if she is.
ZILOV: Whatever for?
VERA: So I can pick up a few tips. Isn't that allowed?
ZILOV: That'd be all I need. Don't talk nonsense. We'll meet tomorrow. That's the end of it.
   [*Enter* SAIAPIN *and* KUSHAK. KUSHAK *is a solid-looking citizen of about fifty. At work he cuts quite an imposing figure: strict, decisive, businesslike. Away from his office he is very unsure of himself, indecisive, and fussy. When visiting he keeps glancing out of the window, like most other car-owners.*]
   Over here, Vadim Andreevich. Take a seat.
KUSHAK: Good afternoon.
VERA: Hullo.
ZILOV: This is Vera.
KUSHAK: Very pleased to meet you . . .
   [WAITER *brings kebabs, and leaves.*]
ZILOV: [*picking up bottle.*] This is for the kebabs. I hope you don't mind.
KUSHAK: Um . . . Well, this is only the lunch-hour . . . [*To* VERA.] We stick to our rules, you know . . .
VERA: One exception won't do any harm.
KUSHAK: You don't think so? Well, I suppose we can make an exception. After all it isn't vodka. [*Looks round.*]
SAIAPIN: We've got good reason, Vadim Andreevich. He's got his flat. It's a big deal.
KUSHAK: Yes, that's a good enough reason.
ZILOV: [*pouring wine for everybody.*] You can count this as a bit of a warm-up for the evening, Vadim Andreevich. I hope you haven't forgotten. We're expecting you at eight, as we agreed.
KUSHAK: I really don't know if I can come. I haven't been feeling

too well, you see, and my wife's away . . . er . . . at this point in time . . .

ZILOV: Vadim Andreevich, you promised.

VERA: Where is your wife, if it's not a secret?

KUSHAK: She's on the Black Sea. On holiday.

ZILOV: So she can take a holiday, but you can't go anywhere?

KUSHAK: You've got a point . . . But on the other hand she's all alone there, and I go out enjoying myself . . . It's . . . sort of . . . unethical. Don't you think so?

VERA: You're a good husband. A real collector's item. A husband like you is allowed to go anywhere, in any company.

ZILOV: She's right. You're coming. That's decided.

KUSHAK: [to VERA.] So you'd advise me to go . . .

VERA: [archly] Definitely. In your position nobody else would hesitate. The nonsense you talk!

KUSHAK: Oh no, don't get the wrong idea. I'm no prude, but . . . well . . . Briefly, I agree. [Plucking up his courage, wags his finger at VERA.] Watch your step. It looks as if you're . . . er . . . seducing me. [Looks round.]

VERA: [conspiratorially] Well, that's still a little way off, but it would be interesting . . . It wouldn't be a bad thing . . .

KUSHAK: [obtusely] Do you think so?

VERA: Sure. I have a weakness for faithful husbands.

ZILOV: Vadim Andreevich! Take care!

VERA: [to KUSHAK.] Drink up. And do you know what? I'll call you Oleg. You don't mind? . . .

KUSHAK: Oleg? . . . But why?

VERA: Don't you like it?

KUSHAK: I really don't know . . .

VERA: Do us a favour . . .

KUSHAK: Oleg . . . Funny . . . But for you . . . If you want to . . .

VERA: And none too soon. [Touching his nose with her finger.] Oleg.

[Pause. SAIAPIN laughs silently, hiding this from KUSHAK. ZILOV watches VERA and KUSHAK with interest. KUSHAK looks round.]

KUSHAK: They don't do a bad meal here, you know. I must admit I haven't been here for a while . . .

VERA: Come here more often. They have music here in the evenings.

KUSHAK: Will there be any today?
VERA: Any what?
KUSHAK: Music...
VERA: Certainly. But aren't you going to a house-warming party tonight?
KUSHAK: And you? Aren't you coming too?
VERA: I'm not invited.
KUSHAK: Really?
VERA: It's quite all right. You only invite your friends to house-warming parties, and Viktor and I... we just went to the same school. And happened to meet.
KUSHAK: Is that so?...
VERA: So why should I be invited? I'm not dropping any hints.
KUSHAK: Er...
   [SAIAPIN *nudges* ZILOV *in the ribs. Short pause.*]
ZILOV: [*to* VERA.] What are you talking about? I simply hadn't had a chance to invite you. Do come.
VERA: Thanks. Only you mustn't think I was hinting.
KUSHAK: Come now. Does anybody think you were?
SAIAPIN: No, nobody.
ZILOV: Everybody'll be pleased. It'll make for a good evening. You were the one thing that was missing. Take the address down.
   [*Light fades, stage rotates, light comes on.* ZILOV's *first memory continues.* ZILOV's *flat.* ZILOV *and* GALINA *wait for their guests to arrive. The furniture consists only of one chair, an iron bed, a suitcase, and the table, around which* GALINA *is fussing.* GALINA *is twenty-six. The delicacy of her appearance is important, like the grace of her bearing, which is not immediately obvious, and must never appear to be deliberate. This feature, which was undoubtedly prominent when she was younger, is now obscured by work, the burden of unrealized hopes, and life with an irresponsible husband. Her face wears an almost permanent expression of concentration and worry. (She is a teacher, and teachers marking exercise-books often have this look.) Now she is wearing a dark dress with an apron over it, and bedroom slippers.*]
ZILOV: [*by the table.*] This is first-class grub, I can tell you. None of 'em deserves grub like this. Except the boss.
GALINA: Everything's turned out all right. But what are they going to sit on?

ZILOV: The women on the bed. I'll sit on the chair. And the rest on the floor.
GALINA: The boss as well?
ZILOV: Yes, on the floor! Next time he can get us a furnished flat.
GALINA: I'm ashamed. Three on the bed, and the chair and the suitcase makes five. And how many are coming? One, two, three . . . six people.
ZILOV: Seven.
GALINA: Seven? How come? . . . There'll be you and me, the Saiapins, Kuzakov, and Kushak. That's all. Kushak's wife won't be coming, you said. That makes six.
ZILOV: There'll be one more.
GALINA: And who might that be? Not that dreadful Dima of yours, surely?
ZILOV: No, he's working tonight. What's so dreadful about him?
GALINA: I don't know, but he is. Even the way he looks at you. I'm afraid of him.
ZILOV: Rubbish. He's a good bloke.
GALINA: But who's the seventh, then?
ZILOV: A certain nice lady.
GALINA: Really?
ZILOV: Haven't I told you about her?
GALINA: Believe it or not, you haven't. It comes as a surprise.
ZILOV: I clean forgot. Her name's Vera. I gather she's nice-looking . . . At any rate Kushak's wild about her.
GALINA: I see. On our very first day here you're turning our flat into a . . .
ZILOV: Not at all. With him it's pure love.
GALINA: Pure love? While his wife stays at home?
ZILOV: His wife's an old bag. By the way he asked me to have a word with you. I forgot.
GALINA: Forgot what?
ZILOV: To ask you to let them meet here.
GALINA: And what if I say no?
ZILOV: Too late now.
GALINA: I don't want our flat to be a . . .
ZILOV: What'll happen to it if poor old Kushak . . . and incidentally, he was the one who got it for us, this flat — what'll happen to it if he has the odd hour here, to relax, daydream, and say

sweet nothings to a nice lady? Will the ceiling come crashing down?

GALINA: I don't like it.

ZILOV: I wasn't thinking of the flat. Don't get the wrong idea. I just felt sorry for Kushak. And you might feel a bit sorry for him too. It won't do to be so heartless.

GALINA: [*laying another place at the table.*] You really do go out of your way to help your friends.

ZILOV: [*hugging her.*] Stop it. Let me give you a hand.

GALINA: Everything's ready.

ZILOV: Perfect. What about a drink?

GALINA: Just the two of us?

ZILOV: Just one glass.

GALINA: No, let's do things properly and wait for our guests.

ZILOV: [*choosing bottle.*] Best to start with some vodka, I think. [*Pours drinks.*]

GALINA: That's not right. The guests'll come and find us tipsy.

ZILOV: What does it matter?

GALINA: Don't get drunk tonight, all right?

ZILOV: Okay, okay.

GALINA: Well then, here's to our new home.

ZILOV: Cheers.

GALINA: Yesterday, when we were moving, I got into the taxi thinking: that's it for good. Goodbye to the back streets; high life — here we come!

ZILOV: Skoal.

[*They drink.*]

GALINA: We'll get on well together here, won't we?

ZILOV: Of course.

GALINA: Just like we did at first. In the evenings we'll read, and talk ...won't we?

ZILOV: Sure.

GALINA: There's nothing worse than being at home without you and not knowing where you are.

ZILOV: We'll get the phone on.

GALINA: I don't like telephones. When you talk to me on the phone I get the feeling you're lying.

ZILOV: That's a mistake. You're wrong to mistrust machinery. After all, the future belongs to it.

[*Pause.* GALINA *goes to window.*]
GALINA: [*looking out of window.*] I got a letter today, you know. Quite unexpectedly. Do you know who from?
ZILOV: Well? [*Fills his glass.*] Who?
GALINA: From a childhood friend. It's amazing that he suddenly thought of me again.
[ZILOV *drinks.*]
Our parents were friends, and we were sweethearts. We parted when we were twelve. [*Laughs*] He was ever so funny. When we were saying goodbye he started crying, and then he said, perfectly seriously, "Galia, give me a farewell bite."
ZILOV: Go on. [*Filling glass.*] Did you bite him?
GALINA: Yes. I bit his finger.
ZILOV: That's funny. [*Drinks*]
GALINA: He says family life hasn't worked for him, and he's going to stay single for the rest of his life.
ZILOV: Not a bad idea.
GALINA: Somebody's arrived. I think it's for us. Looks like them. Yes, it is. Saiapin and the venerable Valeria, and somebody else with them.
ZILOV: [*going to window.*] The boss. That's his car.
GALINA: What about Kuzakov?
ZILOV: He'll come. He won't run off anywhere.
GALINA: And the nice lady?
ZILOV: No problem. She'll come along later. [*Goes into hall.*]
[GALINA *puts on shoes instead of slippers, and takes off apron, but thinks for a moment and puts it on again.*]
[*in hall.*] Do come in.
[*Enter* KUSHAK, SAIAPIN *and* VALERIA. VALERIA *is about twenty-five. Strikingly dynamic. Her outward attractiveness sits uneasily with her forceful, almost masculine drive. Her hair is cut short and dyed. She is fashionably dressed.*]
KUSHAK: [*handing* GALINA *some flowers.*] My warmest congratulations on your move.
VALERIA: [*walking about the room.*] Come on then, let's have a look at it.
SAIAPIN: It'll do. It'll do. Not a bad place.
KUSHAK: A charming little flat, charming. And I wish you every happiness in it.

[VALERIA *goes into kitchen.*]

VALERIA: Hot and cold water? . . . Lovely! . . . Gas? . . . Lovely! . . . [*Reappearing*] Yes, yes . . . And what's in here? . . . Eighteen square metres?

GALINA: Yes . . . I think so.

VALERIA: Lovely!

KUSHAK: Charming little place. [*Goes to window, glances at his car.*]

[VALERIA *rushes into next room.* GALINA *follows her.*]

SAIAPIN: [*wistfully*] Yes, no question about it. This is a decent place. [*Goes into next room.*]

VALERIA: [*from next room.*] A balcony? . . . Facing south? . . . Or north?

KUSHAK: Yes, a flat means a lot. My congratulations again.

ZILOV: Thanks again.

VALERIA: [*from next room.*] Lovely!

KUSHAK: Wonderful, wonderful . . . And is everybody here? [*Glances into next room.*]

ZILOV: [*closing door into next room.*] She isn't here, but you can be sure she won't be long. You've got her intrigued.

KUSHAK: Do you think so?

ZILOV: Don't be so modest. She's fallen for you.

KUSHAK: Viktor! [*Looking round.*] The things you say . . . And you mean to say . . .

ZILOV: I mean to say: don't hang back.

KUSHAK: But look here, is it all right . . . with the Saiapins here, and your wife. Do you think it's ethical?

ZILOV: Nonsense. Just act decisively, without ceremony. You mustn't hesitate. Take the bull by the horns.

KUSHAK: Well I never! I never suspected you of being so frivolous. If you're not careful, Viktor, you'll . . . er . . . corrupt me.

ZILOV: I've always wanted to do you a good turn.

[*Enter* VALERIA, SAIAPIN, *and* GALINA.]

VALERIA: Furniture! Get some furniture! Quick! [*Goes into hall.*]

KUSHAK: Yes, you must have furniture . . . But never mind. You can't do everything at once. You'll get some gradually. [*Goes to window, glances at car.*]

GALINA: In the meantime we'll have to sit on the bed.

[*Sound of toilet being flushed.* VALERIA'*s voice, "Lovely!"*

Then enter VALERIA.]
VALERIA: Congratulations. Now you'll be able to lead a normal life. [*To* SAIAPIN.] Tolia, if you and I don't move into a flat like this within six months I'll leave you! That's a promise!
KUSHAK: Er . . . In six months things ought to . . . er . . . sort themselves out.
VALERIA: [*dramatically*.] Oh, Vadim Andreevich! I'll . . . I'll . . .
ZILOV: You'll what?
VALERIA: I'll worship at your feet! I swear I will!
ZILOV: Down on your knees, my child . . .
SAIAPIN: [*hastily*] Yes. You'll put the T.V. here, the couch here, and the fridge next to it. You'll have beer and stuff in the fridge. Ready for your friends.
[*Doorbell rings.* ZILOV *goes into hall. Pause.*]
ZILOV: [*in the doorway*.] Vadim Andreevich! Come and do the honours.
[KUSHAK *goes into hall.*]
VALERIA: [*to* ZILOV.] Who is it?
ZILOV: A friend of Vadim Andreevich's. A certain nice lady.
VALERIA: [*surprised*.] What sort of lady?
ZILOV: A young and pretty one. [*Goes into hall.*]
VALERIA: Well, good for him!
GALINA: Good for who?
VALERIA: Vadim Andreevich, of course. He must be at least forty.
SAIAPIN: Forty-six.
[*Enter* ZILOV, VERA, *and* KUSHAK. VERA *is holding a large parcel.*]
ZILOV: After you.
KUSHAK: [*to* VERA.] After you.
ZILOV: [*to all*.] Come and meet the people . . .
VERA: I'm Vera.
VALERIA: I'm Valeria.
VERA: Pleased to meet you.
ZILOV: This my wife.
KUSHAK: The lady of the house.
GALINA: My name's Galina.
VERA: Pleased to meet you. Congratulations. This is for you . . .
[*Hands* ZILOV *the parcel.*]
VALERIA: [*to* ZILOV.] Whatever is it?

ZILOV: I think it's a bomb.
VALERIA: Show us. I'm dying of curiosity.
 [ZILOV *opens the parcel and pulls out a large toy cat.* SAIAPIN *suddenly does quite a convincing "miaou".*]
 [*startled*] Oh!
 [*All laugh.*]
 You made me jump! [*Takes cat and examines it.*] Some cat, this!
KUSHAK: What whiskers! Look at them! And what eyes! They look real. [*To* VERA.] A marvellous present!
VALERIA: [*handing cat to* GALINA.] Very nice.
GALINA: [*to* VERA.] Thank you very much.
VERA: Guess what! I've given him a name.
GALINA: Oh yes? What is it?
VERA: I've called him Oleg.
ZILOV: Oh, Lord . . .
KUSHAK: [*reproachfully*] Verochka . . .
VERA: If you like the name, you can call him that.
VALERIA: Oleg. It's a beautiful name. [*To* GALINA *and* ZILOV.] He'll bring you luck.
ZILOV: I can feel it coming.
KUSHAK: And now it's our turn.
VALERIA: Tolia, bring them in.
 [SAIAPIN *goes into hall and returns with several bundles, which he is about to start unwrapping.*]
 No, let him guess!
 [*Doorbell rings.*]
GALINA: It's Kuzakov. [*Goes into hall.*]
ZILOV: [*to* VALERIA.] What am I supposed to guess?
VALERIA: Guess what we're giving you.
 [*Enter* KUZAKOV *and* GALINA. KUZAKOV *is about thirty. Not a colourful figure, he is generally pensive and withdrawn. Speaks little, but listens well. Dresses scruffily. For these reasons he does not stand out in company. He suffers this with dignity, but with some irritation too, which he keeps well hidden.*]
KUZAKOV: Good to see you all in the new flat. [*Comes in, looks at table.*] I hope I'm not late.
VALERIA: Not at all. We're giving them our present.

KUZAKOV: Present? . . . [*To* VALERIA.] Why are you looking at me like that? Do you think I've come empty-handed? [*To* ZILOV.] Vitia! Come and lend a hand!
ZILOV: You need me?
KUZAKOV: You're essential.
VALERIA: Sounds interesting.
[KUZAKOV *and* ZILOV *go out.*]
Can't carry it by himself. Just fancy!
KUSHAK: Verochka, do sit down.
VERA: Thank you, Oleg.
SAIAPIN: [*to* VALERIA, *about the bundles.*] Well? Shall I unwrap them?
[KUSHAK *rushes to window and looks at his car.*]
VALERIA: No. Let's wait and see what he's playing at.
GALINA: Forget about them. Take your seats at the table instead.
[*Door bangs.* KUZAKOV *and* ZILOV *carry in a park bench. All laugh.*]
KUZAKOV: Here you are. From my very own suite.
VALERIA: You scrounger!
GALINA: Thanks, Kuzia. You couldn't have thought of anything better.
ZILOV: [*sitting down on bench.*] Latest style. [*To* KUZAKOV.] Sit down, you old tramp.
GALINA: Put it by the table. The ladies will sit on it.
VALERIA: Now it's our turn. Your attention, please! [*To* ZILOV.] Guess what we're giving you.
ZILOV: I don't know. Give me an island, if you've got one to spare.
VALERIA: Seriously, though.
ZILOV: I don't know.
VALERIA: What do you like most of all? . . . Well?
ZILOV: What do I like? . . . Let me think.
VALERIA: Well, there's your wife, naturally . . .
GALINA: No, he stopped liking me a long time ago . . .
VERA: [*smirking*] His mistress, maybe.
[SAIAPIN *guffaws.*]
KUSHAK: [*astonished.*] Verochka!
VALERIA: [*to* ZILOV.] Well? Can you guess?
ZILOV: I'm trying, but I can't.
VALERIA: What a bonehead! You must know what you like!

GALINA: He likes his friends more than anything else.
VERA: Women. Give him some women.
KUZAKOV: That's all rubbish. What Vitia likes most of all is work.
[*All laugh.*]
KUSHAK: [*his first words drowned in general laughter.*] Why make fun of him like this? . . . He mightn't have much of a nose for business, but he's a capable fellow. Why laugh at him?
VALERIA: No good. We'll get no sense out of him. Right. You don't know, but we know. We know what you like. [*To* SAIAPIN.] Unwrap it, Tolia.
[SAIAPIN *unwraps parcel. It contains various pieces of a sportsman's equipment: hunting knife, cartridge pouch, and several wooden ducks of the type used as lures.* SAIAPIN *displays these to all.*]
ZILOV: Oho! . . .
[*All laugh.*]
SAIAPIN: [*to* ZILOV.] Here you are.
ZILOV: [*taking his presents.*] Just the job! The very thing I wanted. What a fool I was not to guess!
GALINA: Yes, you couldn't have pleased him better.
ZILOV: That's right. It's a fine thing, duck-shooting. [*Puts on cartridge pouch and hooks on the dummy birds. He remains thus attired until the end of this scene.*]
VALERIA: We'll come again in September, and we'll expect some of your game to eat. Don't forget.
GALINA: [*animatedly*] Yes, come and see us. But I warn you, the game'll come from the shop.
KUSHAK: Why's that?
GALINA: Because he never gets beyond talking about shooting and getting ready for it.
ZILOV: Don't listen to her.
GALINA: It's the truth, isn't it? Well, have you ever shot anything? Even once? Own up! Even a tiny little bird, even this big? [*Showing length on finger.*]
KUZAKOV: What's that you're showing him? He couldn't hit one this big, [*Showing with both hands.*] let alone that little thing.
[*All laugh.*]
ZILOV: [*so pleased with his presents that he ignores this banter.*] All right, all right. Wait and see.

SAIAPIN: Vitia! To be quite sure, shoot at these [*Indicates dummies.*] They won't fly away.
ZILOV: Okay now. What do you know about it?
GALINA: [*clapping hands.*] May I ask you all to take your seats at the table?
[*All sit down.* KUSHAK *goes to window and glances at his car.*]
VERA: [*to* KUSHAK.] Why do you keep looking out of the window, Oleg? Left something out there?
KUZAKOV: Just his car.
KUSHAK: [*embarrassed*] No . . . that is, yes. My car.
VALERIA: Don't worry, Vadim Andreevich. We're closer to the window. We can look out. [*To* SAIAPIN.] Keep your eyes open.
[*All are seated except* KUZAKOV.]
VERA: [*to* KUZAKOV.] What about you? [*Squeezes up on bench.*] Sit down, Oleg. Don't mind us.
KUZAKOV: Thank you. [*Sits down.*] But you've got my name wrong. It's Nikolai, and you called me Oleg.
VERA: What's the difference?
KUSHAK: [*surprised*] Verochka! . . .
VALERIA: She's quite right. He looks like that cat. [*To* KUZAKOV.] You do, don't argue. Show him the cat.
[GALINA *shows* KUZAKOV *the toy cat. All laugh.*]
The spitting image.
KUZAKOV: There's no resemblance. You're just asking for trouble.
ZILOV: [*to* KUZAKOV.] Don't argue, old fellow. Take it quietly.
[*Takes bottle and pours wine for all.*]
KUZAKOV: All right. [*To* VERA.] But I'll ask you for an explanation later.
VERA: Fine, I'll give you one.
ZILOV: And now, my friends . . . [*Picking up glass.*] Down the hatch!
SAIAPIN: Bottoms up!
VALERIA: Wait! What's all this — "Down the hatch!" and "Bottoms up!"? Think you're in a bar? I thought we were at a house-warming.
ZILOV: We are. What had you in mind?
VALERIA: Well, there are certain customs and traditions, after all . . . Somebody must know them . . .
[*Silence.* ZILOV *pours wine for all.*]

VERA: I could do a dance on the table. If you like.
KUSHAK: Verochka! [*To* ZILOV.] Her jokes are ... er ... [*To* VERA.] inimitable ...
KUZAKOV: I vaguely remember. Something about drinking four times for the four corners of the house. That's the tradition.
VALERIA: [*mimicking* KUZAKOV.] "I vaguely remember." Fat lot of use you are! [*To* KUSHAK.] Vadim Andreevich, you're our only hope.
KUSHAK: [*rising*] My friends, let's not rack our brains over nothing. You're all young people ...
VALERIA: [*surprised*] And you, Vadim Andreevich?
VERA: Come on, Oleg, don't pretend. You're not that old yet.
KUSHAK: [*to* VERA *and* VALERIA.] Thank you, thank you. We're all young people. What do we want with the traditional wisdom of the old? Let's just congratulate our hosts, and drink to their new flat.
[*Simultaneous cries of "Congratulations!" "Cheers!" "Thank you," etc.*]
ZILOV: Down the hatch!
SAIAPIN: Bottoms up!
[*The same loud, bright music is heard. The lights fade, to come on again seconds later. The music is playing softly. The end of the first memory is accompanied by this music. The same room. The same furniture as for the party. The guests are leaving.* ZILOV *and* VERA. VERA *wearing coat.*]
VERA: I like your wife. I'm surprised you managed to get anyone as nice as her.
ZILOV: I don't know how I managed it, Verochka. It was a long time ago. Six years ago ...
VERA: I can just image what she's had to put up with from you ... You're the biggest Oleg of the lot.
ZILOV: Okay. Phone me at work tomorrow.
VERA: I will ... If I have time.
ZILOV: As you like.
VERA: Looks as if the hearty fellow's hoping for something.
ZILOV: Let him hope. You don't feel sorry for him, do you?
VERA: Maybe I ought to go with him. What do you think? You don't object, do you?
ZILOV: Why keep on about it? He's done what he had to do. Now let him go on his way.

VERA: But maybe I ought to. After all, he's one of the bosses.
ZILOV: Look, you can do whatever you like. You started this whole business.
[KUSHAK *appears in the doorway, the worse for drink.*]
KUSHAK: What an evening! It was enchanting, if I may say so . . . I give thanks to fate for . . .
VERA: You should be giving thanks to him [*Indicates* ZILOV.], not fate.
KUSHAK: Yes, of course! Thank you, Viktor, for all your hospitality and . . . for everything.
[GALINA *comes out of kitchen.*]
And thank you so much, Galina Nikolaevna. I'll remember this evening for the rest of my life!
VERA: So will I.
GALINA: Delighted. I hope you'll come and see us more often. I'd be so glad.
VERA: [*to* GALINA.] My best to you. [*To* ZILOV *and* KUZAKOV.] Bye-bye, Olegs.
KUZAKOV: Bye.
[*Exit* KUSHAK *and* VERA.]
GALINA: I'll see you off. [*Exit.*]
ZILOV: [*to* KUZAKOV.] That's fine then. Everybody's happy. Everybody had a good time. It was a good party.
KUZAKOV: Tell me: who's Vera, and where does she come from?
ZILOV: Fancy her, do you?
KUZAKOV: Frankly, yes.
ZILOV: Then go to work. What's the problem?
KUZAKOV: But I don't understand where Kushak comes into it. What is there between them?
ZILOV: Between them? Practically nothing. Only his drunken fantasies.
KUZAKOV: That's what I thought.
ZILOV: You can take it from me, the poor sod's wasting his time.
KUZAKOV: So all her larking around's just an act, is it?
ZILOV: You think so?
KUZAKOV: Can't you see? Haven't you come across women like that before?
ZILOV: Like what?
KUZAKOV: Like her. They make out they're Christ knows what, when in fact they're . . .

ZILOV: In fact they're what?
KUZAKOV: Vitia, I don't think she's at all like what she pretends to be.
ZILOV: [*clapping* KUZAKOV *on the shoulder.*] You're wrong, as usual, old chap.
[KUSHAK *appears in doorway.*]
KUSHAK: Viktor! . . . Er . . . Can I have a word with you?
KUZAKOV: Of course, of course. I've said all I had to say. [*To* ZILOV.] Bye, Vitia.
ZILOV: See you, Kolia.
[*Exit* KUZAKOV.]
Yes?
KUSHAK: She's . . . er . . . I'm delighted with her! But . . . how do I . . . er . . . go about it?
ZILOV: [*familiarly*] Don't you know? . . . With promises, vows, and threats. The usual way . . .
KUSHAK: Er . . . yes, but . . . what sort of things?
ZILOV: Good heavens! Say you'll crown her with gold, you'll make her your wife, say you'll kill her! What else can you say? Get busy!
KUSHAK: [*starts running out, but returns.*] But are you quite sure it won't lead . . . er . . . to any scandal?
ZILOV: You really are like a child.
KUSHAK: No, don't get me wrong. I'm no prude, but still . . .
ZILOV: Be a man, and everything'll be all right.
[*Exit* KUSHAK. ZILOV *is left alone, looking at his presents. Enter* GALINA.]
GALINA: I think I'm drunk . . .
ZILOV: Sure you are. Drunk as a lord.
GALINA: Am I really? Whatever will the guests think?
ZILOV: Them? I'm sick of them.
[*Short pause.*]
GALINA: Listen, I want to tell you something.
ZILOV: Go on.
GALINA: I want a child.
ZILOV: Oh, that again?
GALINA: It's time we had one, you know.
ZILOV: You think so?
GALINA: I've never wanted one so much . . . What about you? What do you say?

ZILOV: Me? . . . Well, if it's time we had one, I suppose we might as well . . .
GALINA: No, I can see you don't want one.
ZILOV: Now where'd you get that idea? I've nothing against it . . . What are you all upset about? There's no problem. No sooner said than done.
GALINA: You don't want a child.
[*Enter* KUSHAK. GALINA *goes into next room.*]
KUSHAK: [*extremely annoyed.*] Viktor! Viktor . . .
ZILOV: What's the trouble?
KUSHAK: She's . . . She's vanished!
ZILOV: Really? . . . The woman or the car?
[KUSHAK *rushes to window, glances at car.*]
KUSHAK: The woman. She's run away . . . What's the meaning of this? . . . I don't know what to call it . . .
ZILOV: The heave-ho.
KUSHAK: What?
ZILOV: [*irritated*] It's called the heave-ho . . . She's given you the heave-ho. Don't you understand?
KUSHAK: [*suddenly sober.*] Viktor, . . . I'm disappointed in you.
[*The merry music becomes a funeral march. Lights fade, and stage is set as at beginning of play.* ZILOV *drinks beer, perched on windowsill. Suddenly he picks up toy cat and hurls it into corner of room.*]

SCENE TWO

ZILOV's *room. As before it is raining outside.* ZILOV *dials a number on phone.*

ZILOV: Is Kuzakov there, please? . . . No? . . . Right. [*Depresses cradle, dials another number.*] Enquiries? Put Saiapin on, would you? . . . Not there? Not shown up? . . . I see. [*Hangs up.*] Some workers! . . . [*Sits thoughtfully by phone.*]
[*Lights fade. Stage rotates, showing new set when lights come on. Second memory. An office. One window, two stout cupboards, four desks, at one of which* SAIAPIN *is sitting. Enter* ZILOV.]

ZILOV: The boss is doing his nut. [*Comes in, sits down.*] Know what he's after now? Modernization. Stories about new mass-production systems and young, thriving industries. Wants them now.
SAIAPIN: He had that idea last week. Don't you remember?
ZILOV: Have we got any stuff like that to give him?
SAIAPIN: There's the porcelain plant. [*Takes something out of desk drawer.*] But we've had it a year already.
ZILOV: Let's have a look. Uhuh . . . [*Turns pages.*] Reconstruction plans, mass-production system . . . Just the thing!
SAIAPIN: But those are just plans.
ZILOV: Who drew them up? [*Looks*] Smirnov. Chief engineer. I know him. He's the sort you can count on.
SAIAPIN: But we don't need plans. We need facts.
ZILOV: Facts? Where are we going to find facts today? Or tomorrow? . . . Hold on! . . . Hold on! . . . Hold on! . . . Hold on! . . . The chief engineer has set it all down in the present tense.
SAIAPIN: So what?
ZILOV: So what? He writes as if it was all finished. Get it? . . . How long do you say we've had this thing here?
SAIAPIN: About a year.
ZILOV: Excellent. We can reckon that in a year these wonderful plans have been put into effect. The dream has become reality. I'll sign. [*Signs*]
SAIAPIN: Ingenious, but . . . a bit risky.
ZILOV: Rubbish. It'll get through. Nobody'll notice. Why should they? . . . Sign here.
SAIAPIN: I'd be glad to, but . . .
ZILOV: Come on, sign. This is a fine job we have, but you have to admit it's a bit on the dull side. A bit of daring and creative imagination won't do us any harm.
SAIAPIN: We ought to check it, though, ring the plant, the engineer . . .
ZILOV: I'm afraid the engineer might disappoint us. Let's be optimistic, old fellow.
SAIAPIN: This'll be the death of us.
[*Knock at door.* ZILOV *opens it.*]
VOICE: Your mail.
ZILOV: Let's have it.

VOICE: Sign here.
 [ZILOV *tosses bundle of mail onto table.*]
SAIAPIN: [*sorting through it.*] Letter for you.
ZILOV: From a woman?
SAIAPIN: From A.N. Zilov. [*Tosses letter across desk.*] "A letter came for Grandpa Fedia from his little grandson..."
ZILOV: From the old man. Let's see what the old fool's got to say. [*Reads*] Oh, Lord... You don't say! He's dying again. [*Looking up from letter.*] Once or twice a year, on the average, the old fellow lies down to die. Listen to this: [*Reads*] "...this time it's the end, I can feel it in my bones. Come home, son, to see us and comfort your mother. She hasn't seen you for four years." See what he's up to? He sends out letters like this all over the place, and settles down to wait, the old fox. The whole stupid family comes flocking in with ohs and ahs, and he's delighted. He'll lie there for a bit, then before you know it he'll be on his feet, hale and hearty, and drinking vodka again. What do you say to that?
SAIAPIN: Is he retired?
ZILOV: Yes, on a special pension.
SAIAPIN: How old is he?
ZILOV: Over seventy. Seventy-two or seventy-five. Something like that.
SAIAPIN: That's old. You know, he really could die.
ZILOV: Him? No, the old man's got plenty of life in him yet.
SAIAPIN: All the same you might go and visit him.
ZILOV: When?
SAIAPIN: During your holiday, in September.
ZILOV: I can't. September's sacred: the shooting season.
 [*Short pause.*]
SAIAPIN: What about this article then? What shall we do?
ZILOV: I thought we'd decided. We'll give him this. I've signed it.
SAIAPIN: It's easy for you, but for me... Especially now, when I've got this chance of a flat, you understand...
ZILOV: Listen, we'll toss for it. Heads — we give it to him; tails — we admit we haven't got any article.
SAIAPIN: [*sighing*] All right...
 [*Knock on door.*]
ZILOV: Come in. [*Tosses coin.*]

[*Enter* IRINA. *The coin is forgotten.* IRINA *is eighteen. Her direct manner should not on any account be mistaken for naiveté, nor her open-heartedness for simplicity. Nor should her trusting air be shown as stemming from ignorance or flippancy, for her most important characteristic is her honesty. But at the same time it should be borne in mind that she is now taking her very first independent steps in life.*]

IRINA: Hullo.
ZILOV: Good morning.
IRINA: Excuse me, is this the editorial office?
[*Short pause.*]
ZILOV: What can we do for you?
IRINA: I want to get an announcement printed . . .
ZILOV: Announcement? . . . What sort of announcement?
IRINA: You see, I've lost somebody. I was supposed to meet him . . .
ZILOV: Sit down and tell us all about it. Take your time. [*Shows her to seat, winking at* SAIAPIN.] I think we might be able to help you.
IRINA: Really?
ZILOV: We'll do our best.
SAIAPIN: He'll do everything within his power.
IRINA: Really? Thank you so much . . .
ZILOV: Don't mention it. Now what's the problem?
IRINA: I've really got to find him. We were in the same carriage on the train here. He's called Kostia, but I don't know his surname . . .
ZILOV: Go on.
IRINA: I let him down. But it's not my fault. Really it isn't.
ZILOV: What happened?
IRINA: We'd agreed to meet today at twelve outside the central post office.
But at just the same time I had to write the essay paper.
SAIAPIN: What for? An entrance exam?
IRINA: Yes, I'm applying for the Institute of Foreign Languages. If only I'd known where the central post office was, I'd have finished my essay sooner. Anyway, I ran all the way there, but he'd gone . . .
SAIAPIN: Is that all?
IRINA: It's turned out badly.

ZILOV: Yes, I've never heard of anything like it. Nobody in our town behaves like that. Where do you come from?
IRINA: From Mikhalevka.
ZILOV: And where's that?
IRINA: In the north. A long way from here.
ZILOV: And what's your name?
IRINA: Irina.
SAIAPIN: That's a nice name.
ZILOV: Well, Irina, how can you go on living after that?
IRINA: If you'll print an announcement . . .
ZILOV: What announcement? . . .
IRINA: [*eagerly*] I've got it ready! Like this: "Kostia! I was late. Wait for me outside the central post office at twelve on the fifth of August. I'll explain everything. Irina." Won't that do?
SAIAPIN: "Wait for me, and I'll return,
    Only wait for me . . ."
IRINA: Surely it'll do, won't it? . . . He'll read it. He reads all the papers. He bought papers at every station. And he writes poetry.
ZILOV: Oh, so he's a poet. Konstantin Simonov maybe?
IRINA: You're being funny. Simonov's old, and he lives in Moscow.
ZILOV: Not at all. He used to live in Moscow, but now he lives here.
IRINA: [*surprised*] Is that so?
ZILOV: Of course. I've had Moscow up to the back teeth, he says. All the racket and hustle and bustle. How much can a man take? I'll go and live somewhere quiet, he says. You can take it from me.
IRINA: No, he's not Simonov. He's only written two poems, and he wrote another in the train.
ZILOV: And I expect he dedicated it to you, did he?
IRINA: How did you know?
ZILOV: He dedicated his poem to you, and you fell in love with him. Don't tell me I'm wrong.
IRINA: Fell in love? . . . No, not at all . . .
ZILOV: You mean you don't love him?
IRINA: Of course I don't.
ZILOV: Then why do you have to find him?
IRINA: To explain. Otherwise it'll look as if I let him down on purpose.

ZILOV: [*to* SAIAPIN.] What do you say to that?
SAIAPIN: "Love me, my beauty, while I have my freedom,
　　　　Love me, my beauty, while I am yours . . ."
　　　　[*Enter* KUSHAK.]
KUSHAK: Where's that article? What are you doing? . . . What brings you here, young lady?
ZILOV: Her name's Irina. A personal matter.
KUSHAK: I hope you're not going to say she's an old schoolfriend of yours.
ZILOV: [*looking* IRINA *up and down.*] I'm not. If I did nobody would believe me.
SAIAPIN: She's looking for a friend.
KUSHAK: Here? Among you?
IRINA: No. I want to get an announcement printed.
KUSHAK: Announcement? . . . Here? Why here?
　　　　[SAIAPIN *laughs silently.*]
IRINA: But this is the editorial office, isn't it?
KUSHAK: Editorial office? . . . [*Shakes fist at* ZILOV *and* SAIAPIN.] You've made a mistake, young lady. This isn't the editorial office.
IRINA: What?
ZILOV: Don't worry. The editorial office is just next door.
IRINA: [*to* ZILOV.] But why did you tell me this was it? . . . I don't understand . . .
KUSHAK: [*irritably*] Perfectly clear, isn't it? You want the editorial office, and this office is called the C.B.T.I., Central Bureau of Technical Information, if you prefer . . .
IRINA: [*rising*] I'm sorry. [*Goes to door.*]
KUSHAK: [*watching her go. More gently.*] That's all right . . . Must have been the word "information" that misled you. Best of luck.
IRINA: [*to* ZILOV, *from door.*] Why did you do that? . . .
ZILOV: [*going after her.*] Nothing to worry about, Irina. Everything'll be all right. [*To* KUSHAK *and* SAIAPIN *from the doorway.*] Won't be a minute. [*Exit*]
KUSHAK: Do you intend to give me an article?
SAIAPIN: Yes, we do.
KUSHAK: I can see what you intend. Makes me wonder if this place is an office or a house of assignation. How many times do I have to warn you?

SAIAPIN: Why pick on me? You know I'm not terribly interested in women.
KUSHAK: It's a disgrace. After all there's a time and a place for everything. I shan't warn you again. And hurry up with that article. I'll send it off for typesetting this afternoon. [*Exit*]
SAIAPIN: He gets the girls, and I get told off for it. [*Dials a number on phone.*] Editorial office? . . . Kuzakov? . . . Hi. No! This is no time for chess. Is Zilov there? . . . He isn't? . . . What a bastard! . . . No, no, not you . . . Well, you too if you like. [*Enter* ZILOV.]
ZILOV: Well, what do you think of her?
SAIAPIN: Look, you know where you can go with your woman?
ZILOV: No, where? I'd like your advice. I was thinking of the cinema to start with.
SAIAPIN: For crying out loud! He's demanding his article [*Points at door of* KUSHAK'*s office.*] What are we going to do? He won't leave it at that . . . Don't forget, he's got it in for you. Since your house-warming. Surely you haven't forgotten?
ZILOV: As if I care. [*Puts on coat.*] How often do you meet a girl like that? She's one in a million. Don't you see? . . . Maybe I'll love her all my life — who knows? [*Goes to door.*]
SAIAPIN: Stop! Wait a minute, for God's sake!
ZILOV: Be quick then. I've a girl waiting for me.
SAIAPIN: He wants an article. What are we going to do?
ZILOV: That business again! Blast it! Give him that thing, and forget it. Put your signature on it.
SAIAPIN: I'm taking a big risk, you realize.
ZILOV: Damn the risk! Is it the first time? [*Remembering something.*] Hold it! That coin! Where is it?
[*Both search for the coin forgotten twenty minutes earlier.*] What did we say?
SAIAPIN: Heads — we give it to him; tails — we don't . . . There it is. Tails. Look.
ZILOV: What bad luck . . . Hold on though. Haven't you got it mixed up? Tails — we give it to him; heads — we don't . . . Listen, give it here! Tails — we do; heads — we don't! [*Tosses coin.*]
SAIAPIN: It's heads.
ZILOV: [*annoyed*] Hell! . . . Well, that's it then. It's fate. We'll see about writing the stupid thing tomorrow. [*Goes to door.*]

SAIAPIN: [*holding him back.*] Then we'll go and see him together. I'm not going to take the rap all by myself.
ZILOV: What a business . . . Listen! Third time lucky. Let's toss again. Tails — we admit we haven't got anything to give him; heads — we don't. [*Tosses coin.*]
SAIAPIN: It's heads.
ZILOV: [*relieved.*] Thank goodness. That's one thing taken care of. [*Goes to door.*]
[*Phone rings.*]
SAIAPIN: [*into phone.*] Yes . . . Right away . . . [*To* ZILOV.] Wait! It's for you.
ZILOV: Who is it?
SAIAPIN: Sounds like your wife.
ZILOV: I'm not here.
SAIAPIN: I've already said you are.
ZILOV: Idiot! [*Takes receiver.*] What is it? [*Covers receiver with hand.*] Keep her occupied for a moment, would you? There's a good fellow. She's waiting by the entrance. But make sure you act polite. You could scare her off as easy as wink. Off you go . . .
[*Exit* SAIAPIN.]
Well, what's happened? . . . See me? . . . Now? . . . Out of the question . . . There's a flap on. A report . . . They're all on holiday. Just the two of us working flat out here . . . No. No . . . What's all the rush? What's up? . . . Of course not . . . What's happened? . . . What? . . . A baby? . . . You sure? . . . That's great. Congratulations . . . A boy, I'm sure . . . Of course . . . Yes . . . I *am* glad . . . Of course I am . . . Well, what do you expect me to do? Sing a song? Do a dance? . . . See me? . . . We'll see each other tonight. Not going to give birth this minute, are you? . . . What? . . . Just a moment! [*It is clear that the other party has abruptly cut him off. He is a little annoyed.*] Already gone off in a huff. [*Exit*]
[*Lights fade, stage rotates, lights come on.* ZILOV *is sitting by the telephone in his room. He gets up and walks about the room. Stops by wreath and stands looking at it for a moment.*]
ZILOV: The swine have had their bit of fun . . .

ACT TWO
SCENE ONE

ZILOV's *room. It is raining outside.* ZILOV *is talking on the phone.*

ZILOV: [*impatiently*] Phoning you is a waste of time, I can tell you . . . Yes, a waste of time. You always say the same thing: variable cloud, winds light to moderate. What's that? . . . Just look out of the window . . . You call that variable cloud. I call it a downpour . . . I want to know when it's going to stop . . . [*In conciliatory tone.*] Yes, whoever can tell? God knows? . . . You're supposed to be taming the elements and you can't even tell me when it's going to stop raining . . . What do you do there, eh? . . . What? [*Hurriedly. It is apparent that he wants to talk.*] Just a moment! Let's have a chat. Your work's not much use to anyone anyway . . . Don't be angry, young lady . . . You're forty? . . . Well, no reason why you shouldn't recall your youth . . . How old am I? . . . How should I put it? "I'm only a young girl now, but my heart is a thousand years old . . ." You heard that song? . . . What did you say? . . . Oh, you're wanted. Pity. What a pity. [*Hangs up. Lies down on couch on back, with hands under head.*]
[*Lights fade, then come on again. Third memory begins.* ZILOV's *flat. Couch, a few chairs, the toy cat,* VERA's *gift, on the windowsill. Early morning.* GALINA *is asleep, sitting at table on which lamp is burning and a stack of exercise books*

stands. *Latch clicks.* GALINA *wakes and raises head. She is wearing glasses, which she now takes off and lays on the table. Turns towards window. Enter* ZILOV.]

ZILOV: Hullo.

GALINA: Good morning. [*Turns off lamp.*]

ZILOV: Why aren't you asleep? . . . [*Pause*] Too much work? . . . [*Takes off jacket and throws it onto couch.*] Haven't you been to bed at all? . . . [*Short pause.*] It's no good working as hard as that. We're not cart-horses. [*Sits down on couch.*] I'm dead on my feet. [*Yawns*] Yes, I'm going to have to escape from that office. Nothing else for it . . . Call it a job? I ask you. Know where I've been? . . . [*Short pause.*] In Svirsk, if you can imagine. Yesterday after lunch with no warning they pack me off in a hurry to the porcelain plant. What for? I ask. For the splendid occasion of the reconstruction of the workshop. I have to study it, report on it, keep the scientists informed. What about? Their little tinpot factory! That little potting shed. Enough to make you weep . . . No, this isn't the life for me. After all, I'm an engineer . . . [*Short pause.*] I phoned you at school but you were in class . . . Yes, we need a phone at home. We absolutely must get one, don't you think? . . . Galia! . . .

[*Silence.*]

Don't you want to talk to me? . . . That's odd . . . [*Pause. He lies down on couch.*] What's happened? What's the matter? . . . If I've done something, do me the favour of telling me . . . Or haven't you had a letter for a while? From that childhood friend? Has he stopped writing? . . . If so why pick on me? . . . I'm tired. I want to go to bed . . . Do you hear? I've only had two hours' sleep. At the station . . . [*Short pause.*] Well? What is it? Don't you believe me?

GALINA: You were seen in town last night.

ZILOV: What? . . . That's rich . . . And who saw me? . . . In town? . . . Last night? Me? . . . Wonders never cease! [*Short pause.*] What do you mean by "night"? If you mean seven in the evening that's different. That I can explain.

GALINA: I don't believe a word you say.

ZILOV: [*having thought for a moment, and taken offence.*] Are you serious?

GALINA: I don't believe a word you say.
ZILOV: [*calmly*] There's no call for that. A wife ought to trust her husband. That's obvious. The most important thing in family life is trust. Without it family life is unthinkable. Who saw me in town yesterday? Or rather, who claims to have seen me and claims I was in town? . . .
GALINA: It doesn't make any difference who.
ZILOV: No, we must sort this out, to clear up any suspicions. Who saw me? And where?
GALINA: You were seen at the grocer's at ten.
ZILOV: Who by?
GALINA: What does it matter who by? A neighbour.
ZILOV: Maria Vasilyevna? . . . Her? . . . Then it's obvious. She's short-sighted. Now is that likely — she saw me, but I didn't see her? That's absolutely impossible. The old girl saw somebody else. [*Going over to her.*] Galia, you've become too suspicious. You trust the neighbours more than you trust me. Aren't you ashamed of yourself? . . . [*Tries to embrace her.*]
GALINA: [*freeing herself.*] You said you were tired . . .
ZILOV: So what?
GALINA: So you don't have to embrace me. Have a rest if you're tired.
ZILOV: I'm not as tired as all that . . . [*Tries to embrace her again.*]
GALINA: [*walks away.*] No. I'd rather you didn't. [*After pause.*] And you and I aren't going to be doing any more of that.
[*Short pause.*]
ZILOV: [*anxiously*] What do you mean by that? . . . What's wrong with you? Why are you looking at me like that? . . . What is it? . . . You can look at other people like that, you can look at a rapist like that . . . but, like it or not, I'm your husband . . . You're even going to have a child by me . . .
GALINA: No need to worry about that. We're not going to have a child.
ZILOV: What? . . . What do you mean? . . . Have you been to the hospital? [*Short pause.*] [*Menacingly*] Tell me! Have you been to the hospital?
GALINA: Anyone'd think you didn't want me to.
ZILOV: [*losing his temper.*] What have you gone and done? . . . How could you? . . . Why didn't you tell me before? . . . Tell me!

... How dare you do something like that alone? ... Do you know what you're doing? Do you? ... Oh no, I'll never forgive you for that!

GALINA: Cut the clowning.

[*Pause.*]

ZILOV: This is awful ... It's awful that you didn't consult me. [*Short pause.*] What now? You can't bring it back ... [*Goes to her.*] How do you feel? All right? ... [*Short pause.*] Well, don't take it too hard. We can put things right ... Everything'll be fine ... [*Pause*] Everything'll be fine, do you hear? ... And next time you won't take one step without asking me. I'll keep an eye on you all the time, believe me.

GALINA: I don't believe a word you say.

ZILOV: But why not? ... After all, *I* believe what *you* say.

GALINA: But I don't believe you.

ZILOV: Funny ... [*Pause*] Once upon a time we promised to trust each other, remember? Each other, not the neighbours ... Isn't that right? Or have you forgotten?

GALINA: Once upon a time ... So you remember. We said all sorts of things then.

ZILOV: But surely nothing's changed!

GALINA: Nothing? Don't be silly. Everything's over.

ZILOV: Look, let's not panic. [*Goes towards her, she retreats. He sits down on chair in middle of room.*] All right, a few things have changed. Life moves on, but you and I haven't changed. At least my feelings for you are just as they were six years ago. Like that evening. I hope you haven't forgotten.

GALINA: It's morning now, not evening. Forget about that. There's nothing left.

ZILOV: No, no, everything's fine. If something's not quite right, we can bring it all back any time we like. Right now, if you like. It's up to us entirely.

GALINA: We can't bring anything back.

ZILOV: You don't believe me? ... Well, let's see what we can do. Close your eyes, and you'll see. Close your eyes. [*Short pause.*] All right then, keep them open. [*Looks round room.*] Ye-es ... Yes, our room was a bit smaller ... The table was here. [*Moves table.*] The bed was here. [*Moves couch.*] We don't need this. [*Takes toy cat from windowsill and throws it under couch.*] What else? . . . Wine. We had some wine . . . Haven't we got any? . . . Pity . . . Yes! Flowers! We had some flowers . . . Do you remember what sort? . . . I think they were snowdrops. Yes, it was April. Was it April?

GALINA: Stop it. And leave that evening alone.

ZILOV: [*hurt*] Leave it alone? What do you mean? . . . That evening's my holy of holies, the great day of my life. And we'll bring it back, you'll see . . . Flowers! [*Snatches up brass ashtray from table, shows it to* GALINA.] Snowdrops. I've brought you some snowdrops.

GALINA: Are you making fun of me?

ZILOV: Of course not! Can't you understand? . . . Sit down here! . . . Come on, please . . . When I came in you were sitting by the window. Here. Sit down . . . [*Pushes her into seat.*]

GALINA: [*getting up.*] Stop this, will you?

ZILOV: [*pushing her down again.*] You were looking out of the window. Look out of the window . . . It was open. [*Opens window and steps back into room.*] That's it . . . Now what else was there? . . .

GALINA: For heaven's sake, stop.

ZILOV: No, heaven didn't come into it, but there was a church opposite, remember? . . . Yes, the planetarium. Inside it had been converted into a planetarium, but from the outside it was still a church. And you said: "I'd like to marry you in a church." Remember? . . . And what did I say? . . . [*Short pause.*] I think I kissed you, didn't I? . . . Let's do that now: you say what you said about the church, and I'll give you a kiss.

GALINA: Leave me alone, will you?

ZILOV: All right, let's not anticipate matters. You were looking out of the window. Look out of the window. When I came in you looked round . . . Right, so I come in. [*Acting out role.*] You look round. Turn your head . . . No, you must turn your head. When you looked round and we looked into each other's eyes I realized that everything would happen that evening. And you? . . . Didn't you feel that too? . . . Okay, let's keep things in order and not get distracted. I come in, you look round. [*Shouts*] I'm coming in!

[GALINA *involuntarily turns her head.*]

No, that won't do. You're looking at me as if I was a rapist. And you looked at me ever so tenderly then, really . . . Make an effort . . . I'm coming in. [*Acting out role.*] Here I come . . . [*Loudly*] Galia!

[GALINA *looks round.*]

Right . . . That'll do . . . [*Acting*] I hope I'm not late.

GALINA: Yes you are. You should have got here last night, not this morning.

ZILOV: For goodness' sake! You're not here now, you're there. There. Understand? That evening. Come on . . . [*Acting*] I hope I'm not late.

[GALINA *says nothing.* ZILOV *approaches and hands her the flowers, i.e. the ashtray.*]

GALINA: [*ironically*] Thank you.

ZILOV: Who are you watching for? Own up.

GALIAN: [*in mocking tone, after pause.*] Hullo, Vitia. Have you ever been to church?

ZILOV: Yes. Looked in once with some of my mates, when we were drunk. Have you?

GALINA: [*mocking*] I went with my grandmother. To keep her company.

ZILOV: What was it like?

GALINA: [*mocking*] Very nice. I'd like to marry you in a church.

[ZILOV *tries to kiss her.*]

Hands off, if you don't mind.

ZILOV: No, no. You didn't say "Hands off!" then. Don't you remember what you said? . . . [*Short pause.*]

[*In bitterly reproachful tone.*] There you are, you don't remember anything any more.

GALINA: Oh yes I do, you know . . . [*Recollecting aloud in gently mocking tone.*] Think: we go up some steps, go in, and everything's quiet, there are candles burning, and there is such a splendid, festive feeling.

ZILOV: That's it! And then I sat down here [*Sits down.*] and asked you . . . [*Acting*] Is the lady of the house at home?

GALINA: It wasn't like that at all. You were so nervous then . . .

ZILOV: [*acting*] Is the lady of the house in? [*Waits, then prompts her.*] "No, she's on duty . . ." Come on! . . . [*Acting*] Is the lady of the house in?

GALINA: [*thoughtfully*] Yes . . . She was on duty that evening . . .
ZILOV: [*acting*] So she'll be out this evening?
   [ZILOV *puts his arm round her. She pushes him away, but only gently, lost in her memories.*]
   So she'll be out.
GALINA: It wasn't quite like that. I said to you . . . [*In a low voice she repeats her words of long ago.*] Let's go somewhere . . .
ZILOV: [*catching on.*] No.
GALINA: Let's go the planetarium. We've never been there.
ZILOV: No.
GALINA: Well, would you like me to walk you back to your hostel.
ZILOV: Do you want me to go?
GALINA: No . . . I want to go for a walk with you . . . [*Breaking into remembered conversation.*] Well, go on. [*Prompts*] "I'm not going anywhere."
ZILOV: I'm not going anywhere.
GALINA: Why not?
ZILOV: Because . . . [*Stumbles*] Because . . .
GALINA: [*impatiently*] Why not?
ZILOV: [*remembering*] Because I love you.
GALINA: And if we go for a short walk will you stop loving me?
ZILOV: [*uncertainly*] No, but I'd never get over it . . .
GALINA: [*with ease.*] Come on, please. Prove that you love me . . . [*Pause*] What is it now? . . . [*Agitatedly*] Go on, go on!
ZILOV: [*insincerely*] I can't live without you.
GALINA: No, no! That's not it at all! Can't you feel that it's wrong? . . . Can't you?
ZILOV: [*uncertainly*] Darling . . .
GALINA: No!
ZILOV: [*querying tone.*] My love?
GALINA: No!
ZILOV: [*fateful tone.*] My dear!
GALINA: [*pained*] No! No! No! . . . Surely you can remember!
ZILOV: [*racking brain.*] Don't get excited . . . Just a moment, one moment . . . It'll all come back to me . . . [*Finally remembering.*] Got it! [*Taking her hand.*] Come here to me!
GALINA: [*freeing hand.*] No! You haven't said the most important thing.
ZILOV: It doesn't matter. [*Tries to embrace her.*]

GALINA: No! You must remember it . . . Try! Please! [*Short pause, despairingly.*] Are you going to remember or aren't you? [*Pause. She waits.*]

ZILOV: Damned if I know! A man might say all sorts of things at a time like that!

GALINA: [*with something close to hatred.*] You've forgotten everything. Everything!

ZILOV: That's enough of that. [*Roughly*] Come here. [*Forcefully draws her towards him.*]

[GALINA *tears free and slowly backs away. Silence.* GALINA *suddenly collapses onto a chair and weeps.*]

ZILOV: [*after pause, with genuine grief.*] So much for our memories of youth.

[*Lights fade and come on again.* ZILOV *is lying on the couch with his hands under his head.*]

SCENE TWO

ZILOV *walks up and down the room. Stands for a while by the window. Goes to phone, dials number.*

ZILOV: Dima . . . Me here, Zilov . . . I don't think this rain's ever going to stop . . . It's going to go on for forty days and forty nights . . . Why not? It happened once before, I hear . . . What about starting out now, Dima? . . . Why not? We could spend the night at Kliuchi . . . What if it *is* boggy? . . . If we leave the sidecar behind? . . . Without the sidecar we could get the bike across, I guarantee . . . We couldn't? . . . Too bad . . . In a lousy mood, to tell you the truth . . . One thing and another. Now I've got my friends doing their best to cheer me up . . . You haven't heard? Know what they've sent me? . . . A wreath . . . A wreath! . . . Yes, of course — for a coffin, or a grave . . . Their idea of a joke, the swine . . . You think it's funny? . . . I don't think it's very funny at all . . . I'm so sensitive this little joke of theirs'll be giving me nightmares . . . And they call themselves my friends! More like a gang of terrorists. But didn't you know about it? . . . Thank goodness for that. That makes one decent soul at least

... [*Anxiously*] Dima! I didn't by any chance hit you yesterday, did I? No? ... That's good ... [*Agitatedly*] Look, forgive a stupid question, old chap, but what do you think of me? ... [*Listens*] I'll ... I'll tell you. After yesterday's business I'm all alone ... No, I can feel I'm on my own. And you seem to be the closest friend I've got ... [*Forced laugh.*] No, that's not the point ... Anyway, thank goodness we're going shooting together ... [*In his normal voice.*] Yes, I'll be waiting for you to ring ... I'm not going anywhere. I'll be waiting. [*Hangs up, walks about room, stops. Stands facing window.*]

[*Lights fade, stage rotates, lights come on. Next memory begins. The Technical Information Office.* ZILOV *and* SAIAPIN. SAIAPIN *is writing something.*]

ZILOV: Five o'clock. Down tools! [*Puts papers in drawer.*] Stop. You've been working like an automaton lately.

SAIAPIN: What else can I do? It's all very well for you to talk — you've already got a flat ... A flat of your own means a lot, whatever you say. Just take this side of it: when you share a flat everybody knows everything you do. It's all public. Your wife goes on the rampage, and if you're a sensitive fellow you sit quiet and endure it. Even if you feel like thumping her? ... I mean it ... As soon as they give us a flat of our own she'll find out what's what.

ZILOV: [*laughing*] When you have your house-warming party I'll give you a pair of boxing gloves.

SAIAPIN: Yes, once you have your own flat you're a free man. If you don't like this office you can quit and get a job somewhere else.

ZILOV: For example?

SAIAPIN: In a factory, for instance, or teaching. Why shouldn't we?

ZILOV: Forget it, pal. You and I'll never go anywhere.

SAIAPIN: Why not?

ZILOV: Because, in the words of my old man, you're idle and debauched ...

SAIAPIN: What about you?

ZILOV: Me? ... [*Grins*] I could probably still take up something serious. But I don't want to. Don't feel like it.

SAIAPIN: Speaking for myself, this place suits me quite well, but the wife ...

ZILOV: There's no better place for you and me than this office, old fellow. It's just like home.
SAIAPIN: We'll see. [*Clears desk.*] What's your programme for the evening? We're off to the football match.
ZILOV: [*leaning back in his chair.*] Off you go then.
SAIAPIN: [*pulls chessboard out of drawer.*] We've time for a quick game before the match.
ZILOV: Go ahead.
SAIAPIN: The match ought to be a good laugh. We're playing Krasnogorsk. Feel like coming along for a laugh? [*Dials number on phone.*]
ZILOV: Leave the phone. I'm expecting a call.
SAIAPIN: [*into phone.*] Kuzakov? . . . How's life? Want to be check-mated? Come on then, while I've got a bit of time . . .
ZILOV: I'm expecting a call, I said.
SAIAPIN: That's right. My turn to be white . . . Hurry up then. [*Hangs up.*] Who's going to ring you? [*Setting up chessboard.*] Not that girl again, is it?
ZILOV: What if it is?
SAIAPIN: I see you're serious about her.
ZILOV: I like her.
[*Phone rings.*]
[*Picks up phone.*] Ira? . . . Hullo, my dearest . . . Where are you?
SAIAPIN: "My love, my love, my dearest love,
 Why aren't you here with me? . . ."
ZILOV: I've missed you . . . Don't you believe me? . . . Well, how can I prove it? . . . You'll see how I've lost weight . . . Yes, since last night . . . Doesn't take long . . . Where are you? . . . What? . . . In a phone-box? . . . Somebody bothering you? . . . Who's bothering you? . . . Pestering you? . . . [*To* SAIAPIN.] Some boys. There you are, she's just too pretty . . . [*Into phone.*] Tell 'em to get lost. Say you'll call the police . . . And don't you dare smile at them, you hear? . . . I'll be waiting for you at six in the "Forget-Me Not" . . . The "Forget-Me-Not" at six. Don't be late . . . What? . . . Don't you dare talk to them. I forbid you! [*Hangs up.*] Those louts have got a nerve!
SAIAPIN: I can't make out whether you're in love, or just playing games with her.

[*Enter* KUSHAK, *carrying large folder.*]

KUSHAK: Want to get me locked up, do you? [*Short pause.*] Where'd you get hold of this forgery? [*Short pause.*] Which of you tried to plant this blatant piece of disinformation?

ZILOV: What's up, chief?

KUSHAK: Oh, of course, you don't know anything about it.

ZILOV: Why? Found a few slips, have you? [*Points to folder.*]

KUSHAK: Slips? . . . How well you put it! I never suspected you were so modest. Slips! The whole thing's a pack of lies!

ZILOV: What's a pack of lies?

KUSHAK: [*stabbing finger at folder.*] This! This thing here! As if you didn't know!

ZILOV: The porcelain plant? Is it really?

KUSHAK: There's been no reconstruction, and there isn't going to be!

ZILOV: You don't say!

KUSHAK: There's not a word of truth in this!

ZILOV: If that's so it really is awful. Scandalous! However did it happen? We'll have to get to the bottom of it. What shall we do? . . . Hold it . . . Where's our original. [*Rummages in desk.*]

KUSHAK: Which of you dealt with this? [*Short pause.*]

ZILOV: I did.

KUSHAK: Zilov, I like you less and less every day.

ZILOV: What can I do? Change my hairstyle maybe?

KUSHAK: Less of the wisecracks, Zilov. This isn't quite so funny as you think, I'll have you know. Sit down and write an explanation. [*To* SAIAPIN.] You too.

SAIAPIN: Me?

KUSHAK: Yes, you. Who else. You both signed the article, you can both answer for it.

ZILOV: It's nothing to do with him.

KUSHAK: I see. So it's all your doing, is it?

ZILOV: Looks like it.

KUSHAK: Just as I thought . . . Very honourable of you, very honourable indeed. I understand you perfectly. That's the way true friends ought to behave.

ZILOV: Not at all, but I realize I've let him down . . .

KUSHAK: [*ironically*] Aha, so you've let him down. So you ought to

be punished, while he should only be encouraged, if I understand you correctly.
ZILOV: Well, that sounds perfectly logical.
KUSHAK: Yes, yes. You make it all sound so simple. Beautifully simple . . . There's just one thing I don't like . . . Just one thing, my friends, . . . I don't like the way you treat everybody else as stupider than you. Or do you think that's a good thing?
ZILOV: No, it's a bad thing.
KUSHAK: Exactly! A bad thing! It's perfectly clear to all — even to me — why you're shielding him . . . So perhaps you'll tell me why I have to be treated as somebody stupider than you. [*To* ZILOV, *point-blank.*] That's the question that has to be asked, I'm sure you'll agree. Sooner or later.

[VALERIA *appears and stops in the doorway, unnoticed by the others.*]

ZILOV: Yes, an interesting question . . .
KUSHAK: Not half as interesting as the next question. Tell me: do you like working in this office?
ZILOV: [*after pause.*] Yes, perfectly well . . . Why, has it really come to that?
KUSHAK: If the responsibility for this [*Shakes folder in air.*] act of crying irresponsibility is yours alone, I'll sack you. [*Short pause.*] So, my dear friends, you're going to have to tell me the truth . . . Which of you dealt with this? You alone? Or both of you? . . . [*Short pause.*]
SAIAPIN: I don't know about that article. Zilov prepared it. I trusted him.
KUSHAK: I see . . . [*To* ZILOV.] And what have you to say?
ZILOV: I've already told you. I prepared it.
KUSHAK: In that case the matter's closed. [*To* SAIAPIN.] But you still won't get off without a reprimand. From now on never sign anything until you've read it properly. That ought to be obvious. Once upon a time every three-year-old used to know it. Disgraceful!
VALERIA: Hullo!
KUSHAK: Good evening.
VALERIA: [*to* KUSHAK.] What have these two time-servers been up to? They deserve more than a scolding, Vadim Andreevich. They deserve a beating. Too bad I'm only a weak woman . . .

KUSHAK: Yes, I have to inform you that I have cause for complaint. They've committed a serious error in their work. An unforgivable error, in my opinion.

VALERIA: Have they now? . . . Then give them everything they deserve! Kindly punish my husband with all the severity of the law.

KUSHAK: Your husband is somewhat lacking in . . . er . . .

ZILOV: [*prompting*] . . . a sense of principle.

KUSHAK: Precisely.

VALERIA: [*to her husband.*] Rascal. [*To* KUSHAK.] Vadim Andreevich, whatever you do to them, I'll be only too pleased.

KUSHAK: Much as I regret it, this cannot be allowed to pass without repercussions.

VALERIA: Vadim Andreevich! I've had a brilliant idea! You'll never think of a better punishment! Reprimands are no good. They don't care. Even if you sacked them they wouldn't be too sorry. There's only one way . . .

SAIAPIN: What might that be?

VALERIA: [*to* KUSHAK.] Shall I tell you?

KUSHAK: Yes, tell me, Valeria. Thank goodness you've got plenty of common sense.

VALERIA: [*about* SAIAPIN.] What if we deprive him of his football tonight, eh?

SAIAPIN: [*adopting an appropriate tone.*] Now look here!

VALERIA: Yes, yes! Instead of watching the football you can sit here and work. Overtime! Get it? While we go to the match. Vadim Andreevich and I!

ZILOV: Not bad.

VALERIA: [*to* KUSHAK.] Well?

SAIAPIN: [*in same tone.*] You don't give the orders here, you know . . .

VALERIA: [*to* KUSHAK.] Agreed?

KUSHAK: [*with forced laugh.*] That'd be funny, of course . . . but at the same time . . . It's not exactly . . .

VALERIA: Then it's agreed! You're a football fan too, aren't you?

KUSHAK: Me? . . . Well, I'm not that crazy about it . . . Moderately, you know . . .

VALERIA: Then you won't understand what football means to him. Let's go! Let's go! This'll be a real punishment to him!

KUSHAK: Well, I don't know . . .
VALERIA: Vadim Andreevich! Isn't it clear? He's too busy, they're both too busy. And I can't go by myself, can I?
KUSHAK: No, but I . . . Never mind. But look, this might be seen more than one way . . .
VALERIA: Vadim Andreevich! Which way? What's there to think about? [*To her husband.*] Well? Let's have your opinion.
SAIAPIN: Unfortunately, Vadim Andreevich, she's the one who gives the orders. Once she's made up her mind . . .
VALERIA: [*taking* KUSHAK's *arm.*] Vadim Andreevich, we'll be late. And as for Zilov, just postpone his holidays. For a week. He'll miss the start of the shooting season . . .
ZILOV: That's none of your business.
VALERIA: He'll never get over it, you'll see. [*Pulling* KUSHAK, *who looks lost, towards the door.*] Come on, we've got to hurry.
KUSHAK: [*in doorway.*] Now listen, Valeria. If you think they can get off as lightly as that, you're mistaken.
VALERIA: Oh, I quite agree. They should both get their just desserts. They've no right to hope for anything. Business and friendship don't mix . . . [*vanishes with* KUSHAK.]
SAIAPIN: [*not without pride.*] Did you see that?
ZILOV: Yes, with her you're as safe as houses.
SAIAPIN: She's a real friend for life.
ZILOV: Yes, quite a family you make. And you don't do so badly either . . .
SAIAPIN: He won't sack you, old fellow . . . Do you realize? That flat was going up in smoke before I'd even got it! Before our very eyes! Don't you see that?

[*Voice outside door: "Telegram."* ZILOV *goes out and immediately comes in again with telegram in hand. Opens telegram as he walks, and suddenly stops in his tracks. Stands quite still for some time.*]
What is it?
ZILOV: The old man's died. [*Pause. Sits down, lowers head.*] So this time he was right . . .
[*Pause*]
SAIAPIN: When?
ZILOV: Yesterday, at six o'clock . . . [*Short pause.*] Oh, Dad, Dad . . . If only I'd known . . . [*Pause. Rises, dials number on*

phone.] Galia . . . Dad's died . . . Yes . . . yes . . . Got any money? . . . Bring me what you've got. I'm leaving . . . Today. Now . . . Yes . . . I'll be in the office. I'll be waiting . . . [*Hangs up.*]

SAIAPIN: Can you make it in time?

ZILOV: Ought to be able to . . . Five hours on the plane, half a day on the steamer, then the bus . . . I hope I can make it.

SAIAPIN: Ye-es . . . He won't sack you now, that's for sure.

ZILOV: What?

SAIAPIN: He won't sack you, he's got no right to after a thing like that.

ZILOV: Shut up, you idiot!

[*Enter* KUZAKOV *and* VERA. ZILOV *sits with lowered head.*]

KUZAKOV: Hi there, Olegs! [*Short pause.*] Why so sad, what's got you down, proud falcons? Or could it be a drink you want, you alkies? [*Comes into room, takes seat at chessboard.*] Well then, grand master . . .

SAIAPIN: Wait. This isn't the time.

KUZAKOV: What's happened?

VERA: They're disillusioned with life.

KUZAKOV: Well, maybe they're right. Life's more or less over anyway.

[SAIAPIN *shows* KUZAKOV *the telegram.*]

VERA: [*to* ZILOV.] What's the matter with you, Oleg? Got a hangover? Bit of a headache?

ZILOV: Shut up, you fool!

VERA: He really is out of sorts.

ZILOV: I said shut up!

KUZAKOV: [*to* VERA.] Leave him alone!

ZILOV: [*to* VERA.] Why did you come here? What do you want?

KUZAKOV: She came with me.

ZILOV: You might have found something better than her to show round the offices.

[*Short pause.*]

VERA: [*to* KUZAKOV.] Well? What are you going to say to that?

[KUZAKOV *silently hands* VERA *the telegram. Funeral march. Lights fade, stage rotates. Music stops. Lights come on. Memory continues. The Café Forget-me-not.* ZILOV *and* GALINA *stop at entrance.*]

ZILOV: You'd better go now.
GALINA: Will you have time to go home?
ZILOV: What for?
GALINA: To get ready to leave.
ZILOV: Get ready? I'm not going to a birthday party . . . Off you go. Go home.
GALINA: But maybe I . . .
ZILOV: What?
GALINA: Maybe we should go together.
ZILOV: No, we've agreed I'll go alone.
GALINA: I thought it might be better . . .
ZILOV: How?
GALINA: If I went with you.
ZILOV: Why? . . . There's nothing you can do . . . What's the time?
GALINA: Twenty to six.
ZILOV: Goodbye. I've got to catch the plane. I'll just look in here. I need a drop to drink . . . Bye. [*Goes into café. Sits down at table.* GALINA *stands by door.*] Dima!
    [*Enter* WAITER.]
WAITER: [*to* GALINA.] Hi, Galia . . . Come in, be our guest. [*Goes up to* ZILOV.] Hi, Vitia.
ZILOV: Hullo, Dima. Bring us some vodka, would you.
WAITER: [*softly, referring to* GALINA.] Vitia, why doesn't your wife even say hullo to me? . . . Not that I care, but it isn't very polite of her . . . How much vodka?
ZILOV: Two hundred grams.
    [WAITER *goes out.* GALINA *comes over to table.*]
    You still here?
GALINA: I'll sit with you for a bit. [*Sits down.*] Before you leave.
ZILOV: I want to be alone, don't you see?
GALINA: No I don't. I thought this was the time you'd want to . . .
ZILOV: This is the time I want to be alone.
    [*Short pause.*]
GALINA: Yes, I understand. Your father looked on me as a stranger . . . And for a long time I've been like a stranger to you . . . I've been waiting to tell you for some time . . . I've been getting these letters . . .
ZILOV: What letters?
GALINA: I get them every day.

ZILOV: Do you? . . . May I ask who from? Your childhood friend, I suppose?
GALINA: He loves me.
[*Short pause.*]
ZILOV: And how do you feel about him?
GALINA: I don't know . . . But you and I can't go on the way we are . . .
ZILOV: And you choose this day of all days to tell me so?
GALINA: You don't want me. Admit it.
ZILOV: Aren't you ashamed of yourself? . . . You go keeping up this exchange of love-letters and I don't know what else, and you pick today — the day my dad dies — to break the news to me. Thanks for your words of comfort.
[*Short pause.*]
GALINA: I'm sure I'm at fault, but I can't go on like this . . . I'm sorry if I'm in the wrong.
ZILOV: Well, go on, don't stop at that! Tell me what the two of you get up to, and how. Tell me all about it.
GALINA: There's nothing to tell.
ZILOV: Nothing? . . . I don't know about that at all. You keep quiet, so you were cheating on me already. How am I to know what you're really up to?
GALINA: Cut it out. You're inventing things.
ZILOV: Me? Inventing things? You said yourself you don't know who to love.
GALINA: That's not true!
ZILOV: Do you realize how low you've sunk? How can I take a woman like you to my father's graveside? Never! Go away! Get out of my sight!
GALINA: You're crazy! You don't know what you're saying . . .
ZILOV: I said: Go away! And don't come back! You can go and join your friend any time you like. I wish you joy of him!
GALINA: What's the matter with you? . . . I haven't give him any cause for hope. I haven't answered one of his letters for ages . . . I've only written him two letters ever. Only two. So how can you talk like that?
ZILOV: [*suddenly calm.*] All right . . . I blew my top, I'm sorry . . . It's my nerves. You've got to appreciate the strain they've been under . . .

GALINA: It's my fault. I'm sorry . . .
ZILOV: Okay, don't be offended . . . Didn't I say I felt I had to be alone? . . . [*Short pause.*] Run along home now, will you?
GALINA: [*rising.*] All right.
ZILOV: And don't be angry.
GALINA: I'm not angry. When are you coming back?
ZILOV: When? . . . In a week or so, I expect.
GALINA: It's too bad I didn't even get your things ready for you. You haven't even got your raincoat.
ZILOV: Never mind, I'll manage . . . [*Goes up to her and kisses her on the cheek.*] Goodbye.
[*Exit* GALINA. *Pause. Enter* WAITER.]
What's the time?
WAITER: Five to six . . . Don't you want anything to eat with that?
ZILOV: No . . . Have a drink with me, Dima.
WAITER: [*sitting down.*] Thanks, Vitia, but when I'm at work I don't touch a drop. That's a rule with me, you know. [*Pause*] Well, are you counting the days? How many left now? . . . My motorbike's all ready to go . . . We need to give the boat a coat of pitch, though. And you ought to write to old Limper . . . Vitia!
ZILOV: Yes.
WAITER: I'm talking about the boat. You've got to write.
ZILOV: I've done everything already. The boat's in the water.
WAITER: Good for you.
ZILOV: Yes, only eighteen days to go. Hardly any time at all . . . [*Falls silent.*]
WAITER: What's the trouble?
ZILOV: A stroke of bad luck, Dima.
WAITER: What is it?
ZILOV: I'm going to my old man's funeral . . .
WAITER: [*sympathetically, after pause.*] I see . . .
[*Short pause.* ZILOV *drinks.*]
That's a bad business.
ZILOV: Couldn't be worse, Dima . . . I was a rotten son to him. Didn't visit him once in four years . . .
WAITER: I see . . .
ZILOV: Well, I'll see him now . . .
WAITER: Far to go?

ZILOV: [*with affirmative nod.*] I'm afraid I won't make it in time . . . [*Pause*] How much do I owe you?
WAITER: A ruble sixty.
ZILOV: [*taking out his money.*] Oh yes. I owe you three rubles from before . . .
WAITER: Three rubles twenty, Vitia.
ZILOV: Oh, sorry . . . There you are. [*Gives him money.*] Thanks.
WAITER: [*rises, does calculation on abacus.*] Thirty-five kopecks change.
[ZILOV *waves hand to dismiss matter.*]
Thanks.
[IRINA *appears in doorway.*]
ZILOV: [*to* WAITER.] See you, Dima.
WAITER: See you. Keep smiling, mate. Don't let it get you down. [*Exit*]
IRINA: [*approaching*] Good evening.
ZILOV: Come here. Sit down.
[IRINA *sits down, folds her arms in silly way on table, sits up straight, head up, as if at school desk. Laughs.*]
[*Laying his hand on her arms.*] Well? Been a good girl?
IRINA: I'm very obedient. I've been behaving just as you told me to.
ZILOV: Good girl. What about those louts? . . . By the phone box.
IRINA: Oh! It was all I could do to get away. They're crazy. First they wouldn't let me out of the box.
ZILOV: The blighters.
IRINA: They're just crazy. They wouldn't let me out, and I said: "Let me out, or I'll swear at you." And then one of them said: "Don't swear at us, come with us, it's my birthday." I don't expect it was true. And I said: "I'm going to meet somebody." And they still wouldn't give up: "We'll escort you," they said. Don't you think they're crazy? [*Without pause.*] You were fibbing. You haven't lost any weight. Not a bit. But you're sad.
ZILOV: I'm going away.
IRINA: When?
ZILOV: Now. When we say goodbye I have to catch a plane.
[*Short pause.*]
IRINA: Do you really have to?
ZILOV: Yes, really.

IRINA: Off you go then. I'll be waiting. Will I have to wait long?
ZILOV: Yes. A whole week.
> [*Enter* GALINA, *carrying raincoat and briefcase. She hurries in, but after a few steps towards* ZILOV's *and* IRINA's *table she stops. Short pause.* GALINA *looks at them, and then at her.* ZILOV's *hand is still on* IRINA's *hands.* GALINA *goes to nearest chair, leaves coat and briefcase on it, and suddenly walks away. Short pause.*]

IRINA: Who's that?
> [*Short pause.*]

ZILOV: My wife.
IRINA: [*astonished*] Wife? . . .
ZILOV: Yes, I'm married . . . [*Pause*] Yes . . . You're quite shaken. Speechless . . . It's all over for you . . . [*Short pause.*] Well? . . . You can call me a rogue, you can stand up and walk out . . . Do as you like. [*Short pause.*] It's all over, isn't it? . . . Why don't you say something? Eh? . . . Don't you know what to say at times like this? I'll teach you, if you like . . .
IRINA: [*softly*] No . . .
ZILOV: What do you mean: no? I'm married, I tell you . . . Do you think that doesn't change anything?
IRINA: It doesn't change anything . . . It makes no difference . . .
ZILOV: [*takes seat beside her, puts arm round her.*] My darling! You're as white as a sheet. Calm down, and don't let this nonsense worry you. I'm married — that's true — but my wife and I have been strangers to each other for a long time. We're friends, good friends. That's all.
IRINA: Is that the truth?
ZILOV: I could have told you the very first day, but why? What'd be the point? . . . Come on! If I'd intended to deceive you I'd have deceived you just now. I'd have said she was my sister . . .
IRINA: At first I nearly died . . . But then I thought it was all the the same whether you were married or not. And I felt afraid.
ZILOV: Poor girl! My precious! You've no idea how precious you are . . .
> [*Short pause.* ZILOV *kisses* IRINA's *hand. She puts him off, glancing round in embarrassment.*]

IRINA: I'm hungry.
ZILOV: Now there's an idea. We'll have a meal. And a drop to drink with it, eh? [*Loudly*] Dima!

IRINA: What about your flight? Will you catch it? . . .
ZILOV: [*gloomily*] You're right . . . I'll have to hurry . . .
   [*Enter* WAITER.]
WAITER: [*to* ZILOV.] Did you call?
ZILOV: Yes . . . [*Short pause. Indecisively.*] Get us something to eat, and some wine . . . Not too much though.
WAITER: Something to eat? What would you like?
ZILOV: [*to* IRINA.] What would you like?
IRINA: I'll have what you have.
ZILOV: [*with new-found resolution.*] Steak. Something cold, a bottle of wine, and two hundred grams of cognac. That'll be all.
IRINA: Won't you miss your plane?
ZILOV: I'll go tomorrow. [*To* WAITER.] Got that?
WAITER: Yes.
   [*Funeral march, which suddenly breaks off, and after a second's pause is replaced by its merry version. The stage rotates, the music fades, lights come on.* ZILOV *is standing in the middle of the room, his face turned towards the window.*]

SCENE THREE

ZILOV: [*dialling number on phone.*] That the hostel? . . . Could you get me Irina from room forty? . . . What's that? . . . How long ago? . . . Taken her things? . . . Do you know if she was accepted for the institute? . . . Today? . . . Just a moment! Have you got the phone number of the admissions board? . . . Two two one three seven . . . Thank you. [*Depresses cradle, then dials again.*] Two two one three seven . . . Admissions board? . . . Editorial office here . . . Kuzakov . . . Yes, Kuzakov . . . I wonder if you could do us a favour. You had an application from Irina Nikolaevna Rozhkova . . . Rozhkova. Department of English . . . Can you tell us whether she's been accepted or not? Could you find out, please? . . . Yes, it's urgent. Phone number? Five two zero four eight . . . About twenty minutes? . . . Good, I'll be expecting you to call. [*Hangs up. Sits by phone.*]

[*Lights fade, and come on again. Next memory.* ZILOV's *flat. Two rooms can be seen, divided by a wall with a door. In one room* ZILOV *is sitting at a table on which are some scales, various boxes, and cartridges. He is preparing to go shooting. In his room a shotgun, some wooden ducks, and a large photograph of* ZILOV *in the country, in shooting kit, festooned with game, first catch the eye. In the other room, where the house-warming party was held,* GALINA *is busy packing to leave. Here a brand new telephone is prominently displayed.* GALINA *finishes packing, closes suitcase, sits down and waits in silence.* ZILOV *emerges from his room.*]

ZILOV: All ready? ... Well then, let's sit for a while before you go. [*Sits down.*] Have you sent a telegram?

GALINA: Yes ...

ZILOV: Is somebody meeting you?

GALINA: Yes.

ZILOV: Are you quite sure they're at home?

GALINA: They? ... One of them is always in.

ZILOV: Have a good rest. Let them take you out gathering berries and mushrooms ... Does your uncle go out shooting?

GALINA: I don't think so ...

ZILOV: Is it a good place for it? Do you know?

GALINA: I think so. The forest's lovely, and the lakes ... [*Suddenly*] Let's go together.

ZILOV: Go there? Shooting?

GALINA: No, I was joking. I'm not taking you ... What I need is a good rest.

ZILOV: True. We'd do best to go our separate ways. For a little while.

GALINA: Yes, it would be best that way ...

ZILOV: The season opens soon, so it's not a good time to rush off to a new place. I've waited a whole year, and I can't take any risks now.

GALINA: Yes ... Why take risks ... [*Pause. Rises.*] You don't have to see me off, you know. My suitcase isn't heavy ... I'll take a taxi.

ZILOV: As you like ... When should I expect you?

GALINA: Expect me? ... Are you really going to expect me?

ZILOV: Of course. When will you be back?

GALINA: I'll be back . . . sometime.
ZILOV: Sometime? What does that mean?
GALINA: I was joking. I'll be back in a month . . . Well, let's say goodbye.
[*They kiss.*]
All the best . . . Think of me sometimes . . . Well, 'bye then.
ZILOV: Bye . . . When you start back don't forget to send a telegram. All right?
GALINA: [*in doorway.*] Yes, of course . . . [*Exit*]
ZILOV: [*sitting down for two seconds, thoughtful, then walking about the room, looking out of window, walking up and down the room again, then sitting down on couch and dialling number on phone.*] Hostel? . . . Could you get me Irina from Room 40, please? . . . Rozhkova, Irina Nikolaevna . . . Nobody you can send? . . . I don't believe it. I'm phoning from the institute on a business matter . . . Acting vice-chancellor here . . . Yes, the acting vice-chancellor . . . Would you be so kind? . . . I'll hold on . . . [*Lies down on couch. Pause. Changing voice.*] Miss Rozhkova? . . . Irina Nikolaevna, is that the name? . . . Acting vice-chancellor calling . . . There's one little question that's come up here . . . Are you a Komsomol member? . . . You're not? . . . Why not? . . . That's no reason . . . You might even believe in God, for all I know . . . Then what do you believe in? . . . And who do you think ought to know? Not me, I hope . . . You need to take a more serious attitude, Miss Rozhkova . . . Very well, we're accepting you nevertheless into the institute, and awarding you a grant . . . with a bonus. Yes, a bonus. Do you know why? . . . Because of your beautiful eyes . . . They're blue, if my memory serves me right . . . [*In his own voice.*] Hello, my darling . . . [*Laughs*] Yes, of course it's me . . . Did I fool you? . . . No need to scold me . . . That's how it'll turn out, you wait and see . . . I'm at home . . . [*In businesslike tone.*] Know what? Hurry over here and see me . . . Right away . . . Yes . . . I'm alone . . . All alone . . . She's left . . . For a month, to start with . . . No excuses, I'm expecting you . . . Dead easy. Didn't I show you? . . . Yes, second after the stop . . . Green balcony, that's it . . . Fourth floor, flat twenty . . . Twenty . . . I'll be waiting . . . [*Hangs up, walks about room, perches on windowsill.*]

[*Enter* GALINA.]
What's wrong? . . . Forgotten something?
GALINA: No, I've come back to tell you the truth. I'm going for good.
ZILOV: For good?
GALINA: Yes. [*Short pause.*]
ZILOV: You mean forever? For all time?
GALINA: Yes, forever, for all time.
ZILOV: Seriously? [*Short pause.*] Did you make up your mind a long time ago?
GALINA: Yes.
ZILOV: So you were prepared to go off without a word to me?
GALINA: As you see, I couldn't . . .
ZILOV: And you're quite sure . . .
GALINA: [*interrupting*] My taxi's waiting. Goodbye.
ZILOV: Hold on. That's no way to go about it. You're leaving me for good, and you don't even want to know my opinion on the subject.
GALINA: Let's not talk about it any more, please. What's the point? We've said everything we had to say . . . over the last six years . . . I can't take any more . . . Goodbye.
ZILOV: No, that won't do. All this "for good", "forever", "goodbye" — forget all that. You're going for one month, exactly one month.
GALINA: I'll miss my train.
ZILOV: To hell with your train! Promise me you'll come back. Otherwise I won't let you go . . . Promise, and leave me your address, do you hear?
GALINA: Which address?
ZILOV: Which? . . . Yours, of course. Your uncle's. Which one do you think?
[*Short pause.*] I'm not going to my uncle.
ZILOV: What? . . . Then where are you going? To that childhood friend of yours? [*Short pause.*] To him?
GALINA: Yes.
[*Short pause.*]
ZILOV: [*boiling with rage.*] So that's it . . .
GALINA: Stop it. You've been pretending long enough. It makes no difference to you where I'm going or who I'm going to see.

And don't pretend you care. You haven't cared about anything for ages. Nothing matters to you. Nothing in all the world. You've no heart, that's the trouble with you. No heart at all . . .

ZILOV: *[shaking her.]* And what about you, you bitch? Have you got a heart? Have you? Where is it? Where is it? I want to know! If you've got one, show it to me!

GALINA: Let me go! . . . Let go.

ZILOV: Oh, of course. You're in a hurry . . . You can't wait to make a cuckold of me . . . Well, you're not going to, damn you! *[Drags her into next room.]* It isn't quite as easy as that! *[Pushes her onto chair in next room.]* Sit down and don't move! You slut! *[Goes onto balcony. Shouts.]* Hey, chief! . . . Chief! . . . Hey! Would you mind calling the driver? . . .
[GALINA sits with head lowered.]
When he shows up, tell him to come up to the fourth floor . . . Would you mind?
[GALINA suddenly gets up and goes into other room.]
And tell him to bring the suitcase! . . . Thanks! . . . *[Turns round, runs to the door, but GALINA has already locked it.]* Open up! *[Knocks]* Open the door at once! *[Charges the door with his shoulder, to no avail.]* Open the door! Open it, or it'll be worse for you! . . .
[GALINA sinks to the floor in front of the door, weeping.]
[Stands for a moment in silence.] I'm asking you to be kind enough to open the door . . . Don't try my patience, or you'll regret it . . .
[GALINA weeps louder.]
[Knocks for a time, then stops. Stands in silence.] Come on, open it. I won't touch you . . . But as for that friend of yours, I'll kill him . . . Open the door! . . . You're not going anywhere . . . It's out of the question.
[GALINA rises, wipes away tears.]
Don't forget that you're my wife . . . I'm surprised I didn't strangle you on the spot when you told me what you were up to. *[Pause]* Listen! I want to have a frank talk with you. We haven't talked frankly for a long time, that's the trouble . . .
[GALINA quietly goes out.]
[With sincerity and feeling.] It's all my fault, I know. I

brought you to it myself . . . I tormented you, but I swear the kind of life I was leading was just as sickening to me as to you . . . You're right, I don't care about anything at all. I don't know what's happening to me . . . I don't know . . . But surely I have a heart! . . . No, I have nothing, except you. I realized that today, do you hear? What have I got besides you? . . . Friends? I haven't got any friends . . . Women? . . . Yes, there've been a few, but for what? I don't need them, believe me . . . What else? Not my job, surely! Good grief! How on earth can anyone take any of that seriously! I'm absolutely alone. There's nothing in my life except you. Help me! Without you I'm finished . . . Let's go away somewhere! Start again . . . We're not that old yet . . .
[*Enter* IRINA.]
Do you hear me? . . .
[IRINA *stops*.]
Do you hear?
IRINA: Yes . . .

ZILOV: I'll take you out shooting. Would you like to go?

IRINA: Yes, I would.

ZILOV: Fine . . . Do you know what you'll see? . . . You'll see things you've never dreamed of, I promise you. That's the only place you can feel you're really a person. I'll take you out in the boat, do you hear? You've never ever seen it, have you? I'll row you across to the other side! Would you like that?

IRINA: Yes . . . [*Sensing his agitation, she stands immobile by the door.*]

ZILOV: But remember, we have to get up early, before dawn. You'll see what a mist there is in the morning. And we'll start out in the boat — it's as if you were dreaming, and didn't know where you were going. And when the sun comes up it's just like being in church! Even better than a church . . . And the nights! Heavens! You've no idea how quiet it is! It's as if you weren't even there, do you understand? As if you hadn't been born, and there's nothing there. And never was. And never will be . . . And you see lots of duck. Plenty of them. Of course, I'm no crack-shot, but that's not the point . . . I'd never take a woman out shooting with me. Except you . . . And do you know why? . . . Because I love you . . . Do you hear? . . . Come on, open the door!

IRINA: Open it? . . . Are you locked in?
[ZILOV *charges door.*]
So you are. [*Turns key.*]
[ZILOV *flings door open. Pause.* ZILOV *is stunned and at a loss for words.*]
Why are you looking at me like that?
[*Short pause.*]
ZILOV: I'll be damned! . . . You look like a queen! . . . What a dress! It's wonderful! Where did you get it?
IRINA: This dress? . . . But it's old . . . I was wearing it yesterday and the day before . . .
ZILOV: You couldn't have been . . . All the same, today you look special . . . I've never yet seen you looking like that.
IRINA: [*pleased*] Really? . . . But who locked you in?
ZILOV: Locked me in? . . . Oh, my neighbour . . . A grown man and still likes fooling around.
IRINA: Do you really love me that much?
ZILOV: How much?
IRINA: As much as you said just now.
ZILOV: [*embracing her.*] Do you doubt it?
IRINA: No . . . How did you know it was me? Surely you can't tell my footsteps?
ZILOV: Of course I can.
IRINA: [*happily*] I can hardly believe it . . .
ZILOV: Why not? I was expecting you . . . But, to be quite honest, I saw you from the balcony.
IRINA: When you go shooting do you go a long way?
ZILOV: What? . . . Oh, yes, a very long way. Ever so far.
IRINA: My father used to take me shooting as well . . . I'll go with you, whatever happens. Whether I'm accepted or not. But when?
ZILOV: When what?
IRINA: When shall we go shooting?
[ZILOV *suddenly starts laughing.*]
What are you laughing at?
[*He laughs so hard he cannot answer.*]
What is it? . . . Why are you laughing?
ZILOV: [*through his laughter.*] No, no . . . Don't take any notice. I just . . . remembered something . . . Just a moment . . . One moment . . . [*Stops laughing.*] That's better.

IRINA: [*frightened*] You weren't laughing at me?
ZILOV: Don't be silly. Of course not. I simply remembered something . . . A joke. I heard it in the office yesterday. And suddenly I remembered it. It happens like that sometimes.
IRINA: Tell me.
ZILOV: Tell you what?
IRINA: The joke.
ZILOV: It's not worth it.
IRINA: No, go on. Tell me.
ZILOV: Oh, all right . . . A husband goes off on a business trip . . . Or was it the wife? . . . The hell with it!
IRINA: No, go on.
[ZILOV *shakes head.*]
Why not?
ZILOV: It's not for your ears. It's a dirty joke.
IRINA: But when are we going shooting?
ZILOV: Soon. We'll go soon.
[*Lights fade. Phone rings in darkness. Lights come on.* ZILOV *is sitting by the phone, which is ringing.*]
ZILOV: [*awaking from daydream, seizes receiver.*] Yes . . . Yes . . . What? She's taken her papers? . . . Failed the exam? Are you sure about that? . . . Just a moment! When did she collect her papers? . . . Yes . . . No, one moment! I've a favour to ask . . . Do you know her? . . . Well, if she happens to call in again could you tell her . . . *If* she does! . . . Tell her Zilov rang . . . Zilov. And that he'd like her to phone him . . . Yes, *begs* her to phone him. Tell her that . . . [*Hangs up.*] So she's gone.

ACT THREE

ZILOV's *flat. On the table a huge rucksack and a shotgun in a canvas case. Rain is still falling outside.* ZILOV *is talking on the phone. Now he is wearing a pullover, wide trousers, and a cap. He is barefoot. A quilted jacket is lying on the couch, and on the floor are his hunting boots.*

ZILOV: No, I can't stand it any longer . . . Dima, I might be a bad shot, but God knows I'm a good friend to you, and I wouldn't do that . . . No, I won't wait . . . I can't . . . Okay, to hell with you and your motorbike! . . . Yes, right away . . . Yes, in the rain . . . One way or another . . . By bus to Kliuchi, then walk . . . Walk. Don't you know that word? . . . That's it, so you haven't forgotten . . . What? . . . The boat? . . . Of course you can, as usual . . . So what if it *is* mine? Don't we always share? . . . No, I don't care about it, you needn't worry . . . Just a sec, Dima! Just a sec! . . . I wanted to ask you . . . One question . . . Wait! . . . Yes! Listen, it wasn't you who gave me a punch in the face yesterday, was it? . . . I've been trying, and I just can't remember . . . No, why should I suspect anything? I'm just asking . . . If I knew I wouldn't be asking . . . Okay, I'm sorry, never mind . . . Still, I'd like to know . . . Okay, sorry. Don't take offence . . . Right, see you there . . . So long . . . See you. [*Hangs up. Gets ready to go. Sits down and pulls on boots.*]
[*Knock at door.*]
Yes!
[*Voice outside: "Telegram".*]

[*Gets up, goes into hall, returns, unfolding telegram, reads it aloud.*] "Dear Oleg . . . Please accept this expression of our deepest sympathy on the untimely death of our best friend, Viktor Alexandrovich Zilov . . . From his friends . . ." [*Pause*] From his friends . . . How about that? [*Slowly tears telegram up.*]
[*Music is heard: a bizarre combination of the funeral march alternating with its merry version. In the darkness the stage rotates. Lights come on. Music stops. Last memory begins. The Café Forget-me-not. Two tables moved together.* ZILOV *and* WAITER. WAITER *is laying table.* ZILOV *sitting at head of table. He is wearing a black suit, looking solemn and keyed up.*]

ZILOV: Right . . . And a couple of bottles of champagne. Naturally, today's a big day, isn't it?
WAITER: How many people are coming?
ZILOV: Seven.
WAITER: Who are they?
ZILOV: The same crowd. My friends! Who do you think? . . . To be quite honest, I don't want to see them at all.
WAITER: Had a quarrel with them?
ZILOV: Quarrel? . . . Something like that . . . Or maybe not . . . Do we ever really know? . . . Take you and me. We're friends, but say I take you and sell you for a kopeck. Then we meet and I say to you: "Look, mate, I've got this kopeck. Come with me. You're my friend, and I want to have a drink with you." And you go with me, and we have a drink, and embrace and bear-hug, although you know full well where I got that kopeck. But you go with me because you don't give a damn and it's all one to you how I came by that kopeck . . . And you meet me the next day, and we start all over again . . . That's how it is. "Quarrel" you say . . . I simply don't want to see them . . .
WAITER: Then why did you invite them?
ZILOV: Because it does my heart good to see them.
WAITER: I don't understand.
ZILOV: It'll make my happiness complete. Just think of the difference: today I stare at their ugly mugs, and tomorrow I'll be out shooting.
WAITER: You're fooling around, old fellow . . .

ZILOV: Tomorrow we'll get started as early as possible, right? About six, eh, Dima? . . . If we leave early we'll be there by evening.

WAITER: We'll have time. Officially the season opens the day after tomorrow.

ZILOV: That's the point. That means we have to be there tomorrow. For sure. Or else we'll miss the first morning.

WAITER: No need to worry, we'll make it in time.

ZILOV: Can you imagine, — damn it! — another twenty-four hours and we'll be out in the boat? In the silence. In the mist. Drink up, Dima! Let's drink to the first morning of the season.

WAITER: Don't try to talk me into it, Vitia. I'm at work.

ZILOV: But this is your last evening. You can count yourself on holiday already.

WAITER: I said no. I have to turn in the takings, and besides, you know my rule.

ZILOV: Oh, forget your rule. [*Hands* WAITER *glass.*] Just one. To the first morning.

WAITER: Not a drop. Tomorrow I'll have as many as you like — a hundred glasses.

ZILOV: Okay . . . To tell you the truth this caff makes me sick. We won't be seeing it for a whole month, thank God . . . Well, here's to duck-shooting.

[*Drinks*] I've got a feeling I'll be lucky this time.

WAITER: Forget your feelings. If you can't shoot, feelings won't help. You'll go on missing just the same old way.

ZILOV: Dima, how long can I go on missing? Surely not this time too?

WAITER: Vitia, if I've told you once I've told you a hundred times: you'll go on missing until you learn to relax.

ZILOV: What is all this: "relax", "don't get excited"? Are you making fun of me, Dima? I know you need a good eye, and a steady hand, like yours . . .

WAITER: Vitia, there's nothing wrong with your eye, and your hand's perfectly all right, you know all you need to know about shooting, but when it comes to the crunch you can't shoot. Why? Because the most important thing in shooting is your attitude to it, — whether you're relaxed or not, and how nervous you are . . . And when the duck settle on the water what do you do?

ZILOV: [*rising*] What do you mean: what do I do?
WAITER: [*interrupting*] As soon as they're down you jump to your feet. Now what's the good of that? You know how it's done? You've got to be steady, calm, and precise about it. No hurry.
ZILOV: What about when they're in flight? No hurry then either?
WAITER: Hurry? What's the point? You've got to shoot fast, but you've still got to keep a cool head . . . How can I put it? . . . As if they weren't real duck in the wild, but duck in a picture.
ZILOV: But they're not in a picture. They're alive.
WAITER: They're alive for a bad shot. But for a good shot they're already as good as dead. You follow?
ZILOV: [*thoughtlessly.*] I get it . . . I'll have another drink. Here's to keeping a cool head. [*Drinks*] This time everything's going to be spot on. [*Gives thumbs-up sign.*] Just wait and see . . .
WAITER: [*derisively*] Yes, we'll see . . . As long as we get some decent weather.
ZILOV: We're bound to. God forbid it should rain . . .
[*Short pause.*]
WAITER: I hear your wife's left you, Vitia. That right? . . . I hear you're on your own.
ZILOV: You mean that business about the key? . . . I'm not alone. I've got my fiancée staying with me.
WAITER: Fiancée. [*Smirks*] That's a nice way of putting it . . .
ZILOV: [*suddenly annoyed.*] What are you smirking about? You haven't slept with her have you?
WAITER: [*taken aback*] Of course I haven't . . . What's up with you?
ZILOV: Nothing. Don't smirk at the wrong moments . . . I said fiancée and I mean it. I'm going to marry her. Got that?
WAITER: Do you think I mind? . . . [*Finishes what he was doing, takes a step back, flicking a napkin at the same time.*] Now we're ready.
ZILOV: You know what you can do? [*Pulls out money and hands some to* WAITER.] You can bring me a couple more bottles. I've the right to have a fling once a year, don't you think?
WAITER: Sure you have, Vitia. The customer is always right.
[*Enter* VERA *and* KUZAKOV. VERA *is holding some asters.*]
KUZAKOV: 'Evening, Olegs!
ZILOV: Hullo, hullo . . .

WAITER: Hi.
ZILOV: Sit down.
VERA: [*about* ZILOV.] Look how he's tricked out today.
KUZAKOV: Quite a dandy.
VERA: A birthday-boy.
KUZAKOV: A prince.
ZILOV: All right. That's enough of your chatter. Sit down.
VERA: [*handing flowers to* WAITER.] Put these in a vase, would you, Oleg?
WAITER: [*mockingly*] At your service. [*Exit*]
KUZAKOV: [*to* VERA, *about* WAITER.] Do you know him?
VERA: Yes, unfortunately.
ZILOV: You'd do better to ask who she doesn't know.
KUZAKOV: I don't like him.
VERA: Neither do I, Kolia. But why should I pretend I don't know him?
ZILOV: Nonsense, he's a perfectly good fellow. [*To* KUZAKOV.] You seem to be guarding her jealously.
KUZAKOV: [*drawing* VERA *to him.*] You're right. I am.
VERA: And what's wrong with that? [*Giving* KUZAKOV *a slight hug.*]
ZILOV: Well I'm damned! We're all lovey-dovey, are we? . . . [*To* KUZAKOV, *in mocking tone.*] Listen. Why don't you marry her?
KUZAKOV: You know, I really will.
ZILOV: [*surprised*] No kidding?
KUZAKOV: Have you got any objections?
ZILOV: [*mockingly*] Objections? . . . Of course not. On the contrary. I'll bless the union.
SAIAPIN: Hi there, Olegs!
[*All greet one another.* WAITER *brings flowers and wine, and goes out.*]
ZILOV: Welcome, everybody. Take your seats at the table, please. You sit here, Vadim Andreevich.
KUSHAK: Right, I'll put myself here. [*Sits down next to* ZILOV.] Next to our happy holiday-maker.
ZILOV: Now we're all here. And my fiancée will be along in a moment . . . [*Waits for comments.*]
VALERIA: Fiancée?
ZILOV: Why? . . . Don't you like the idea?

VALERIA: Well, let's say it's news to us, at any rate . . .
VERA: Are you engaged?
ZILOV: Sure. If you're engaged why shouldn't I be? . . .
VALERIA: [*interrupting*] That's all very well. So you're engaged. But don't you think that once you'd invited us you might have waited before having a drink? You could have refrained for a while.
ZILOV: Well, here we are. My fiancée'll be here in a minute and we'll have a drink. It's a long time since we had a drink together, isn't it, Vadim Andreevich?
KUSHAK: [*obviously feeling ill at ease.*] Yes, it is . . . [*Looking round.*] But in these matters I'm not specially . . .
ZILOV: How are we to know? If you ask me, you drink at home, at night.
VALERIA: What rubbish! Vadim Andreevich is the only man here who can't be called a drunkard.
SAIAPIN: Friends! What's this I see? Look at the table!
ZILOV: What is it?
SAIAPIN: Crabs!
VALERIA: Crabs? . . . Lovely! What a luxury!
KUSHAK: Yes, crabs really are a great find these days.

[*Enter* IRINA. *She looks bright and cheerful in a light-coloured dress.*]

IRINA: Good evening.

[*All greet her.*]

ZILOV: [*rather gloomily.*] Where've you been? [*His tone immediately has its effect on* IRINA's *cheerful mood. She says nothing.*] Okay, come here.

[IRINA *comes closer.*]

[*To all.*] Here she is. I'll ask you all to love and cherish her. Her name's Irina. [*To* IRINA.] I'll introduce you. This is Vadim Andreevich.

KUSHAK: How do you do?
ZILOV: He's my boss. The director, if you like. Very broad-minded, he is.

[IRINA *nods to each in turn.*]

[*Introducing his friends with sweeping gestures.*] Saiapin . . . Another prominent figure . . . His lady and comrade-in-arms. Proceeding on . . . Kuzakov. Engaged to be married, as I've just discovered . . . [*Of* VERA.] And so is she . . . as you see . . . All of them are my best friends.

IRINA: [*gently*] Very pleased to meet you.

ZILOV: They're very pleased too. [*To all.*] Or are you displeased? [*Short pause.* SAIAPIN *is unable to restrain a giggle.*] You're all pleased? That's what I thought. And now let's have a drink. To duck-shooting. [*Short pause.* ZILOV *drinks alone.*]

KUZAKOV: [*mockingly*] Well? Did it go down nicely?

ZILOV: Beautifully.

KUZAKOV: Did you invite us here to watch you getting drunk?

ZILOV: Not at all. I invited you so as to have some sober people to look at.

VALERIA: And do you intend to look at us for long?

ZILOV: I've already finished. You can have a drink. To duck-shooting. I warn you, that's the only thing you're going to drink to tonight. Nothing else.

[*Short pause.*]

KUSHAK: [*cautiously*] I know shooting's your hobby, Viktor, but still . . .

ZILOV: [*interrupting*] Shooting a bloody hobby? Nothing of the sort! [*Snorts*] Hobby indeed! Let's have less of these banalities, and drink to the new season.

VALERIA: [*to* ZILOV.] Listen, you've got your shooting on the brain.

KUSHAK: It's true, Viktor. I should think we've all got our own interests, but you can't go on like that about yours . . . We're your guests, after all . . .

ZILOV: Rubbish. You're going to drink to duck-shooting, and that's the end of it. And if not, why did you come? [*Despite what he has drunk* ZILOV *is still sober and thinking clearly.*]

KUZAKOV: I don't understand what you're after. Do you want us to leave?

SAIAPIN: No, no! Vitia's joking. As usual. Don't you know what he's like?

ZILOV: [*to* IRINA.] Just take a look at this crowd. See how serious they all are. They aren't drinking, nor eating anything. They're thinking of something quite different. They came here to tell me how to run my life.

VERA: I've had enough of this.

ZILOV: Had enough? Oh, of course! You're not used to a lot of preliminary chat.

IRINA: [*at a loss; softly to* ZILOV.] Stop it . . .
ZILOV: Wait a bit! You don't know them. These people are so respectable that they're ashamed to sit at the same table as me. [*To* VERA.] Isn't that right, Verochka? You're dying of shame, admit it. After all, you're engaged to be married. [*Laughs*]
KUZAKOV: [*rising*] Look here! As long as I've known you you've always been a small-time mischief-maker. What's happened? Now I see you've broken into the big league. If you're not careful you'll really kick up a shindy.
VERA: And are we going to wait? Hadn't we better leave?
ZILOV: No, why leave? Don't hurry. Let us feast our eyes on you. You make such a splendid couple. They ought to put you on T.V. Specially the bride-to-be.
KUZAKOV: Have you quite finished?
ZILOV: Bride-to-be! Don't make me laugh. Ask her who of us she hasn't been to bed with.
IRINA: Viktor!
[KUZAKOV *rises and makes towards* ZILOV. SAIAPIN *rises and approaches from the other side.*]
VERA: [*jumps up and screams.*] Don't touch him.
[KUZAKOV *and* SAIAPIN *stop. Short pause.*]
You can't beat up a drunk . . . And besides he's . . . He's telling the truth.
VALERIA: [*to* VERA.] How can you! He's lost any shame he ever had. He thinks he's out on the marsh with his double-barrelled gun!
KUSHAK: [*to* ZILOV.] Viktor! You're forgetting yourself. You're not out in the forest. This is a public place. There are families here, and young girls . . .
ZILOV: Oh yes! Of course! Family, friend of the family, bride-to-be, I crave your forgiveness! . . . [*Gloomily*] Cut it out. Who are you trying to fool? And why bother? For the sake of decency? . . . You can stuff your decency. Do you hear? I'm sick to death of your decency.
IRINA: [*shaking* ZILOV.] Viktor! . . .
KUSHAK: [*indignant*] Now look here! I'm no prude, but this is a bit much!
[*Rises*]

ZILOV: [*to* KUSHAK.] Oh, of course! You came to spend a quiet, respectable evening here, and what did you get? Is that it? Why did you come? Tell me frankly. Why? . . . Nothing to say? Then I'll tell you why you came. You wanted a girl — that's why you came along.

KUSHAK: Stop that, you fool!

IRINA: Viktor!

[*Enter* WAITER.]

WAITER: Vitia, less noise, old fellow. It's not allowed . . .

ZILOV: [*breaking clear; to all.*] You've fooled around enough! How much can a man take? If it's a girl you want, say so.

VALERIA: He's an out-and-out monster.

ZILOV: [*to* KUSHAK.] If you want one, help yourself! Take your pick! Her [*points to* VERA.] or her [*points to* VALERIA.] You're a friend of the family, so what's the problem? [*Points to* SAIAPIN.] He'll let you have her. He'll be only too glad!

IRINA: [*shaking* ZILOV.] Stop it. Stop it! Or I'm leaving.

VALERIA: Monster! [*To* SAIAPIN.] What are you waiting for? He's insulting us, don't you hear?

[SAIAPIN *makes towards* ZILOV, *but the* WAITER *holds him back.*]

WAITER: Steady now . . . That's not allowed in here.

ZILOV: [*to* KUSHAK.] Well, what's the problem? Take your pick!

IRINA: [*in despair.*] I'm going to leave, do you hear?

VALERIA: Monster! [*To* KUSHAK *and* SAIAPIN.] Let's go!

[VALERIA, KUSHAK, *and* SAIAPIN *make for the door.* VERA *and* KUZAKOV *follow.*]

ZILOV: [*shouting*] Wait!

[*They stop.*]

[*Grabs* IRINA *by the arm and hustles her out from behind the table.*] Here's another one! Here! Take her with you!

IRINA: [*screaming*] Viktor!

ZILOV: Can't speak too highly of her! Eighteen years old! A delightful creature! My fiancée! Well? Why are you looking so lost? You don't think it'll work? Nonsense! You can take it from me, there's nothing to it!

WAITER: Steady on, now. Steady . . . [*Shepherds* ZILOV *towards the table.*]

[IRINA *looks at* ZILOV, *aghast.*]

KUZAKOV: [*to* IRINA.] Come with us . . .
ZILOV: That's the way. Take her with you and clear out . . . [*Shouting*] I said: clear out! Get out of here!
VALERIA: [*in doorway.*] Chump!
SAIAPIN: Poacher!
   [*Exit* VERA, KUZAKOV, VALERIA, *and* SAIAPIN. WAITER *ushers* ZILOV *to seat at table.* IRINA *stands in middle of room, looking as if struck dumb.*]
ZILOV: [*at departing company.*] That's better! You can all go to hell! And I hope I never see you again! Scum! . . . Olegs! May you all rot! [*Pours himself some vodka and drains the glass. Only now does he become hopelessly drunk. Turns to* IRINA.] You can clear out with the rest of them.
WAITER: If there's one person you shouldn't be insulting it's this girl. If I were you I wouldn't talk like that to such a nice girl.
ZILOV: And just who do you think you are? . . . A flunkey . . . Giving advice like everybody else. She's yours if you want her. I don't give a damn . . . She's as worthless as the rest. Or if she isn't now she soon will be. She's got plenty of time ahead of her . . .
WAITER: [*to* IRINA, *as if apologizing on his own behalf and* ZILOV'*s.*] He's out of it. Doesn't know what he's saying.
ZILOV: [*to* IRINA.] Why are you staring at me like that? What do you want? [*To* WAITER.] Listen to me, flunkey. Take her out of here! And go away. I want to be alone . . . I don't believe any of you. Understand? . . .
   [IRINA, *walking like a sleepwalker, goes slowly to door and disappears.* ZILOV *drops his head onto table.*]
WAITER: [*going up to* ZILOV, *pokes him in the side, then lifts his head.*] So I'm a flunkey, am I?
ZILOV: [*vaguely*] What do you want? . . .
WAITER: Did you say I was a flunkey?
ZILOV: You? . . . Yes, of course. What else do you think you are?
   [WAITER *looks round, then punches* ZILOV *in face.* ZILOV *falls between the chairs. Without pausing,* WAITER *starts clearing table. Enter* KUZAKOV *and* SAIAPIN.]
SAIAPIN: Where is he?
WAITER: [*pointing*] He's had it. Not moving a muscle.
SAIAPIN: Quite a champion.

KUZAKOV: [*picking* ZILOV *up, to* SAIAPIN.] Give us a hand.
WAITER: Good thing you came back. I wasn't going to haul him out. My duties stop short of that. [*Exit with tray.*]
   [KUZAKOV *and* SAIAPIN *sit* ZILOV *on chair and bring him round.*]
KUZAKOV: Wake up, you trouble-maker.
ZILOV: What is it?
KUZAKOV: Time to go home.
ZILOV: Home? . . . What for? Have I left something behind? . . . No, I don't want to go home. I don't want to go anywhere. I'm staying here. And that's final!
SAIAPIN: [*loudly, into* ZILOV's *ear.*] It's night, you dummy. The café's closing. Night, do you hear? Night!
ZILOV: Night? . . . [*With sudden animation.*] Where's it night? What are you talking about? It'd be dark if it was night. And what do you call that? [*Points at open door, through which the brightly-lit street can be seen.*] What's that? . . . Call that night, do you? It's as bright as day! Some bloody night that! Oh, all this makes me sick . . . [*Suddenly drooping.*]
KUZAKOV: Dead drunk . . . [*To* ZILOV.] Can you walk? . . .
ZILOV: Yes, I can still walk . . . But let's have a drink first. We'll have a drink, and then go . . . [*Suddenly*] Wait! Where's my fiancée?
SAIAPIN: He's noticed!
ZILOV: Where's my fiancée? Where's she gone? Bring her back! Bring her back! We'll get married in the planetarium . . .
   [*The sound of rain is heard, starting to fall outside.*]
SAIAPIN: It's started raining.
KUZAKOV: So we'll have to drag him along in the rain. Let's go.
   [*They pick* ZILOV *up. He resists.*]
ZILOV: Where are you taking me?
SAIAPIN: To the planetarium. To swear your marriage vows.
ZILOV: [*resisting*] I don't want to.
KUZAKOV: [*to* SAIAPIN.] Hold it . . . [*Loudly, to* ZILOV.] Listen, you hooligan! You're going shooting tomorrow. Have you forgotten?
ZILOV: Shooting? . . . [*Cheering up.*] That's right! I'll be damned! Got to hurry. [*Rises, almost falling.*]
   [*They seize him and support him.*]

KUZAKOV: He's like a dead body. Let's take his arms.
SAIAPIN: Dead body?
KUZAKOV: Sure, like a corpse. I'm afraid we'll have to carry him.
SAIAPIN: [*rubbing his hands.*] A corpse! [*Laughs*] I've got a brilliant idea! [*Laughs*] We'll arrange something for him tomorrow!
KUZAKOV: Arrange what?
SAIAPIN: A dirty great surprise! He gave us one today. We'll arrange one for him tomorrow! Corpse! [*Guffaws*] Let's go!
[*They take* ZILOV *by his arms and lead him away. The noise of the rain grows louder. Funeral march. The lights go out for one second, after which, as in first scene, two spotlights come on one after the other. The weak light of the first shows* ZILOV *standing by the door, as we left him at the beginning of this scene. The second, brighter, marks a circle in the middle of the stage, in which* ZILOV's *visions from the first scene are re-enacted. This time this scene is accompanied from start to finish by the funeral march. The behaviour and speech of the characters now reappearing in* ZILOV's *imagination must this time show no tendency towards clowning or exaggeration. They must behave as if all this were really happening, and as* ZILOV *remembers it.* KUZAKOV *and* SAIAPIN *emerge into the brighter spotlight.*]
SAIAPIN: He isn't. I don't believe you. He couldn't have done.
KUZAKOV: It's a fact.
SAIAPIN: Must have been another of his little jokes. You know what he's like, don't you?
KUZAKOV: Not this time, unfortunately. This time there's no joking.
SAIAPIN: I bet it's just a rumour he's put about, and he's sitting quietly in the "Forget-me-not."
[*Enter* VERA *and* VALERIA, *then* KUSHAK.]
VALERIA: Just imagine! Yesterday he was getting ready to go out shooting, cracking jokes . . . Only yesterday! And now this! . . .
VERA: I'd never have thought it of him. He was the dearest Oleg of them all.
KUSHAK: What a shame! I'd never have believed it, but you know, lately he'd been acting . . . I'm no prude, but he'd been acting most . . . er . . . reprehensibly. That sort of behaviour never does anybody any good.

[VERA, VALERIA, *and* KUSHAK *vanish. Enter* GALINA, *followed by* IRINA.]
GALINA: I can't believe it, I can't, I can't! . . . Why did he do it?
IRINA: Why?
GALINA: [*to* IRINA.] Did he love you?
IRINA: I don't know.
GALINA: We lived together for six years, but I could never work him out. [*To* IRINA.] You and I are going to be friends, aren't we?
IRINA: Yes.
[*They embrace and weep.*]
GALINA: I'm leaving . . . For good . . . Will you write to me?
IRINA: [*through tears.*] Yes . . .
[GALINA *vanishes. Enter* KUSHAK *and* WAITER.]
KUSHAK: [*to* IRINA.] How nice to see you . . .
WAITER: You shouldn't be alone in your state, Miss.
KUSHAK: No, but . . . Of course she shouldn't . . . All the same . . .
WAITER: We'll expect you at six in the "Forget-me-not." Will you come?
IRINA: [*through tears.*] Yes . . .
[*All vanish. Enter* KUZAKOV.]
KUZAKOV: [*thoughtfully*] Who's to tell? . . . When you come to think about it, life's over and done anyway . . . [*Vanishes*]
[GALINA, KUZAKOV, SAIAPIN, VALERIA, KUSHAK, IRINA, *and* WAITER *pass across the stage in a funeral procession. Last comes the boy carrying the wreath. Both spotlights suddenly go out, the music breaks off. For two or three seconds the stage is in darkness. Lights come on.* ZILOV *is alone in the room. He stands still by the window for a long time. Rain is falling outside. He moves to close the window, but suddenly flings it open and leans out.*]
ZILOV: [*shouting*] Vitka! . . . Where are you going? . . . How are your lessons? . . . All right? . . . Good lad . . . What? Don't worry, everything'll be okay . . . Okay . . . 'Bye, Vitia . . . 'Bye. [*Closes window. Takes off cap and throws it onto floor. Goes to phone, dials number.*] Dima? . . . Listen, I'm not going . . . No, no, I wanted to let you know: I'm not going at all . . . Changed my mind . . . Can't I change my mind? . . . I've got other plans . . . Yes, a different place . . . Nonsense,

how can I compete with you? . . . Listen, what are you doing now? . . . I just wanted to invite you . . . To a wake . . . My own . . . I got tired of her. Or she got tired of me. One of the two . . . Anyway, you're invited to a wake, as a neighbour . . Why not? Too lazy to cross the street? Anything to drink? Of course there is. What did you think? . . . Coming? . . . Right, see you then. [*Hangs up, then takes receiver again, dials number.*] Can I speak to Saiapin . . . Hi. Zilov here . . . Yes, still alive . . . I got it, thanks. Very funny . . . Kuzakov there too? Good . . . Good for you. I'm dying of laughter . . . Of course . . . Quite right there, fellows . . . Well then, come to the wake . . . Sure. Got to see the business through . . . That's why I'm inviting you to the wake . . . What? What'll you do? Eat and drink, of course. The usual thing . . . Yes, right away . . . Coming? . . . Good. [*Hangs up, takes seat at table, takes paper and pen, and writes something. Rises, takes shotgun, removes case, assembles it, and leans it against table. Undoes rucksack, takes out cartridge pouch, loads shotgun. All this is done fairly hastily. Sits down on chair, stands shotgun on floor, and leans on muzzles with chest. Measures distance to trigger with one hand, then with other. Moves chair closer to table, sits down, resting butt of gun against table with muzzles against his chest. Sets gun aside, pulls off right shoe and sock, and again positions gun between table and his chest. Feels for trigger with big toe . . .*]
[*Phone rings. He sits motionless. Phone goes on ringing long and insistently. He rises, goes quickly to phone and takes receiver, holding it in one hand and the gun in the other.*]

ZILOV: Yes . . . Go ahead, I'm listening . . , Go ahead. Speak! . . . [*Extremely agitated.*] Who is it? . . . Look here, I'm in no mood for jokes . . .

[KUZAKOV *and* SAIAPIN *appear in doorway without knocking. The sight of* ZILOV, *shotgun in hand, with one shoe on, and his tone of voice alert them to the situation, and they do nothing to betray their presence, stopping in the doorway.* ZILOV *has his back to them.*]

Who's ringing? Answer me! [*For a moment he holds the receiver before his eyes, then puts it to his ear again, then slowly lowers it. He stands by the phone for a while with gun*

and receiver in his hands. Without looking he throws down the receiver, missing the phone. Returns to table, replaces chair at correct distance from it, but the moment he sits down KUZAKOV *rushes at him from behind and snatches the shotgun out of his hands.* ZILOV *jumps up. Short pause.*]
Give it here! [*Hurls himself at* KUZAKOV. *They wrestle.*]
SAIAPIN: Vitia . . . Vitia . . . What's the matter with you?
[*The two of them overpower him and sit him down on the couch.*]
KUZAKOV: [*with gun in hand.*] You nut! This is some toy to play with!
ZILOV: [*breathing heavily.*] What a bloody nerve!
SAIAPIN: You're saying *we've* got a nerve?!
ZILOV: You might have knocked, damn you!
SAIAPIN: He's off his head. [*Takes note from table and reads it aloud.*] "I ask that nobody be blamed for my death" . . . What's this, Vitia, old fellow? Have you gone round the bend?
KUZAKOV: [*breaking the shotgun, draws out a cartridge, and looks at it.*] You really have gone crazy.
SAIAPIN: [*takes cartridge and puts it in his pocket. To* ZILOV.] For a stunt like that you can get . . . [*To* KUZAKOV.] What if we'd decided to walk, eh? What then? [*To* ZILOV.] Surely you wouldn't have . . .
ZILOV: You've come too soon. Go away.
KUZAKOV: We're not going anywhere.
SAIAPIN: [*sitting down.*] We'll sit here for a while, have a rest, and a smoke, won't we, eh, Kolia? . . . What a business. [*To* KUZAKOV.] And you said: let's walk there. But I looked and saw a taxi, and said: No, let's go by cab. As if I sensed something.
KUZAKOV: [*to* ZILOV.] Snap out of it, there's a good fellow. Get a grip on yourself . . . Put your shoe on, to start with.
[*Pause*]
ZILOV: Go away.
KUZAKOV: We aren't going anywhere, so forget about that.
ZILOV: As you like. I'm in no hurry.
KUZAKOV: What happened? Doesn't life mean anything to you?
ZILOV: Don't try to talk me round. You're wasting your time. I'll see it through.

[*The room now appears slightly brighter. In the square of sky seen through the window occasional blue patches show.*]

KUZAKOV: [*goes to phone, lifts receiver, dials number.*] That the shop? . . . Can I speak to Vera? . . . Vera? . . . Don't wait for me, I'll be late . . . Unexpected delay . . . What time? I don't know exactly. Stay in, will you? . . . See you. [*Hangs up.*]

SAIAPIN: Not upset about the wreath, are you, Vitia? . . . Eh? . . . Not because of us, surely?

ZILOV: Why the hell did you have to get into that cab? Who asked you to? Was four blocks too far for you to walk?

KUZAKOV: But what happened? What's the matter with you? . . . What's the trouble? What else do you want? You're young, fit, you've got a job, and a flat. You're popular with women. Why can't you just live and enjoy life? What more do you want?

ZILOV: I want you to go away.

SAIAPIN: Vitia, do you realize what you're saying? We're your friends, aren't we? So how can we go away now? How can we leave you at a time like this? Come off it!

ZILOV: I'll see this thing through. And nobody — blast you! — nobody on earth'll stop me. Is that clear? . . . That's final!
[*Pause*]

SAIAPIN: Why don't you say something, boys? . . . Let's talk about something, eh? [*Short pause. Ingenuously.*] Vitia, have you noticed? Your floor's drying out. Have to get it seen to. [*Rises, goes to kitchen partition and taps on it.*] Cardboard . . . Cardboard and plaster . . . There's some shoddy building these days . . . [*Goes to other wall.* ZILOV *watches him with growing interest.*] What about this one? [*Knocks*] The same . . .
[*Short pause.*]

ZILOV: Go on. Why have you stopped? Go on, mate, keep it up. Go through all the rooms, think out what to put where.

SAIAPIN: Vitia! What do you mean? Surely you don't think I'm staking any claim . . .

ZILOV: Staking a claim? No, old fellow, you're not simply staking a claim, you've come for the keys. Well, here they are. [*Takes keys from pocket and tosses them to* SAIAPIN.] Take them . . . Don't hesitate, take them.

SAIAPIN: You're off your head!
KUZAKOV: Hold it, you've misunderstood.
SAIAPIN: What do you take us for?
ZILOV: Drop it, fellers! No need to get all sentimental. Admit it, this way suits you both, doesn't it? . . . So what's keeping you? Why the hell are you waiting here? Give me the gun, and get out. I haven't changed my mind yet.
KUZAKOV: What are you on about? Come to your senses. Who needs your death? Think about it. Does he need it? . . . Do I? . . . You don't need it yourself. And if you don't like the way you live, that's fine — you can live some other way. Who's to stop you? . . . And don't judge others by your own measure. Don't think the worst of everybody.
ZILOV: All right, that'll do. [*To* SAIAPIN.] Tolia, throw this paragon of virtue out of your flat.
SAIAPIN: Why do that? I agree . . .
KUZAKOV: As for the wreath, I'm quite prepared to apologize to you.
ZILOV: Shut up. I don't believe you.
KUZAKOV: I had nothing to do with it, but I knew about the wreath, and since it's here I share the blame.
ZILOV: I don't believe you. Understand? . . . So go away.
KUZAKOV: I won't go away. I won't go until you put this stupid idea of suicide out of your mind.
[*Enter* WAITER.]
WAITER: Hi . . . What's all the fuss about?
SAIAPIN: Ah, lucky you've come. Take a look at him, and listen to what he's been getting up to.
WAITER: What about the wake?
ZILOV: I didn't have time to get everything ready.
WAITER: What about the booze?
ZILOV: I'm not master in this house any longer.
SAIAPIN: [*to* WAITER, *holding finger to head*.] Don't you see? Look at this. [*Hands him* ZILOV's *note*.] And tell him what you think . . .
WAITER: [*reading*] "I ask that nobody be blamed for my death . . ."
SAIAPIN: He's had one go already. Right before our eyes.
WAITER: Has he?
KUZAKOV: It's true.

SAIAPIN: Here. [*Hands* WAITER *a cartridge.*] I took this out of the gun.
WAITER: [*examining cartridge.*] Duck-shot . . . Your percussion caps aren't reliable. Get some ordinary ones. They never fail.
ZILOV: Thanks for the advice.
WAITER: [*sitting down.*] Make sure you change them. It's stopped raining. [*Takes shotgun.*] In an hour [*Breaks shotgun.*] we'll be able [*Playfully, with two movements loads shotgun.*] to leave. Understand? Cut out the chatter, and I'll come and pick you up in an hour.
ZILOV: I'm not going anywhere. I've told you already. [*To* KUZAKOV *and* SAIAPIN.] No need to worry, you're onto a winner.
SAIAPIN: Vitia! Stop acting crazy! Get ready to go shooting.
KUZAKOV: Put your shoes on. [*Picking up rucksack.*] Put this on. [*To* SAIAPIN *and* WAITER.] Let's take him outside.
[KUZAKOV *and* SAIAPIN *approach* ZILOV.]
ZILOV: Don't touch me. Keep your hands off.
WAITER: Give us a straight answer. Are you going to go on acting crazy or are you coming shooting?
ZILOV: I'm not going anywhere.
WAITER: Well, what can I say to that? . . . Only that you're a fool. [*Rises*]
SAIAPIN: Not leaving, are you?
WAITER: What can I do here? Nothing. Can't you see that?
ZILOV: That's the way, Dima. You're a scoundrel, Dima, but I like you best of all. At least you don't pretend to be anything you're not, like these . . . Give us your hand . . . [*He and* WAITER *shake hands.*] Say hello to 'em all from me . . .
WAITER: See you, Vitia. Pity we're not going together. You've picked the wrong time to be out of sorts . . . But if you get over it, come along . . .
ZILOV: Okay, Dima. So long.
WAITER: Hold on, where's your boat?
ZILOV: The Limper's got it.
WAITER: In his shed?
ZILOV: Yes.
WAITER: So I can . . .
ZILOV: [*hoarsely*] Sure, take it.
WAITER: Thanks, Vitia. And if anything happens . . .

ZILOV: [*voice quavering*] You can treat it as your own . . . Take it . . . Take everything . . .
SAIAPIN: Vitia, think what you're saying . . .
ZILOV: You've already shared out my things. You're glad about my death. Oh, so glad!
KUZAKOV: That's a lie!
ZILOV: [*with sudden venom.*] I'm still alive, and you're already here waiting. Flocking in like vultures. Haven't you got enough things of your own? Haven't you got enough rooms? . . . Scavengers!
[*He rushes at them. They wrestle.*]
KUZAKOV: That's a lie! . . . That's a lie!
WAITER: Easy now . . . Get a grip on yourself! . . . Can you do that?
ZILOV: [*suddenly stops resisting*] Yes . . . [*Calmly*] Yes, I can . . . But now you won't get anything from me. Not a thing. [*Suddenly takes shotgun from* SAIAPIN *and steps back.*] Get out. [*Short pause.*]
WAITER: [*surprised*] Are you serious?
ZILOV: [*calmly*] Go away.
WAITER: Drop it, old fellow . . .
ZILOV: Clear out of here.
[SAIAPIN *backs to door.* KUZAKOV *holds his ground, facing* ZILOV. WAITER *stands behind him, closer to door.*]
[*To* KUZAKOV.] Get out.
KUZAKOV: I'm not going. I told you: I'm not going till . . .
ZILOV: Get out.
KUZAKOV: No.
ZILOV: I'll shoot. [*Levels gun at* KUZAKOV.]
KUZAKOV: Go ahead and shoot.
WAITER: It's loaded.
ZILOV: So much the better.
[SAIAPIN *disappears.*]
WAITER: Come on. [*Grabbing* KUZAKOV *and bundling him out of the door.*] Better this way . . . And now put that gun down.
ZILOV: You clear out too.
[*For a moment they look each other in the eye.* WAITER *retreats to door.*]
Quick!
[WAITER *holds back* KUZAKOV, *who has reappeared in door-*

way, and they both vanish. ZILOV *stands motionless for a moment, then slowly lowers right arm with gun. He paces about room with gun in hand. Goes up to bed and throws himself onto it face down. Shudders. Shudders again. His shudders become more frequent. It is impossible to tell whether he is laughing or crying. For a long time his body is shaken spasmodically, as if he were laughing very hard, or crying. This lasts for a quarter of a minute. Then he lies still. By this time the rain has stopped, the sky is turning blue, and the roof of the house opposite glows in the pale early-evening sunshine. The phone starts ringing again. He lies still. Phone stops ringing. He rises, and we see his calm face, but we still cannot tell by his face whether he was laughing or crying. Takes phone, dials number, speaks in an even, businesslike tone, with voice slightly raised.*]

ZILOV: Dima? . . . Zilov here . . . Yes . . . Sorry, mate. I got a bit carried away . . . Yes, better now . . . Perfectly calm . . . Yes, I want to go shooting . . . You leaving now? . . . Fine . . . I'm ready . . . Yes, I'm coming.

Provincial Anecdotes
A tragi-comedy in two parts

translated by Kevin Windle

FIRST ANECDOTE

THE COMPOSITOR

CHARACTERS

VIKTORIA   a girl looking for work
POTAPOV   a compositor, travelling on business
SEMION NIKOLAEVICH KALOSHIN   manager of the Hotel Taiga
MARINA   Kaloshin's wife, a waitress in the hotel dining-room
OLEG KAMAEV   a young man, teacher of physical education
BORIS RUKOSUEV   a doctor, friend of Kaloshin's

Whatever anybody says, such things do happen — not often, but they do happen.

N.V. Gogol

A single room in a provincial hotel. A bed, a table, a cupboard, two armchairs, a night table with a telephone and a radio on it. The far wall is hung with cheap, gaudy curtains.
   The latch clicks and enter Viktoria, an attractive girl of about twenty. Without stopping she slips off her coat and shoes, opens the cupboard door, and, unseen behind it, changes her clothes in a flash. She emerges in slippers and a thin dressing-gown.

She goes to the far wall and draws the curtains apart. Behind them is a window, through which can be seen lighted windows on the other side of the street, and right beside her window is the reverse side of a neon sign saying "Hotel Taiga". Viktoria looks out of the window for a moment, then turns, crosses the room, locks the door, takes a book from the table and opens it. Without raising her eyes from the book she goes to the bed, pulls off the bedspread, kicks off her slippers, and lies down.
An impatient knock at the door.
Viktoria jumps up, puts her slippers on, straightens her bed and her hair.
Another knock. Viktoria opens the door.
Enter POTAPOV, *a short, wiry man of about forty. He is wearing grey trousers, a light-coloured shirt, a tie, and a cheap velvet jacket. This modest-looking man is now clearly excited.*

POTAPOV: Hello! Is your radio working?
VIKTORIA: Radio?
POTAPOV: [*impatiently*] Yes, your radio!
VIKTORIA: Why?
POTAPOV: Is it working?
  [VIKTORIA *switches on the radio. A voice is heard giving a running commentary on a football match.* POTAPOV *comes into the room and steals towards the set.*]
COMMENTATOR: Khusainov has the ball, he passes to Yankin, Yankin crosses to the right . . .
  [POTAPOV *stands beside the radio, listening.*] . . . he is tackled, he passes . . . No, his shot goes wide . . . and now Shalimov moves into the attack . . . Shalimov passes, but Khusainov intercepts . . . Khusainov has the ball again . . .
VIKTORIA: Football, and I thought it was something . . .
POTAPOV: Shhh!
COMMENTATOR: Khusainov gets past Shalimov . . .
VIKTORIA: You had me worried . . .
POTAPOV: [*sternly*] Quiet!
COMMENTATOR: . . . the full-backs move in to tackle him . . .
VIKTORIA: Won't you sit down?
COMMENTATOR: Khusainov sends the ball into the penalty area . . .

VIKTORIA: Sit down . . .
POTAPOV: [*furiously*] Can't you keep quiet?
COMMENTATOR: . . . But there's nobody there, . . . too bad, nobody but a "Torpedo" full-back . . . And there's the referee's whistle now . . . So the first half has ended with no score . . . nil all . . . The teams go off for a break, and we'll take a short break too, listeners . . . We'll be back in fifteen minutes to see who'll come out on top in this tense, exciting contest.
ANNOUNCER: We now broadcast some light music.
[*Music.*]
POTAPOV: [*sitting down.*] If they lose this time I'll . . . I don't know what I'll do!
[*Short pause.*]
VIKTORIA: [*cautiously*] May I say something?
POTAPOV: What? . . . [*Suddenly very politely.*] I'm so sorry! Really . . . I can't think how I could . . . Football, you see . . .
VIKTORIA: No, I don't see. It's not so bad if you can watch it, but listening like this . . . I don't understand.
POTAPOV: Sorry to disturb you.
VIKTORIA: That's all right, you needn't worry . . .
POTAPOV: I have the room next door, you see, and I was sitting there listening, and suddenly the radio packed up, just at the most important moment. I ran out into the corridor, and up and down it. Past eleven already . . . no lights on, except yours, so I burst in here without even thinking what I was doing. [*Backs towards the door.*] Terribly sorry.
VIKTORIA: Wait a minute. [POTAPOV *stops.*] Where are you going? Where are you going to hear the rest of the game?
POTAPOV: I don't know. I'll find somewhere . . .
VIKTORIA: If you like you can take my set, and give it back in the morning.
POTAPOV: You don't mind?
VIKTORIA: Take it.
POTAPOV: Thanks very much. [*Takes radio.*] Terribly sorry. Good night.
[*Exit* POTAPOV, *but no sooner has* VIKTORIA *got ready for bed again than another knock is heard, this time a polite one.* VIKTORIA *opens the door. Enter* POTAPOV. *The door is left open.*]

POTAPOV: Sorry. It won't work in my room. [*Hands radio back to* VIKTORIA.]
VIKTORIA: What a shame.
POTAPOV: Must be the wiring.
VIKTORIA: What'll you do now?
POTAPOV: I've no idea. Thanks very much . . . [*Hesitates*] Shall I go and look for somebody . . . ?
VIKTORIA: Oh, forget it. [*Turns on radio.*] Sit down and listen.
POTAPOV: Can I really?
VIKTORIA: Why shouldn't you? Otherwise you'll have to chase all over the hotel.
POTAPOV: But you have to get your sleep.
VIKTORIA: Don't worry. I go to bed late. [*Moves armchair up to radio.*] Come and sit closer.
POTAPOV: Well, thanks very much. [*Sits down.*] May God send you a good husband for your kindness.
VIKTORIA: Thanks.
[SEMION NIKOLAEVICH KALOSHIN *appears in the doorway. He is about sixty, bald and round with an imposing air. He is short, but erect. His head is almost always thrown back, his brows usually knitted, and his eyes slightly narrowed. All this gives him a fairly impressive presence, and he does not notice people taller than him. He is dressed in a good-quality, dark suit, which hangs rather baggily on him. Before speaking he casts a critical eye over* VIKTORIA *and* POTAPOV.]
KALOSHIN: It's eleven o'clock, ladies and gentlemen. All visitors out, please.
[*Short pause.*]
VIKTORIA: There aren't any here. This gentleman's staying in the hotel too.
POTAPOV: Yes, I'm in the next room.
KALOSHIN: Makes no difference. According to the rules everybody must be in his own room after eleven.
VIKTORIA: All right, but the thing is . . .
KALOSHIN: [*interrupting*] Whatever it is, you can do it tomorrow. But now will you please go to your own rooms.
POTAPOV: Look here . . .
KALOSHIN: [*interrupting*] I don't want to hear about it.
VIKTORIA: All right, all right. He'll leave the room.

KALOSHIN: Come on there, look sharp about it.
VIKTORIA: Yes, yes. He'll go. Right away.
KALOSHIN: I warn you, I'll check up. [*Exit*]
VIKTORIA: Best not to argue with him.
POTAPOV: Yes, I'd better go.
VIKTORIA: No, you don't understand. Lock your door and come back here.
POTAPOV: You know, it'd be better to keep out of his way.
VIKTORIA: We'll lock the door, turn the radio low, and there'll be no trouble. Now go and lock up your room.
POTATOV: Well, if you say so . . . [*Goes out, and returns immediately.*] Done it.
VIKTORIA: You know why it all started? Because we left the door open. [*Turns down volume of radio.*] They rook you for all you're worth, and then force you to sneak around on tiptoe!
POTAPOV: You here on business?
VIKTORIA: Me? No. I'm just staying here one night, and tomorrow I move into a hostel. I've come to work on the building site. What about you?
POTAPOV: I'm on a business trip. [*Sits down.*]
VIKTORIA: Where are you from?
POTAPOV: Moscow.
VIKTORIA: All right. You listen to your programme, and I'll read my book. And we'll lock the door . . . [*Goes to door to lock it.*] [*Door suddenly opens. Enter* KALOSHIN.]
KALOSHIN: [*amiably*] I see. Locking ourselves in, are we? . . .
VIKTORIA: His radio's stopped working . . .
KALOSHIN: [*ambiguously*] Of course.
VIKTORIA: He'll just listen to the football, then leave.
KALOSHIN: [*playfully*] Football, you say?
POTAPOV: Yes, that's right. Football.
KALOSHIN: [*merrily*] Football?
VIKTORIA: Yes, of course.
KALOSHIN: I see. Football, you say.
POTAPOV: Yes, football! Can't you understand that?
KALOSHIN: Oh yes. I understand perfectly. I'm not a child.
POTAPOV: What's that? What do you mean by that?
KALOSHIN: You know what I mean.
POTAPOV: What exactly do you mean?

KALOSHIN: I mean you can try and fool somebody else, but not me.
POTAPOV: Meaning what?
VIKTORIA: Well? Explain . . .
KALOSHIN: And will you explain something to me? Football, did you say?
POTAPOV: Yes, football.
KALOSHIN: Here we go again . . . Then why did you want to lock yourselves in, may I ask? Why lock the door to listen to a football match?
VIKTORIA: Oh, this is too much . . . To keep you out! You! So you wouldn't come in bothering us . . .
KALOSHIN: [*interrupting*] "Bothering you"? That's what I thought — so I wouldn't bother you. Nobody likes being bothered, do they?
POTAPOV: Oh, it's impossible to talk to you!
KALOSHIN: It's perfectly possible to talk to me. But I'm afraid you just don't know how to go about it. [*In an official tone.*] Now kindly return to your own room.
POTAPOV: All right. I'll go, but . . .
VIKTORIA: [*interrupting*] No, don't go. [*To* KALOSHIN.] *You* go! [*Opens door.*] *He* can go.
KALOSHIN: What do you mean?
VIKTORIA: Just what I say. Clear out, that's all. We can get on perfectly well without you. This is my room, and I'll do as I please.
KALOSHIN: What?
VIKTORIA: Nobody asked you to come here and talk to us.
KALOSHIN: My dear lady, don't you know the rules?
VIKTORIA: No.
KALOSHIN: You don't? Then I can tell you them.
POTAPOV: Listen . . .
KALOSHIN: [*interrupting*] You don't know them either? I can tell you too.
VIKTORIA: Go on, we're listening.
KALOSHIN: First you register your names together, and then you can lock yourselves in. Then you can do what you like — feel free. You didn't know? Well now you do. And now will you kindly leave this lady's room?
VIKTORIA: Oh! This is impossible!

POTAPOV: All right. I'll go. But you must apologize to this girl.
KALOSHIN: Whatever for?
POTAPOV: For insulting her. Don't you realize you've insulted her?
KALOSHIN: [*angrily*] *I'm* not going to apologize! You're the one who's going to apologize, and not to her, but to your own lawful wedded wife. But in the meantime, kindly go to your own room. And go quietly.
[*Music from radio stops. The hum of the football ground is heard.*]
POTAPOV: I've heard enough! Now I'm not going anywhere.
VIKTORIA: Quite right.
KALOSHIN: You will go.
POTAPOV: No, I won't. [*Sits down in the armchair by the radio.*]
COMMENTATOR: Here we are back at the Dynamo ground where the two Moscow teams, Spartak and Torpedo, are competing for the national cup . . .
KALOSHIN: You think you're not going, but if you're not careful you're going to get thrown out of this hotel altogether.
[*Sound of stadium crowd.*]
POTAPOV: No, I'm not going. Do what you like. Call the police, but I . . . I'm going to listen to the game.
COMMENTATOR: As you know, the first half ended with no score and . . .
KALOSHIN: [*goes to radio and turns it off.*] That's all.
POTAPOV: I'd advise you not to get in the way. [*Turns on radio.*]
COMMENTATOR: The forwards and backs . . .
[KALOSHIN *switches off radio.* POTAPOV *switches it on.* KALOSHIN *switches it off again and seizes* POTAPOV *by the arm.*]
POTAPOV: Don't touch!
KALOSHIN: [*dragging* POTAPOV *towards the door.*] If you don't understand when people talk to you politely . . . won't go quietly . . .
POTAPOV: Don't you dare! [*resisting*]
VIKTORIA: [*helping* POTAPOV.] You've no right!
POTAPOV: Let me go!
[*Struggle in the doorway.* KALOSHIN *ejects* POTAPOV *by the scruff of his neck.* KALOSHIN *and* POTAPOV *stand facing each other across the doorway. Both breathing heavily.*]

KALOSHIN: Didn't I warn you? . . . I did . . .
POTAPOV: You'll answer for this!
VIKTORIA: Yes, you will!
POTAPOV: I give you my word I won't let matters lie.
KALOSHIN: Get along, get along . . .
POTAPOV: You won't forget me in a hurry.
VIKTORIA: You won't forget him!
POTAPOV: I promise you that. [*Exit*]
KALOSHIN: On your way, on your way . . . I've seen your sort before . . . Casanovas.
VIKTORIA: Go away.
KALOSHIN: Now wait a minute . . . [*Goes to armchair, sits down.*] Oof! . . .
VIKTORIA: [*scornfully*] What's this? Feeling tired?
KALOSHIN: What do you think?
VIKTORIA: But happy? . . . However can you, a man of your age . . .
KALOSHIN: It's a way to earn a living . . .
VIKTORIA: You ought to be ashamed . . .
KALOSHIN: Some job! What a position to be honoured with. Going from floor to floor, day in, day out! And these arguments to boot . . . You tell me, just tell me, how's anyone supposed to handle you lot, hotel guests? How? Try being polite, and you don't understand. Start laying down the law, and you get all uppity. And he nearly dislocated my shoulder.
VIKTORIA: And what about you? Didn't you push him?
KALOSHIN: Teach him a lesson.
VIKTORIA: What if he'd hit his head against the wall?
KALOSHIN: Wouldn't have done him any harm. He'd have rubbed it and gone on his way. He's only small fry.
VIKTORIA: How do you know?
KALOSHIN: I've got eyes. There's five hundred people here, and if they all started taking offence, where'd it all end? . . . Why did he get up in arms? Couldn't he have gone quietly? Doesn't he know the ropes?
VIKTORIA: What ropes?
KALOSHIN: You might be forgiven, on account of your age, but he ought to know better.
VIKTORIA: It's your own fault. You started talking all that nonsense.

He didn't lay a finger on you. He's just a football fan, but he's perfectly decent. He's come here from Moscow . . .
KALOSHIN: [*quickly*] From where?
VIKTORIA: Moscow.
KALOSHIN: [*somewhat mistrustfully*.] What do you mean — from Moscow?
VIKTORIA: Just what I say — from Moscow. Why? Got the wind up?
KALOSHIN: Don't talk nonsense . . . So he's from Moscow. There's plenty of riff-raff even there.
VIKTORIA: But what if he's one of the high-ups?
KALOSHIN: You telling me you don't know him?
VIKTORIA: Of course I don't.
KALOSHIN: You're not having me on?
VIKTORIA: I tell you I don't know him. [*Mischievously*] What if he's one of the high-ups?
KALOSHIN: Him? . . . Don't talk nonsense. Some little schoolteacher more likely.
VIKTORIA: Just suppose.
KALOSHIN: [*becoming anxious*.] Why "suppose"? No question about it. Velvet jacket, cheap little tie . . . I can spot 'em.
VIKTORIA: You mean you treat all guests according to their clothes?
KALOSHIN: What do you think? In this job you don't get far without sharp eyes. If you had to run and check what everyone wrote on his registration form you'd wear yourself out double quick.
VIKTORIA: What do clothes tell you? Plenty of important people dress modestly, and if you ask me . . .
KALOSHIN: [*getting up*.] I won't ask you, and don't try and pull my leg. [*Goes to telephone, dials number*.] I'm tired, and the wife'll probably be out looking for me by now . . . Nobody's asking you . . . [*Hangs up, dials again*.] Yes, it was a black day when I took on this hotel job, a black day. Could have had a nice, quiet job, but I chose to go after the money . . . [*into telephone*.] Desk? Manager here . . . Take a look in the book and tell me who's in room 211 . . . 211. Potapov? . . . Who is he? Where's he from? . . . Moscow? . . . What does he do? . . . Eh? What? . . . A compositor? . . . What's that? . . . [*To* VIKTORIA.] What's a compositor?

VIKTORIA: [*sincerely*] I don't know.
KALOSHIN: [*into telephone.*] Find out what a compositor does . . . And hurry . . . How'd he get in — had he an official warrant? . . . Business trip? . . . What's he come here for? Which organization is he visiting? . . . Not in the book? . . . How many times have you been told to get those forms filled in from top to bottom . . . Disgraceful . . . When did he book in?. . . Today? . . . Who is he? . . . I'm asking you what that means. What is a compositor? . . . What? Nobody knows? . . . How come? . . . Find out, and be quick about it . . . No, no! Don't ask him . . . If he comes and talks to you, be polite . . . [*Hangs up.*] Compositor . . . What's that?
VIKTORIA: [*guilefully*] A compositor . . . I think it's somebody from the fraud squad.
KALOSHIN: [*scared*] Come off it! What an idea . . . Compositor . . . Funny sort of word . . . Damned if I know it! . . . Maybe it's something to do with the trade union.
VIKTORIA: What if he's a deputy of the Supreme Soviet?
KALOSHIN: Come off it, will you? Go easy . . . He'd have taken a de luxe suite, and . . . we'd have got notice in advance . . . They always give notice.
VIKTORIA: That doesn't mean a thing. This one just decided to turn up, without notice. To see what you were up to.
KALOSHIN: Now wait a minute! You'd better keep a watch on your tongue, you know! . . . Compositor . . . Rings a bell . . . Something like that in tsarist times, wasn't there? At the tsar's court?
VIKTORIA: I think there was.
KALOSHIN: Damned if I know . . . [*Dials number on telephone. Speaking into it.*] Dining room? . . . Get me Muza Khananovna . . . Who's speaking? Look, you wouldn't happen to know what a compositor is, would you? . . . No, how could you . . . I said, how could you? . . . Kaloshin . . . Hold on . . . Has my wife left yet? . . . Still at work? . . . No, don't bother. She wouldn't have a clue . . . Okay, thanks . . . [*Hangs up.*] Nobody knows! What sort of place is this? Ignorance all round . . . And I could have had a job on a newsreel team . . . educated milieu, . . . and I end up here . . . [*Dials another number.*] Andrei Vasilyevich? . . . Good

evening ... Kaloshin here ... Sorry to disturb you so late but ... Business call, yes ... That is, not exactly ... Yes, a business matter, Andrei Vasilyevich ... I was wondering, Andrei Vasilyevich, whether you might be able to tell an ignoramus like me what a compositor is .. Com-pos-it-or ... Never come across it? ... We've got this little problem here ... No, no, nothing serious. Terribly sorry, ... terribly sorry ...Good night. [*Hangs up.*] And he's been to two colleges. Doesn't know anything! Just goes to show! At the newsreel studios any cloakroom attendant would be able to tell you, but not in this place. [*Dials another number. Speaking into telephone.*] Desk? ... Well, found out yet? ... What's a compositor? ... Eh? From a paper? ... You think? Couldn't you find out for sure? ... They have editors and correspondents, but what does this one do? ... You don't know? Then what the hell do you mean by ... Find out ... At once! [*Hangs up.*] Looks like he's from a newspaper.

VIKTORIA: A newspaper?

KALOSHIN: [*scared, and not troubling to conceal it.*] I wonder which paper ... "Trud"? Hope it isn't "Izvestia" ... What if he's in charge of all of 'em at once? What'll happen then, eh? What'll he do to me? ... He could ... He could do whatever he liked ... All he's got to do is snap his fingers and I go flying, and not come down, ever!

VIKTORIA: Got you worried now, hasn't he?

KALOSHIN: Where is he? ... I'll apologize! I'll go and apologize this minute! [*Goes out hurriedly.*]

[*From corridor* KALOSHIN'*s voice is heard saying, "Mr Potapov," as he knocks on his door. Very polite knock: "Mr Potapov ... Mr ... er ... compositor ..."*]

KALOSHIN: [*entering the room*] Where is he? Where did he go? Which way?

VIKTORIA: I don't know. To the police, maybe.

KALOSHIN: What shall I do?

VIKTORIA: How should I know? You've made your bed, now you can lie in it.

KALOSHIN: But what'll happen now? ... If he's ... and if he goes to the police ...

VIKTORIA: Serves you right. I don't feel one bit sorry for you.

KALOSHIN: But why? What have I done to him? . . . Why didn't he say anything. Why didn't he tell me who he was? It's not right. He could treat me like a human being — I'm not a donkey. Running about here all day long. I've got sclerosis and high blood pressure . . . three years till retirement. And my nerves are forever playing up. Maybe I . . . [*Stops, as if grasping at a thought. Continues decisively.*] No! all kinds of things have happened to me, but I've never yet had to go to court. And I won't have to this time! [*Forcefully, but in a pleading tone.*] Be a darling, go and find him for me! . . . Will you?

VIKTORIA: Me? Why should I go looking for him?

KALOSHIN: Find him for me! Talk to him! Tell him the manager's on his knees, eating his heart out, feels so bad he daren't look him in the face . . . Won't you? For friendship's sake!

VIKTORIA: Since when were you and I friends? Run after him yourself. It's my bedtime.

KALOSHIN: Look, I've got to make a phone-call. Go after him, there's a dear! I really mean it. I'll apologize. To him . . . and to you! I'll apologize to you right away!

VIKTORIA: As if I needed your apologies!

KALOSHIN: I won't forget it . . . At once, though, eh? My fate could be hanging by a thread now. [*Seizing telephone.*]

VIKTORIA: All right. But don't imagine I'm doing it for your sake. Make your call and get on your way. I want to go to bed. [*Exit*]

KALOSHIN: [*dialling number.*] Lies . . . lies . . . lies . . . You don't beat me that easily! [*Into telephone.*] Katia? Kaloshin here . . . Husband in? . . . On duty? . . . All right, Katia, that'll be all for now. [*Presses on receiver-cradle, dials two digits, speaks into telephone.*] Ambulance station? . . . Get me Rukosuev! . . . Yes! Boris Petrovich! [*Waits*] Lies! . . . You don't beat me that easy . . . [*Into telephone.*] Boris? . . . Semion here . . . Boris, help me! . . . Save me! . . . Me! . . . Trouble . . . At the hotel . . . Put my foot in it! . . . Get me to hospital! . . . Yes, I'm all right, but I need a certificate . . . That I'm not well! . . . Not well, I said, get it? . . . That I'm crazy, get it? Epileptic! . . . No, of course not! I'm all right! . . . All right, I said! . . . But pretend I'm not! . . . Looks like the cops are coming . . . Could end up in court . . . In court, I said . . . That clear? Get going right away! . . . Eh? No ambulance? . . . Have one soon? . . . Hurry, though, Boris. Hurry! . . . I'm up to my neck . . . As good as had it . . . Grateful all my life! I'll be waiting! . . . At the hotel . . . First floor . . . Two hundred and ten . . . Boris! Boris! Hold it! . . . What's a compositor? . . . Com-pos-it-or? . . . You don't know? . . . What? . . . Into bed? . . . Right . . . Boris! Boris! Hold it! . . . [*Lowering his voice.*] Maybe I should . . . er . . . act a bit crazy, eh? You know . . . Kick up a bit of a shindy or . . . No? Not too much? . . . Okay, not too much . . . Got it! . . . I'll be quiet about it then . . . Go to bed . . . Right . . . But be quick! Be quick! [*Hangs up, wipes his brow.*] Lies! [*Dials number. Speaks into telephone.*] Desk? Found out yet? . . . I know that already! I want to know what exactly he does there . . . Drop everything and find out immediately! . . . My wife hasn't called yet, has she? . . . When she does, tell her to go home . . . Yes, without me . . . I'm staying behind . . . important business . . . No, she needn't wait . . . Needn't wait! . . . When you've found out what a compositor is, ring room two hundred and ten . . . His position. Position! Exactly! [*Hangs up.*] Lies! . . . Whoever you might be, brother, you'd better not take on Kaloshin with your bare hands. I might not be a compositor, but I'm nobody's skivvy either . . . [*Takes off his jacket, tie, and shoes, lies down on the bed and draws the blanket over him. Gets up again, tosses his clothes about the room, thinks for a moment, undoes his collar, and pulls his shirt tails out over his trousers.*] I'll put on such a show, my friends, such a performance, that you won't know what to say! [*Lies down again, but sits up at once and looks thoughtfully round the room, wondering what else to do. Reaches for his glasses, puts them on, takes a book from the night table, opens it, and lies down.*]

[*Enter* VIKTORIA.]

VIKTORIA: [*from the doorway.*] Can't find him any . . . any . . . [*Presuming she has come to the wrong room.*] Awfully sorry! [*Hurries out and closes door.*]

KALOSHIN: Hasn't found him . . . Never mind, Mister Compositor!

Now we'll see who does the apologizing . . .
[*Enter* VIKTORIA, *this time opening the door very gingerly.*]
[*Calmly*] Who are you looking for?
[VIKTORIA, *thoroughly baffled, closes the door.*]
[*Satisfied*] She doesn't recognize me.
[*Enter* VIKTORIA *for the third time.*]
Looking for me? . . . Do come in.

VIKTORIA: What's all this?
KALOSHIN: Come right in. Don't be afraid.
VIKTORIA: What's all this?
KALOSHIN: What's what?
VIKTORIA: What are you doing?
KALOSHIN: Me? . . . Just lying down, as you see.
VIKTORIA: Yes, but . . . What are you doing here?
KALOSHIN: Nothing. Just lying down . . . Thought I'd rest for a bit, have a lie down, take a look at a book. What's so funny about that?
VIKTORIA: But that's . . . that's . . . Very odd indeed!
KALOSHIN: What's odd? I don't see.
VIKTORIA: It's . . . it's simply . . . I don't even know what to call it!
KALOSHIN: Call what! I don't see what's bothering you. If you mean I've taken your place, then just say so. I can move over.
VIKTORIA: What?
KALOSHIN: I can move over. Any time.
VIKTORIA: What? Are you serious? . . . Are you playing the clown or are you really off your rocker?
KALOSHIN: Not at all. I'm only small fry, not one of your compositors. I can move over. [*Moves over.*]
VIKTORIA: [*softly*] He's off his head . . . [*Louder*] What's wrong with you? . . . How are you feeling?
KALOSHIN: Roger! Feeling fine, thanks. Switching to "receive". Over!
VIKTORIA: [*softly*] He's crazy! [*Louder*] I'll call a doctor, all right?
KALOSHIN: Fine.
VIKTORIA: [*goes to telephone. Stands with her back to Kaloshin, dials number, speaks softly.*] Ambulance?
[KALOSHIN *sits up in bed, listens to the conversation.*]
Come to the hotel . . . There's a man here in a bad state . . . I think he's gone mad . . . Come quickly! . . . Room Two

Hundred and Ten . . . What? No ambulances free . . . Will you have one soon? . . . Right . . . [*hangs up.*]
[KALOSHIN *lies down.*]
[*turning to* KALOSHIN, *speaking in a tone usually reserved for children.*] There we are. He'll be here soon.
KALOSHIN: Who'll be here soon?
VIKTORIA: The doctor.
KALOSHIN: Why?
VIKTORIA: Why? . . . [*Cautiously*] Just visiting.
KALOSHIN: Visiting? . . . Good, let him come visiting. In the meantime I'll read my book. You don't mind, do you? [*Opens book, reads aloud.*] "At dawn arising from the lake, the geese their southward course did take . . ."
[*A knock at the door. Door opens. Enter* MARINA, KALOSHIN'*s wife. She is a little over thirty, not unattractive, but too heavily made up, with a hint of vulgarity. She is wearing stylish shoes, gaudy stockings, a raincoat, and a waitress's lace bonnet. At her entrance* KALOSHIN *half rises, but lies down again at once. Pause, during which nobody knows what to do or say.*]
KALOSHIN: [*finding nothing better to do, continues reading.*] "Behind the skein across the sky, a flock of . . . er . . . quail did southward fly . . ."
MARINA: What on earth is the meaning of this?
KALOSHIN: Of . . . er . . . what?
MARINA: *This!*
KALOSHIN: [*uncertainly*] I think it means autumn's coming on . . .
MARINA: What are you people doing here — I want to know? [*Shouting*] Tell me, you brazen creatures.
VIKTORIA: Wait a minute . . .
MARINA: [*interrupting*] What do you call this?
VIKTORIA: There's no need to shout . . .
MARINA: [*to* KALOSHIN.] What do you call this? Is this the "important business" you told me about? Is it?
KALOSHIN: Yes . . . It's very serious.
MARINA: Serious?
VIKTORIA: Listen . . .
MARINA: The shame of it! I don't know!

VIKTORIA: Listen to me! He's not normal!
MARINA: What?
VIKTORIA: Not normal, I tell you. He's gone crazy . . .
MARINA: And ain't you pleased! Instead of giving him a slap in the chops you . . .
VIKTORIA: [*interrupting*] Stop shouting, I tell you! He's not right in the head!
MARINA: And are you right in the head? Getting mixed up with an old man! Hussy!
VIKTORIA: Stop it! Try and understand before you . . .
MARINA: Shut up, you tart!
VIKTORIA: Look here!
MARINA: Shut up!
VIKTORIA: Look here!
MARINA: Will you shut up, you good-for-nothing!
VIKTORIA: [*losing her temper.*] Good-for-nothing yourself!
MARINA: Scum!
VIKTORIA: *You* call *me* scum?
MARINA: I'll tear all your hair out by the roots!
VIKTORIA: Shouting her head off, as if anyone was afraid of her!
KALOSHIN: Come on now, keep it down . . .
VIKTORIA: What are you yelling about? Who are you?
MARINA: Me?! Who am I?
VIKTORIA: Yes, you, you! Who are you! [*To* KALOSHIN.] Who is she? Your wife?
KALOSHIN: [*bravely*] Her? . . . I don't know . . . Never set eyes on her before. [MARINA *gasps and falls silent for a moment, eyes wide, mouth open.*]
VIKTORIA: So there's no reason to shout. First you have to try and understand, and then . . .
MARINA: [*bearing down on* KALOSHIN.] You . . . you . . . What are you up to? Damn your shameless face! Do you know what you're saying, or don't you?
VIKTORIA: That's the trouble, he doesn't.
MARINA: Who am I? . . . Well?
KALOSHIN: You? . . . You must be . . . er . . .
MARINA: [*coming closer.*] Who am I?
KALOSHIN: [*moving away.*] You? . . . You're . . . er . . .
MARINA: Well? [*Snatching book out of his hands.*] Don't you recognize me?

KALOSHIN: [*scared*] Yes, yes, I do! . . . [*Thinking again.*] I think I've . . . er . . . seen you somewhere, but . . . [*To* VIKTORIA.] I can't think who she is.
MARINA: You what?? [*Taking a swing at him with the book.*]
KALOSHIN: I remember, now I remember!
MARINA: Well? Who am I? [*Taking another swing at him.*] Answer me!
KALOSHIN: My wife, my wife! [*To* VIKTORIA.] She's awfully like my wife.
MARINA: Awfully like her?
KALOSHIN: Two peas in a pod! [*To* VIKTORIA.] But my wife's not that stupid . . .
MARINA: What's that?
KALOSHIN: Oh, no. My wife's an intelligent woman . . .
VIKTORIA: [*to* MARINA.] But just who are you? Are you his wife or not?
MARINA: Tell her, you scoundrel!
KALOSHIN: [*firmly*] She's not my wife.
VIKTORIA: There. Do you see what I mean?
MARINA: What do you think you're doing, you old devil? Are you trying to make a fool of me?
KALOSHIN: Less noise. You're a dab hand at raising hell, and saying all sorts of rude things. But what about telling me what a compositor is? Do you know that?
MARINA: Look, Semion! Drop all this! Stop playing the idiot.
VIKTORIA: He's not playing anything. He got into bed while I was out of the room.
MARINA: What?? . . . Just what do you take me for?
VIKTORIA: I keep telling you, he's flipped! Surely you can see that by now!
MARINA: I can see all right, don't worry! I can see right through him, the bounder! Flipped indeed! Expect me to believe that?
VIKTORIA: Oh, it's hopeless talking to you. Still, the doctor'll be here soon . . .
MARINA: What did you say?
VIKTORIA: I said the doctor will be here soon, and then . . .
MARINA: [*interrupting*] Have you called a doctor?
VIKTORIA: Of course.
MARINA: [*panic-stricken, to* KALOSHIN.] On your feet now! . . . Get up and get out of here! Hurry!

KALOSHIN: No. Nothing doing.
MARINA: Do you mean you can't get up?
KALOSHIN: No, I can't.
MARINA: What a disgrace! Needing a doctor, I don't know! What a thing to get up to in your old age, and with your weak heart! Damn your shameless eyes!
VIKTORIA: I can't bear any more of this . . .
MARINA: Do what you like, but get up! All we need is to have people see you in that bed! Get up this minute!
KALOSHIN: No, no . . . I can't! . . . Impossible . . . Do you know who I am? I'm an insect, a beetle, a ladybird. If I get up now the wind will blow me away!
MARINA: [*trying to lift him up.*] Get up, you rogue!
KALOSHIN: [*clutching at the bed.*] No, no, no . . .
MARINA: [*to* VIKTORIA.] Give me a hand!
VIKTORIA: Don't touch him.
MARINA: Get up, Semion! Or it'll be worse for you . . .
KALOSHIN: It can't be worse!
MARINA: Are you making fun of me? . . . As if this wasn't enough you have to make me look a fool? Put me to shame all over the town? . . . Well, it won't work. I'll get the better of you! [*Goes to telephone, dials number.*] You think I'm all alone so you can make fun of me as much as you like? . . . Well, you're wrong. [*Speaking into telephone.*] Muza? . . . Marina speaking . . . Muza, would you look and see if Oleg's still there?
KALOSHIN: [*making to sit up.*] Oleg who?
MARINA: [*into telephone.*] He usually sits at the last table . . . Can I have a word . . . [*To* KALOSHIN.] You'll have only yourself to blame for this.
KALOSHIN: Who's Oleg?
MARINA: [*defiantly*] Just a friend of mine. [*into telephone.*] Oleg? . . . Marina speaking . . . Come up to room two hundred and ten, would you? . . . Right away. [*Hangs up.*]
KALOSHIN: [*indignantly*] You told him to come here?
MARINA: You don't like that, eh?
KALOSHIN: [*more indignantly.*]Him? Here?
MARINA: Why? I see you're feeling better.
KALOSHIN: [*remembering his role, calmly.*] So you've told him to come here. [*Lies down.*] Very well . . . The more the merrier.

VIKTORIA: I can imagine. Couldn't we manage better without him?
MARINA: That's none of your business. He's my friend, do you understand? I'm a great believer in men and women being friends. Not like some people I know. [*To* KALOSHIN.] As from today he's going to come calling on us, so there.
[*Knocks at door.* KALOSHIN *shudders.*]
[*Opening door.*] In you come, Oleg.
[*Enter* KAMAEV, *a young man of about thirty. He is healthy-looking, rosy-cheeked, and quite well dressed. His usual manner is a kind of chivalrous familiarity. He is carrying a wrapped package — clearly a bottle.*]
KAMAEV: Evening all!
MARINA: Come in, Oleg . . . Let me introduce you. This here, with the book, is my husband.
KAVAEV: Your husband?
MARINA: That's him.
KAMAEV: [*puzzled*] Well . . . good . . . How do you do? [*Bows*] I'm Kamaev . . . A teacher . . . You . . . not feeling well?
MARINA: He's a bit tired.
KAMAEV: Oh . . . Then he'd better have a rest . . . [*To* KALOSHIN.] This your daughter?
MARINA: No, no, it's her room we're in.
KAMAEV: Oh yes? How do you do? [*bows*] Oleg . . . Kamaev. A teacher . . .
VIKTORIA: So you said.
KAMAEV: What's she so cross about?
MARINA: Can't you see?
KAMAEN: No. I'm a happy sort of fellow, I . . . What exactly am I supposed to see?
MARINA: I came and disturbed them, if you can imagine it.
KAMAEV: You what?
MARINA: I disturbed them.
KAMAEV: Them? [*Looking in surprise at* VIKTORIA, *then at* KALOSHIN.] Impossible! . . .
MARINA: Don't you believe me?
KAMAEV: Seriously?
MARINA: Oleg, you innocent!
VIKTORIA: Don't you think this has gone on long enough?
KAMAEV: [*to* VIKTORIA *and* KALOSHIN.] Well. Good for you! [*To* KALOSHIN.] Up you get! This is something to drink to.

MARINA: He can't get up. Believe it or not.
KAMAEV: Really?
MARINA: You'll have to help him.
KAMAEV: Can't get up? You're kidding! [*Looking* VIKTORIA *up and down.*] Good for you!
KALOSHIN: [*in low voice, but restraining himself with difficulty.*] Just a minute . . .
MARINA: What did you say?
KALOSHIN: Just a minute, children, only wait a while. You shall have a whistle, and a treasure isle . . .
KAMAEV: What's all that about?
MARINA: Believe it or not, he's pretending to be mad.
KAMAEV: Really? . . . Why's that?
MARINA: To get out of trouble, of course.
VIKTORIA: He's not pretending. He *is* mad. And you . . .
MARIAN: [*interrupting*] You keep quiet. [*To* KAMAEV.] You should have heard the yarn she spun me. Trying to tell me he got into bed while she was out of the room. Can you imagine? [KAMAEV *laughs.*]
VIKTORIA: I can't put up with any more of this . . . To hell with you! [*Sits down with her back to the others.*] Sort it out yourselves.
KALOSHIN: Just a minute, children . . .
MARINA: Listen to him.
KALOSHIN: . . . only wait a while . . .
MARINA: Anybody who didn't know him might believe he really was mad.
KAMAEV: I can see you've been having lots of fun here.
VIKTORIA: Too true!
KAMAEV: Well then, I'll join in. But first let's have a drop to drink.
MARINA: No, first we've got to get him up.
KAMAEV: What for? Let him rest.
MARINA: No, no! The doctor'll be here any minute now.
KAMAEV: So what?
MARINA: What do you mean — so what? Just think of the gossip there'll be if . . .
KAMAEV: I see.
MARINA: It'll be all over town, and we can do without that.
KAMAEV: Yes, nobody wants that. [*To* KALOSHIN.] She's right. You'll have to get up.

KALOSHIN: Just a minute, children . . .
KAMAEV: No point waiting.
KALOSHIN: . . . only wait a while . . .
KAMAEV: Even if you are mad it wouldn't do you any harm to think about your reputation.
KALOSHIN: . . . you shall have a whistle, and a treasure isle!
KAMAEV: Hurry up. Get up while there are no strangers here, and we can keep the whole business private. As soon as anybody else shows up . . . Just think how people will look at you . . .
MARINA: All right. No good talking to him any more. Take hold of him and lift him up.
KALOSHIN: [*clutching at the bed.*] No, no! . . . Don't touch me . . . I'm an insect, I'm a gnat, but I . . . I can sting! Better not touch me.
MARINA: [*to* KAMAEV.] Take him by the collar and don't listen to him.
KAMAEV: Now why do it the hard way? [*To* KALOSHIN.] We can do things for ourselves, can't we? We're men of education, aren't we?
KALOSHIN: I'm an insect, I'm a gnat . . .
KAMAEV: That'll do. You're a man of culture, and you understand as well as I do what "moral turpitude" means. Get up.
MARINA: Oleg, you're wasting your time.
KAMAEV: Come on now. Don't make us use force. I'm a man of good upbringing but . . .
KALOSHIN: [*suddenly sits up in bed, speaking with suppressed fury.*] If you're a man of good upbringing . . . [*Louder, and in higher pitch.*] if you're a man of culture . . . [*In a piercing voice, shaking his fists.*] if you're a man of education! . . . then . . . [*Stops, lowers fists, then speaks in pleading voice, desperate, but subdued.*] then tell me what a compositor is!
[*Brief pause.*]
VIKTORIA: [*getting up.*] I can't stand any more of this. [*To* KAMAEV.] Tell him, if you know. He's got it on the brain.
KAMAEV: Got what on the brain?
VIKTORIA: The compositor!
KAMAEV: How come?
VIKTORIA: It's like this. A man came into my room, and this one came along and kicked him out.

KAMAEV: I see . . .
VIKTORIA: And then he had second thoughts. Started wondering who he'd kicked out.
KAMAEV: I see . . .
VIKTORIA: Who could he be? He phoned the desk, and they said he was a compositor. But nobody knew what a compositor was.
KAMAEV: I see . . .
VIKTORIA: Who could he be? Where could he have come from? What if he was from somewhere high up? That's when he really got the wind up. Phoned everybody, and nobody knew. Somebody said he was from a paper, but didn't know any more. That really finished him off.
KAMAEV: I see . . .
VIKTORIA: So there you are. He went off his rocker. From fright.
MARINA: She's lying.
KAMAEV: [*to* MARINA.] Wait. [*To* VIKTORIA.] So nobody knows what a compositor is?
VIKTORIA: That's the whole point! If you know, tell him! It might help, you never know.
KAMAEV: [*amusing himself.*] I hardly think so. I'm afraid it might make things worse . . .
[KALOSHIN, *who has been listening avidly to the conversation, can now no longer conceal his alarm.*]
Insulting a compositor . . . you know . . .
VIKTORIA: [*impatiently*] But who is he?
KAMAEV: Um . . . [*To* KALOSHIN.] You didn't hit him, I hope?
KALOSHIN: [*deadly serious.*] No! No!
KAMAEV: You're among friends here, you can make a clean breast of it. Did you lay hands on him?
KALOSHIN: N-nothing like that! I swear!
VIKTORIA: He threw him out.
KAMAEV: Threw him out? . . . That's bad . . . What about your language?
KALOSHIN: Eh?
KAMAEV: Did you swear at him? . . . Use any bad language?
KALOSHIN: Not once!
VIKTORIA: He called him a Casanova.
KAMAEV: Called the compositor a Casanova? . . . Hmm . . . that's . . . That's too bad.

VIKTORIA: But what is a compositor?
MARINA: Yes, what is it?
VIKTORIA: Do you know or don't you?
KALOSHIN: [*trembling*] What is a compositor?
KAMAEV: I see your reason has returned. All the worse for you. You'd do better to stay mad.
KALOSHIN: [*panting*] What's a compositor?
KAMAEV: A compositor is . . . a . . . Yes, my dear fellow, things look black for you.
VIKTORIA: Don't drag this out!
KAMAEV: A compositor, my friends, is nothing less than a man from the ministry. From high up . . . [*Short pause.*] Yes, my friends, that's who he is. Too late now . . .
   [*Knock at door.* KALOSHIN *shudders and lowers himself back onto the bed. Another knock.* MARINA *cautiously opens the door slightly and peeps out.*]
MARINA: Boris? . . . That you? [*Opens door wide.*]
   [*Enter* RUKOSUEV, *a man of about* KALOSHIN's *age. He is wearing a white coat and glasses. He is carrying a white box.*]
   We're in luck. It's Boris, his old friend.
KAMAEV: I'm Kamaev . . . A teacher . . .
RUKOSUEV: [*entering room.*] Now then, where's the patient? In bed? [*Slightly quizzically.*] Must be serious . . . [*Sits down on bed.*] What's up with you then, Semion, old chap?
   [KALOSHIN *lies still.*]
   What's happened to you?
MARINA: Nothing to worry about. He's putting on a bit of an act.
RUKOSUEV: [*feigning surprise.*] An act? . . . Why should he do that?
MARINA: He's got himself into a fix, and now he's trying to wriggle out of it.
RUKOSUEV: Semion, . . . Semion!
MARINA: Gone deaf, have you?
RUKOSUEV: Semion!
   [MARINA *shakes* KALOSHIN. *He groans.*]
MARINA: Quit playing the fool!
RUKOSUEV: [*in slightly mocking tone.*] Semion, you're overdoing it.
MARINA: Quit playing the fool, do you hear? This is Boris, don't you see? . . . Has he gone deaf?
RUKOSUEV: Semion . . . You're taking things a bit far, chum . . .

KAMAEV: Quite an actor, isn't he? . . .
VIKTORIA: Get up. You've had your bit of fun.
RUKOSUEV: Semion . . . [*Takes* KALOSHIN's *hand, checks pulse.*] What's up with you?
MARINA: Answer him, you clown!
RUKOSUEV: [*suddenly serious, and alarmed.*] Hold on!
MARINA: I never thought he'd have that much gall . . . I don't know!
RUKOSUEV: [*sternly*] Quiet! [*Short pause.*] He's ill.
MARINA: What?
RUKOSUEV: He's unconscious.
KAMAEV: Are you serious?
RUKOSUEV: I'm not joking. [*Takes syringe, etc. from box.*]
MARINA: How's that?
RUKOSUEV: Quiet! [*Pause, he takes* KALOSHIN's *blood pressure.*] He's had a heart attack.
MARINA: Look where his little games have led him . . .
   [RUKOSUEV *gives* KALOSHIN *an injection. All stand in silence.* RUKOSUEV *again checks* KALOSHIN's *pulse and heart.*]
VIKTORIA: Well?
MARINA: How is he?
RUKOSUEV: Quiet . . . He . . . Yes, he's dying.
MARINA: [*loudly*] Dying?
   [KALOSHIN *groans.*]
   Semion!
KALOSHIN: [*suddenly*] What did you say? . . . Boris? Is that you? . . . Did you say that?
MARINA: Semion!
KALOSHIN: I heard . . . She said I was dying . . . Is it true?
RUKOSUEV: Steady, Semion. Don't try to talk.
KALOSHIN: Yes, it's true . . . I can feel that I'm dying . . .
MARINA: [*tearfully*] Semion, my dear one!
KALOSHIN: Stop pretending, Marina . . . You've been pretending all your life, and now you can stop.
RUKOSUEV: Semion! You mustn't talk.
KALOSHIN: Boris, give it to me straight . . . I've had it . . . You said so yourself . . .
MARINA: Semion, you mustn't! I don't want . . .
KALOSHIN: You're lying . . .
MARINA: Semion . . .

KALOSHIN: All these six years . . .
MARINA: Be quiet, Semion . . .
KALOSHIN: You've been waiting for this.
MARINA: You mustn't talk . . .
KALOSHIN: And now you can enjoy it.
RUKOSUEV: Quiet, Semion. Quiet.
KAMAEV: Doctor, I expect you want everybody out except relatives.
KALOSHIN: Is he still here? [*Raising head.*] You still here?
KAMAEV: You talking to me?
KALOSHIN: Get out, you ponce!
RUKOSUEV: Steady now, please!
KALOSHIN: Out!
MARINA: Semion . . .
KALOSHIN: And you, you snake . . . Out of here!
RUKOSUEV: Quiet, quiet!
KALOSHIN: [*to* MARINA *and* KAMAEV.] Get out! . . . I want to die among decent people!
[*Exit* KAMAEV.]
MARINA: Semion . . .
KALOSHIN: Out!
RUKOSUEV: [*leading* MARINA *out.*] Off you go. It'll be better that way. [*closing door.*] Semion, I forbid you to talk.
KALOSHIN: Does it matter . . . I've kept silent too long as it is.
RUKOSUEV: You're not to get excited. Calm down. [*Tests* KALOSHIN's *pulse.*]
[*Knock at door.* VIKTORIA *goes to door.*]
KALOSHIN: Who's there?
RUKOSUEV: Don't open the door.
KALOSHIN: It might be the compositor.
RUKOSUEV: Don't open it for anybody.
KALOSHIN: Why not? Let him come in . . . Compositor or not, as if I care . . . I don't give a damn . . . Turning up like that . . . Decent folk don't just turn up that way. Only crooks and swindlers show up like that. [*Another knock.*]
Open it . . . I'll tell him a thing or two, in parting. I want him to hear . . .
RUKOSUEV: Calm down, Semion.
KALOSHIN: His turn'll come too, even if he is a compositor.
VIKTORIA: [*at the door.*] It's not the compositor, it's your wife.

KALOSHIN: Don't let *her* in. She gave me no peace in life. The least she can do is let me die in peace.
[*Telephone rings.*]
VIKTORIA: [*picking up receiver.*] Yes, two hundred and ten . . . You want Semion Nikolaevich?
RUKOSUEV: He's not to talk. Put it down.
VIKTORIA: [*into telephone.*] He's . . . he's busy . . . What's the message? . . . Compositor? . . . From where? . . . A print-shop? . . . What? . . . Typesetter? . . . You're quite sure? . . . All right, I'll tell him . . . [*Hangs up.*] A compositor works in a print-shop.
KALOSHIN: A print-shop?
VIKTORIA: It means a typesetter.
KALOSHIN: A typesetter? [*Brief pause, then he starts laughing, but immediately groans.*] A typesetter! [*laughs and groans.*] A print-shop rat . . . Midget! . . . Louse! . . . And what a scare he gave me . . . Frightened me to death . . .
RUKOSUEV: Stop that, Semion! You mustn't move.
KALOSHIN: Well, what an idiot I am! . . . Frightened of a word, a sound . . . like a creaky cartwheel . . . The shame . . . The disgrace . . .
RUKOSUEV: Quiet, for goodness sake.
KALOSHIN: I must have deserved it . . . Live like a fool, die like a fool . . .
RUKOSUEV: Lie still . . . [*Gives him injection.*] Water!
[VIKTORIA *hands him a glass of water.*]
KALOSHIN: What's the use? . . . I'm dying, Boris. It's no good now . . . My heart . . . I can feel it stopping . . .
RUKOSUEV: [*handing him medicine.*] Drink this.
KALOSHIN: No use . . . All a waste of time . . .
RUKOSUEV: Drink it, Semion.
KALOSHIN: No, Boris. There's no escaping your fate, that's plain . . .
[*Short pause.* RUKOSUEV *stands the glass of water on the night table.*]
Ages ago, when I was managing a bath-house, I was told — and by somebody who knew what he was talking about — "You've got what it takes to go a long way," he said, "but your ignorance will be your downfall." And so it was . . . I tried to avoid my fate: covered my tracks, twisted and turned,

back-tracked, hopped from one place to another. I changed jobs time and again, managed all sorts of people, all sorts of places . . . Warehouses, bath-houses, registry offices, restaurants. Been in trade-union work, in footwear, in supply, in sports — any line you care to name. Had to deal with all sorts — tourists, invalids, thugs too. True, I never made the big league, but still . . . At one time I even ran a cinema . . . And everywhere I worked something would happen: they'd discover a shortage somewhere, or my shortage of education . . . All kinds of things happened, but I was lucky, always came through all right. One minute you're in it up to your ears, next minute you look around — you're in the clear . . . My fate was the one thing that stopped me. Try as I might to avoid it, I ended up with this hotel. And then with this compositor . . . [*Short pause to get his breath back.*] I was always afraid of the bosses, Boris . . . Not afraid of anything else, only the bosses. And that's not the end of it: I was so afraid of 'em that when they made me a boss I started being afraid of myself. I used to sit in my office and wonder if it was really me sitting there. Used to think, "If I'm not careful I'll end up suing myself in court." . . . Got used to it eventually, of course, but all the same . . . Come to think of it, all my life I've lived with this nervous tension. At home I'd be okay, but the moment I got to work it'd start. With one lot of people you act one part, with another lot — another part. And all the time you're watching yourself, so you don't sell yourself cheap. But you can't get above yourself either. It won't do to sell yourself cheap, but getting above yourself's even worse . . . Day and night I used to have it on my mind. I tell you frankly, Boris, it's only now I can breathe freely . . . Now that I'm dying . . .

RUKOSUEV: Wait a minute, Semion . . .

KALOSHIN: No, Boris, my song is sung . . . It's all up . . .

[*Another knock.* VIKTORIA *goes to the door again.*]

If you see my wife . . . my first wife, Klava . . . and my daughter, tell them I died thinking about them . . .

[VIKTORIA *opens the door slightly, and somebody, evidently* MARINA, *whispers to her.*]

RUKOSUEV: Close the door.

KALOSHIN: Ah, Boris! The only time we really lived was when we were young . . . Remember? . . . Remember how we worked on the river . . . Remember that tug, the *Grigory Kotovsky*? . . . And the *Lieutenant Schmidt*? [*Weeps.*] Remember . . .
RUKOSUEV: Yes, yes, I remember. But don't get excited.
KALOSHIN: And the *Ivan Turgenev*? [*weeps.*] Ah, Boris . . . My life's over . . . all over . . . And who's to blame? That compositor? [*Another knock.*]
My new wife?
RUKOSUEV: Nobody's to blame. Lie still. [*Tries to get hold of* KALOSHIN's *hand.*]
KALOSHIN: [*pulling his hand away.*] No, Boris. I'm to blame . . . It's all my own fault.
[*Another knock.*]
VIKTORIA: [*at the door.*] Your wife wants to come in.
KALOSHIN: Let her in.
RUKOSUEV: No, don't.
KALOSHIN: Let her come in . . . She hasn't done anything. And I knew all about it, all along . . . Only pretended I didn't . . . She's young, pretty, wants to enjoy herself. She's only half my age, after all. You could say I ruined her life . . . Let her in, it's time we said our goodbyes.
[VIKTORIA *lets* MARINA *in.*]
MARINA: Semion! . . . How is he? . . . Semion, how are you?
KALOSHIN: Marina, bless you, I forgive you . . . And you must forgive me. Don't think ill of me . . . Bury me and get married again . . . Never mind. Get married, while there's still time . . .
MARINA: [*surprised and touched.*] Semion! What are you talking about?
KALOSHIN: Marry him, marry that . . . If you like him. [MARINA *bursts into tears.*]
Let him come in.
MARINA: [*weeping, opens door.*] Oleg! . . . Come in, Oleg . . .
[KAMAEV *appears in doorway.*]
KALOSHIN: Come in. [KAMAEV *comes in and stops beside* MARINA.]
Well, Boris? . . . Take a look at them . . . What do you think?
MARINA: [*loudly*] Sem-ion! . . . We'll think of you as long as we live!
KALOSHIN: And good luck to you . . . Live in peace.
KAMAEV: [*stunned*] What?

KALOSHIN: Get married, of course . . . Don't tell me you don't want to.
KAMAEV: Me? . . . No, I . . . I must say I hadn't thought about it.
MARINA: [*stops crying.*] You what? . . . Hadn't thought about it? . . . You always said . . .
KAMAEV: Did I say anything?
MARINA: Of course you did, Oleg . . .
KAMAEV: Well, I suppose I must have done. But I hadn't thought about it.
MARINA: What are you saying, Oleg? Do you mean to say you were deceiving me?
KAMAEV: [*recovering self-possession.*] Not at all, but . . . This won't do. With a man dying here we can't go talking about marriage . . . It isn't right.
KALOSHIN: Don't mind me . . . Let Klava have the cottage, and you two can take the flat. And live in peace. Don't chase after money, nor after rank . . . The main thing is to keep a clear conscience . . .
RUKOSUEV: Hold on, Semion . . . [*Tries to take his wrist in order to test his pulse.*]
KALOSHIN: [*taking his hand away.*] That'll do, Boris . . . I know what I have to do . . . It's all up . . . My heart's . . . going to burst any minute . . . [*To* KAMAEV.] And a compositor is *not* a man from the ministry . . . He's a typesetter, . . . works in a print-shop . . . Don't you forget it.
KAMAEV: You don't say.
KALOSHIN: Live and learn, eh, young man?
[RUKOSUEV *finally succeeds in taking his wrist and testing his pulse.*]
If I could live my life over again . . . I'd live it quite differently.
RUKOSUEV: Hold on a minute . . .
KALOSHIN: Marina . . . Put up a headstone for me . . . just a little one, they don't cost much.
[MARINA *bursts into tears again.*]
And carve on it . . .
RUKOSUEV: Hold on . . . I can't understand this . . .
KALOSHIN: No . . . Don't carve anything. Just my name, in full, and dates of birth and d . . .
RUKOSUEV: [*excitedly*] Semion! You . . . Your . . . Yes, your pulse

is normal! [*Brief pause.*] It's perfectly normal! . . . Just a minute! We'll check your blood pressure . . . [*Checks his blood pressure. Pause.*] Semion! You're better.

KALOSHIN: How's that?

RUKOSUEV: Just like that! You've got over it.

KAMAEV: [*to* RUKOSUEV.] You serious?

RUKOSUEV: This is no time for joking. He's going to live.

MARINA: Semion . . .

KALOSHIN: Live? . . . [*Sits up in bed.*] But . . . but how come?

RUKOSUEV: You're going to live, Semion . . . Don't you like the idea?

KALOSHIN: But . . . Where does that leave us?

KAMAEV: What are you worried about? Live, and enjoy yourself. You've been lucky.

MARINA: Yes, of course, Semion . . . enjoy life . . .

KALOSHIN: But what do I do now about . . .

KAMAEV: What's the problem? If it's your will you're worrying about, you've no need to. Leave everything as it was. I, for one, won't bear you any grudge.

MARINA: Oh, really?

KAMAEV: [*To* KALOSHIN.] To tell you the truth, I actually prefer it that way.

MARINA: But you . . . you always said . . .

KAMAEV: What did I say? Listen, how did you get that idea in your head? And this really isn't the time. He's going to live, and we ought to be rejoicing . . . and what are you doing? I can't understand you.

VIKTORIA: I can't bear any more . . .

MARINA: [*to* KAMAEV.] But I believe I understand you now.

RUKOSUEV: Semion, what's wrong? Aren't you glad?

MARINA: Oh no! We won't leave everything as it was! . . . Semion! Forgive me! [*Drawing close to* KALOSHIN.] Forgive me, Semion . . . I . . . If you can . . . I'll stay with you! And as for him . . . I never want to see him again!

KAMAEV: Thank the Lord for that.

MARINA: Semion! Forgive me . . .

RUKOSUEV: [*to* KALOSHIN.] Pull yourself together!

MARINA: Semion! Look at me! Say something . . .

[*Knock at door.*]

VIKTORIA: Who can that be? . . . I can't bear this . . .
[*Another knock.*]
Come in!
[*Enter* POTAPOV, *very excited.*]
POTAPOV: You can offer your congratulations. They won . . . What's going on here? . . . Everybody in the hotel's gathered in this corridor.
KALOSHIN: Everybody in the hotel? . . . [*Decisively*] To hell with the hotel! I'm starting a new life. In the morning I'm joining the newsreel team.
VIKTORIA: No, I can't bear it any longer!

SECOND ANECDOTE

TWENTY MINUTES WITH AN ANGEL

CHARACTERS

VIKTOR UGAROV a dispatch clerk from Lopatsk, travelling on business
FIODOR GRIGORYEVICH ANCHUGIN, (Fedia) a driver, also from Lopatsk
ANNA VASILYEVNA, (Vasiuta) hotel cleaner
BAZILSKY a violinist on tour
GENNADY MIKHAILOVICH KHOMUTOV an agronomist, also from Lopatsk
STUPAK an engineer
FAINA a student, Stupak's bride

A double room in the same hotel. The room is untidy, with empty bottles on the table. The curtains are still drawn, and the room is lit by a cheap lamp.

Various sounds are heard from neighbouring rooms: phrases played on a violin, and from time to time a woman's voice laughing.

Ugarov is sitting on one of the beds. He has only just woken up, and is now sitting nursing a hangover, his head bent. He stands up, rummages in the night tables and looks under the bed. He is dressed, but has only one shoe on.

UGAROV *is in his early thirties, active, quick-moving, and usually has an optimistic air, though at the moment it is less apparent than usual.*

He studies the bottles and sees that they are empty. Drinks water from the jug, with an expression of disgust. After drinking his fill and getting his breath back he starts going through his pockets. He finds no money in them, and suddenly realizes why not. He stands up and walks across the room. He draws back the curtains. Broad daylight outside.

UGAROV: [*loudly*] Wakey-wakey!
  [ANCHUGIN *wakes, raises his head slightly, and looks blankly at* UGAROV. *He is morose, sluggish, slow in his movements. Any energy he has is dormant.*] Rise and shine!
ANCHUGIN: [*realizing where he is and what has happened.*] Give me a drink. [*Reaches out his hand towards the table.*]
UGAROV: A drink? Any time, as much as you want. [*Hands him the jug of water.*]
ANCHUGIN: [*pushing aside* UGAROV'*s hand with the jug.*] Give me a drink.
UGAROV: You don't want it? Then what would you like? [*Bitterly*] Vodka, beer, or perhaps some brandy?
ANCHUGIN: Vodka.
UGAROV: [*after pause.*] I see. You prefer vodka.
ANCHUGIN: Isn't there any? . . . Nothing at all? [*Sits up and studies the empty bottles.*] Have we got any money?
UGAROV: [*tossing* ANCHUGIN'*s jacket to him.*] Look and see.
ANCHUGIN: [*going through his pockets, then shaking the jacket.*] Not a hope . . . What about you?
UGAROV: Not a kopeck . . . Here, where's my other shoe? [*He walks up and down the room, looking for his shoe.*] Where's it got to? . . . Not seen it? . . . [*Silence*] Do we know anybody in this town?
ANCHUGIN: I don't.
UGAROV: Neither do I. First time I've been here. [*Short pause.*] We'll have to think up something. Just three rubles would do.

ANCHUGIN: Three sixty-two.
UGAROV: Plus a bite to eat . . .
ANCHUGIN: [*pause*] Where can we raise the cash?
UGAROV: At the plant?
ANCHUGIN: I suppose so. There's nowhere else.
UGAROV: [*considering*] Not a good idea . . . The first time . . . Working relationships, and all that. You know . . .
ANCHUGIN: Ring 'em up.
UGAROV: What a fix . . . Okay, I will. [*Pulls telephone towards himself. Hesitates.*] It's a breach of protocol . . .
ANCHUGIN: Stuff your protocol!
UGAROV: Not a good idea . . . You know how they do things. The dispatch clerk gives things to everybody, and nobody gives him anything. That's the law . . . Oh all right. [*Dials number.*] No answer . . . [*Gets out his notebook.*]
ANCHUGIN: [*standing bottle beside him.*] Thirty-six kopecks on the empty.
UGAROV: Five seven one five, head of marketing. She doesn't stand for any nonsense . . . [*Dials*] No answer.
ANCHUGIN: Thirty-six, and a bottle of beer costs thirty-seven. No good.
UGAROV: Five seven three four, main gate. [*Dials*] Porcelain works? . . . Why doesn't the office answer? . . . That so? . . . [*Hangs up.*] Well, Fiodor Grigoryevich, today's Sunday.
[*Silence, then a violin in the next room.*]
ANCHUGIN: Uhuh, . . . Fine state of affairs . . .
UGAROV: Look here, where's my other shoe got to? Has somebody stolen it or something? [*The violin in the next room warms up.*]
ANCHUGIN: [*nodding towards the wall.*] Hasn't a care in the world, that guy. Keeps on sawing away.
UGAROV: What do you expect? He's a musician. He won't want for anything.
ANCHUGIN: I'm sick of him.
[*Woman's voice laughs.*]
And her too, the cow.
UGAROV: The couple in that room don't need any booze. They're happy enough without any. [*Hopefully*] Fiodor Grigoryevich! Who was drinking with us yesterday?

ANCHUGIN: I don't remember. [*Pause*] It was a disaster for me to be sent here with you. I hadn't had a drink for three months, and you've made a complete write-off of me in three days, you snake.

UGAROV: Okay, okay, Fiodor Grigoryevich. Grousing won't get you anywhere. Where are we going to find that money?

ANCHUGIN: Where *can* we find any?

UGAROV: Borrow it.

ANCHUGIN: Who from?

UGAROV: That's the question. We've got to think, use our heads.

ANCHUGIN: I can't think. I've got a headache.

[*Silence. Violin is heard.*]

[*Suddenly jumping up.*] Will he shut up or not? [*Is about to pound on the wall with his fists, but* UGAROV *restrains him.*]

UGAROV: Steady on, Fiodor Grigoryevich. That won't do you any good either.

ANCHUGIN: He's getting on my nerves.

UGAROV: That's his job. No need to kick up a fuss about it. On the contrary, musicians deserve respect. They rake in the money. [*Pretends to be playing the violin.*] One push of the bow, and in comes a ruble; one pull, in comes another. [*Suddenly*] Think he'll give us three rubles?

ANCHUGIN: Him?

UGAROV: Why not? We'll just say: Look, it's like this, we wondered if you might lend us a bit till tomorrow. We'll send off a telegram today, and we'll have the cash to pay you back tomorrow. What do you say? Come on, Fiodor Grigoryevich, get moving.

ANCHUGIN: Why me? Why not you, for instance?

UGAROV: Oh, Fiodor Grigoryevich! I am your boss, after all.

ANCHUGIN: Some boss! [*Pause*] I won't go.

UGAROV: Fiodor Grigoryevich! Take a good look at me. How can I go? I've only got one shoe! . . . I can't appear in public like this. I'm not decent.

ANCHUGIN: I won't go.

UGAROV: All right. You can go to the newly-weds, and I'll see about the musician. So be it. Well, let's get going . . . They're rich, . . . rolled up in a car, and being alone together they'll be in a good mood. Just knock, apologize for bothering them, introduce yourself, and ask if you can have a word with the husband in the corridor . . .

ANCHUGIN: What does he do?

UGAROV: Him? He's an engineer, I think. Ask to have a word in the corridor . . . No, wait. Better to ask in front of the woman. Better with her there . . .

ANCHUGIN: Go and teach your grandmother to suck eggs. [*Gets up.*] All right, the hell with it! I'll try him. [*Goes out.*]

UGAROV: [*dialling number on telephone.*] Is that the violinist? . . . [*Familiarly*] Good morning . . . How are things? . . . Slept well? . . . [*Less familiarly.*] So sorry . . . Your neighbours . . . We're really more in industry . . . No, no, neighbours in this hotel, in the next room . . . Yes . . . Me and my friend here have been listening to you playing and enjoying it so much . . . Pardon? . . . Yesterday? . . . Oh yes, it was rather. [*Titters*] I must admit . . . [*Apologetically*] That was our visitors, you know . . . All their doing . . . Simple folk, not much refinement . . . start singing and dancing as soon as they get half a chance . . . I quite agree. Quite right . . . Point taken . . . What do we want? . . . It's a bit of a ticklish question, you know, a bit tricky, you might say . . . The point? All right, to come to the point . . . We were wondering if you might give us a loan — just a small one? Naturally I'm terribly sorry, but we're due for some money tomorrow . . . What's that? . . . I see . . . [*It is clear that the conversation is over. He throws down the receiver.*] Bloody scrooge!

[*A knock at the door. Enter* VASIUTA *with a mop. She is an elderly, tired-looking woman with a shrill, angry voice.*]

VASIUTA: [*looking round the room.*] Can I clean up?

UGAROV: Yes. Or you can leave it. As you please.

VASIUTA: How many days have you been drinking? [*Tidying room.*]

UGAROV: How many? . . . This is the third, Anna Vasilyevna, begging your pardon, of course.

VASIUTA: What's it all in honour of? And whose fortune are you spending?

UGAROV: Our own, Anna Vasilyevna. Our own hard-earned pay.

VASIUTA: Lord save us! The things people do with their money! I can't bear to see it!

UGAROV: See what?

VASIUTA: All this. Take me, for instance. I have to save every kopeck to dress my grand-daughter, and here you go splurging hundreds and hundreds on booze. Makes me furious. [*Tidies the wardrobe.*] What's this? Lord save us! It's a disgrace!

UGAROV: What's a disgrace, Anna Vasilyevna?

VASIUTA: A shoe in the waste-paper basket! Ain't never seen the like of it!

UGAROV: You don't say! How did it get there?

VASIUTA: That's what I'd like to know.

UGAROV: Can't understand it myself.

VASIUTA: Disgusting ... [*Pause. She goes on cleaning.*] Oh yes, before I forget: a reminder from the manager's office. You haven't paid for the room for three days, and you smashed a jug the day before yesterday. Better have your money ready.

UGAROV: Anna Vasilyevna, have a heart.

[*Enter* ANCHUGIN.]

Anna Vasilyevna, Anna Vasilyevna ... I quite understand, your grandchildren need looking after, but sometimes you just can't help it. You *have* to have a drink. Now take him, Anna Vasilyevna [*Indicating* ANCHUGIN.] Look at him, just look at him ...

VASIUTA: [*looking up from her cleaning.*] Well? ... What's there to look at?

UGAROV: Don't you see he's not well? He's a sick man ... [*Suddenly*] Anna Vasilyevna, dear Anna Vasilyevna! Save us. Lend us three rubles till tomorrow.

VASIUTA: [*quickly*] Oh no. Nothing doing. [*Testily*] Have you no shame at all? Tossing hundreds away and then coming and asking me of all people! No! No! Don't even think about it. [*Exit*]

ANCHUGIN: She'd sooner hang herself than give us any.

[*Pause*]

UGAROV: How'd it go with the neighbours?

ANCHUGIN: Who? [*Points*] Them? ... You're kidding. The guy's no fool, been to college. We're on our honeymoon, he says. Big expenses. Sorry chum, he says, and close the door when you go out. Cut me short. [*Points the other way.*] What about him?

UGAROV: Refused. Just the same.

ANCHUGIN: This is hopeless. Nobody'll give us any. [*Sits down on bed and takes head in hands.*] I can't stand it. My skull's splitting.
[*Female laughter has ceased. Sound of violin.* ANCHUGIN *gets up and pounds on the wall.* UGAROV *restrains him.*]

UGAROV: Don't make trouble, Fiodor Grigoryevich. What's the point?

ANCHUGIN: He's boring holes in my brain, damn him!
[*Enter* BAZILSKY, *after quick knock, irate, bow in hand. He is about fifty.*]

BAZILSKY: What's the meaning of this? Why are you knocking on the wall?

ANCHUGIN: I've had enough of your music.

BAZILSKY: So I'm bothering you, am I? I do apologize! I'm preventing you from yelling, bellowing, roaring and carrying on. I *am* sorry!

UGAROV: [*condescendingly*] Well, seeing this is the first time I think we might . . .

BAZILSKY: I'm so sorry, I forgot. Yesterday you were even squealing. You [*Points to* ANCHUGIN.] were actually squealing. How you manage it is more than I can understand.

UGAROV: But he does.

BAZILSKY: And now you bang on the wall as well. Don't you think that's a bit much, my friends?

ANCHUGIN: We've had enough of your music. [*Pause*] It gets on my nerves.

UGAROV: Yes, we haven't got nerves of steel.

BAZILSKY: Nerves? You mean to tell me you've got nerves?

UGAROV: We certainly have. Do you think nobody has any but you?

BAZILSKY: Well, well. I never would have thought it. [*Pacing up and down the room.*] You know, I really can't imagine you having nerves, or what good they'd do you. [*Standing still.*] But if you've actually got some, what the hell do you mean by banging on the wall?

ANCHUGIN: Your music's been driving us nuts.

UGAROV: You're not in the Palace of Culture now, you know. This is a hotel, and some people are on holiday in it.

ANCHUGIN: That'll do. We don't want to hear another peep out of you. Is that clear?

UGAROV: We'll come to your concert. Then you can play as much as you like, but here . . .
BAZILSKY: [*losing his self-control.*] What? You? At my concert? . . . What for? What on earth for?
UGAROV: What do you mean — what for? To listen to the music. And enjoy it.
BAZILSKY: Enjoy it? Don't try to scare me, dammit! Don't do that! [*Running up and down the room.*] You've never been to a concert in all your lives, and whatever you do don't ever go as long as you live! Do us a favour! Go to a puppet-show or a bar instead! Off you go! Now!
UGAROV: [*slightly puzzled.*] What have you got against us?
BAZILSKY: But not to my concert! Don't do that! You won't see anything funny there! Nothing! And nothing to enjoy! I'd rather play to an empty hall! And stop preventing me working, blast you! [*Rushes out.*]
[*Short pause.*]
ANCHUGIN: Bit on the shirty side, that guy.
UGAROV: You can tell nobody goes to his concerts, and the cash isn't coming in.
ANCHUGIN: He's got cash. But he isn't letting go of it.
[*Violin starts up again.*]
UGAROV: [*inspecting the bottles.*] Thirty-six kopecks. Shall we send a telegram?
ANCHUGIN: Who to?
UGAROV: We have to think about that. If we send it to head office it's bound to be three days before they do anything. If I send one to my wife she won't understand. That leaves my mother . . .
ANCHUGIN: Your mother. Of course. She can't let you down.
UGAROV: [*writing in a notebook.*] "Lopatsk. Two Perov Street. Ugarova. Send forty. Urgent. Central Post Office, Belorechensk. Poste restante. Love Viktor." [*He counts the words.*] One, two, three . . . Three kopecks each . . . We can afford that.
ANCHUGIN: [*clutching his head.*] Three rubles — that's all we need. When I was working with geological expeditions I thought nothing of three rubles. Wouldn't pick it up from the road. I'd spit on it and grind it in. [*Contemptuously*] Three miserable rubles! [*Pause*] And now I could drop dead for want of 'em.

UGAROV: Less of your moaning, Fiodor Grigoryevich. We'll think of something. Not out in the forest, are we? Don't tell me there are no kind people around. We'll find some. [*Stands up and throws open the window.*] Look at all those people. A whole street full . . .

ANCHUGIN: [*goes to window.*] Well? Go ahead and ask them. [*Pause*] Why don't you? Go on.
[*Both look out of window.*]
They're all ever so kind when *you* have money. But not when you haven't. I'll show you. [*Shouts out of window.*] Citizens! Good people! Your attention for one moment!

UGAROV: What are you doing? What's the use?

ANCHUGIN: [*to* UGAROV.] Just watch what happens. [*Shouting*] Good people! Help! A terrible misfortune! A desperate situation!

UGAROV: What do you think you're doing?

ANCHUGIN: [*to* UGAROV.] Wait a bit. [*Shouting*] Citizens! Who will lend us a hundred rubles?

UGAROV: [*laughing*] Cut it out, Fiodor Grigoryevich. The police don't like that sort of joke.

ANCHUGIN: Look at them. They're laughing . . . [*To somebody in the street.*] What are you grinning at? [*To* UGAROV.] Look at him, bloated with good living . . . And the rest pretend not to hear . . . That fat one's put on speed. [UGAROV *laughs.*] That's your "good people" for you.
[*Both walk away from the window.*]
Money's a terrible thing when you haven't got any.
[*Pause*]

UGAROV: Joking apart, where are we going to find three rubles?

ANCHUGIN: What about flogging my cardigan? It's new.

UGAROV: Or this blasted watch!

ANCHUGIN: Watches don't fetch much these days. My cardigan's a better bet.
[*Knock at door.*]

UGAROV: Yes! Come in.
[*Enter* KHOMUTOV. *Aged about forty. Tidily dressed. Modest, even diffident manner. At moments he seems suddenly pensive, absent-minded, inattentive in conversation. But he will have little opportunity to ignore the conversation.*]

KHOMUTOV: Good morning.
UGAROV: Good morning.
KHOMUTOV: Was that you asking for money?
   [*Pause*]
   Just now, from the window . . . Was it you?
ANCHUGIN: What if it was?
KHOMUTOV: Well I . . . If you really need money I . . .
UGAROV: What?
ANCHUGIN: [*sneering*] Perhaps you'd like to give us some?
KHOMUTOV: Yes. I can help you.
   [*Pause*]
ANCHUGIN: Wouldn't care for a belt round the ear, would you?
KHOMUTOV: Belt round the ear? . . . What for?
ANCHUGIN: Just for fun.
KHOMUTOV: [*smiling*] No, I don't want a belt round the ear.
UGAROV: Then what *do* you want?
KHOMUTOV: I wanted to help you. But I see you were joking . . . Well, maybe it was funny . . . Sorry I bothered you. [*Goes towards the door.*]
ANCHUGIN: Wait a minute. Why did you come here?
KHOMUTOV: [*stops*] I've told you: I was going to help you out.
ANCHUGIN: [*sneering*] You wanted to give us some money?
KHOMUTOV: Yes.
   [*Brief pause.*]
UGAROV: Are you joking? . . . Or making fun of us?
KHOMUTOV: Not at all. It looks as if you were making fun of me . . .
UGAROV: We're in no mood for jokes, you know. We haven't even had breakfast yet . . .
KHOMUTOV: [*after a pause.*] I don't understand. Do you need money or don't you?
UGAROV: [*to* ANCHUGIN.] He's offering to chip in and split the price of a bottle.
KHOMUTOV: I'm offering nothing of the kind.
ANCHUGIN: Then cut out the funny business and tell us what brought you here.
KHOMUTOV: I wanted to help you, but I won't insist. [*Goes towards the door, but* ANCHUGIN *calls out to him.*]
ANCHUGIN: Listen, chum . . . [*Goes up to* KHOMUTOV.] Look here. Could you really find it in your heart to part with just three

little rubles? You couldn't, could you? . . . That's what I meant.

KHOMUTOV: I'm surprised at you, and insulted even . . . [*Takes out money.*] There. Take it.

UGAROV: What's this?

KHOMUTOV: Take it. Take it.

UGAROV: What do you mean? [*Takes money.*]

KHOMUTOV: Take it, take it, and do what you like with it. I'm serious. I hope you'll do the same for me, if I ever need help . . . [*Thoughtfully*] We all have our difficult times, and we must all help one another. There's no other way . . . [*Brief pause.*] All right then. If you've got scruples about it. I'll leave you my address. [*Goes over to table. Writes address.*] There you are. Return it if you feel you must. But you don't have to.

UGAROV: What do you mean — don't have to?

KHOMUTOV: Just that. You don't have to. Be seeing you. Goodbye. [*Exit*]

[*Silence. Then* UGAROV *fearfully counts the money.*]

ANCHUGIN: How much?

UGAROV: A hundred! [*Throws the money onto the table. Pause.*] Look, I don't like this . . . [*brief pause.*] There's something fishy about it . . . I have the feeling somebody's coming to beat us up . . . What about you, Fiodor Grigoryevich?

ANCHUGIN: [*counting the money.*] A hundred . . .

UGAROV: Listen, I think I've seen him somewhere. Haven't you seen him somewhere? Was he here yesterday? . . . No? . . . I don't think so . . .

ANCHUGIN: Wait a sec! [*Hurries out.*]

UGAROV: [*sitting down at the table in front of the money.*] Everything was fine till he showed up . . . [*Looks round room, hastily, furtively makes the beds, tidies the room, and covers the money with a newspaper.*] Damned if I know . . . [*Thinks. Opens door and looks out into corridor. Then calls in loud voice.*] Anna Vasilyevna!

[*Enter* VASIUTA. *She stops at the door.*]

Anna Vasilyevna, you're an intelligent woman, tell me what you think . . . Suppose a complete stranger came to see you, said hello nicely, chatted away, and then suddenly pulled out a bundle of notes and said: "You need a hundred rubles — here you are." And left. Could that happen, do you think?

VASIUTA: The rubbish you talk . . . Why did you call me? I won't give you any money, so don't ask.
UGAROV: Thank you, Anna Vasilyevna. That'll be all. You're an intelligent woman. God grant you good health. May you live another hundred and fifty years.
VASIUTA: Ain't you drunkards got nothing better to do? [*Exit*]
[UGAROV *pushes door to, goes over to the table again, counts the money again and examines the notes against the light. Enter* KHOMUTOV, *led by* ANCHUGIN.]
ANCHUGIN: Here. [*Shows* KHOMUTOV *his money.*] Take your loan and get the hell out.
KHOMUTOV: But I've given it to you. It wouldn't be right. And besides, if you need it, why . . .
UGAROV: [*interrupting*] Tell me, have they let you out for good, or just . . . for a while?
KHOMUTOV: Out of what?
UGAROV: Er . . . out of the house . . .
KHOMUTOV: For a week. What's that got to do with it?
UGAROV: A whole week, and without supervision. Sounds irregular.
KHOMUTOV: This money . . . How shall I explain? . . . To put it briefly, I've got money, and I don't need this lot.
ANCHUGIN: What if this money isn't yours at all, eh?
KHOMUTOV: Then whose do you think it is?
UGAROV: Begging your pardon, are you sure it's not forged?
KHOMUTOV: What on earth is this? This is stupid! Can't you understand, I'm giving something in all good faith?
ANCHUGIN: Tell us straight: was it Mica Trust or Lena Gold?
KHOMUTOV: What are you talking about?
ANCHUGIN: Who paid you the advance, the expenses? Which firm?
KHOMUTOV: I don't know what you're on about, for God's sake!
UGAROV: I see . . . By the way, do you believe in him?
KHOMUTOV: In who? God? . . . No, but . . .
UGAROV: But? . . . You don't belong to some sect, by any chance?
[KHOMUTOV *spreads his hands.*]
Just who are you? What do you do?
KHOMUTOV: Me? . . . I'm an agronomist.
ANCHUGIN: An agronomist?
KHOMUTOV: Yes.
ANCHUGIN: Go in for sowing and reaping, do you?

KHOMUTOV: Sure.
ANCHUGIN: On a filthy-rich collective farm, naturally.
KHOMUTOV: It's rich, yes . . .
ANCHUGIN: Short-handed, naturally?
KHOMUTOV: Yes, it's a bit short. What of it?
ANCHUGIN: Should have said so straight away. So you'll naturally build us a house and give us a cow, won't you?
KHOMUTOV: Cut it out! I'm simply giving you some money. To help you out. Why won't you believe me?
[Short pause.]
[Suddenly] Tell me, are your parents still alive.
UGAROV: Why? Why do you ask?
KHOMUTOV: Just curious . . .
ANCHUGIN: From the police, are you? [Takes out his papers.] There — take a look.
UGAROV: Or maybe State Security? Why bother with us. He's only a driver, and I'm a dispatch-clerk. Why bother with us?
KHOMUTOV: What a lot of nonsense! I'll say it again. I'm simply giving it to you . . . With no thought of gain . . . Will you take it?
ANCHUGIN: We'd rather not.
UGAROV: I've got a feeling that if I take that money I'll answer for it for a long time to come.
ANCHUGIN: [handing KHOMUTOV the money.] Here you are. Count it.
KHOMUTOV: [putting it in his pocket.] I see you can't understand ordinary human sympathy. Too bad . . . Well, goodbye. Think of me sometimes. [Goes towards door.]
ANCHUGIN: [stopping him, laying his arm across his shoulders. It looks as if he is embracing him.] Listen, chum. Don't keep us in the dark. Tell us before you leave. Come clean. Or I won't be able to sleep a wink. Honest I won't. Handing over a hundred rubles just like that, just for the asking — who'd believe you? Judge for yourself . . .
KHOMUTOV: [after pause.] I wanted to help you.
ANCHUGIN: You're lying. [Suddenly twists KHOMUTOV's arms.] Give us a towel!
[UGAROV binds KHOMUTOV's hands with a towel.]
KHOMUTOV: [stunned] Hey! . . . What's going on? [Tries to break free]

ANCHUGIN: Don't struggle . . . Tell us everything, right from the beginning.
KHOMUTOV: What are you doing?
UGAROV: Easy . . . easy . . .
   [*They struggle. Another towel is used to tie his hands to the head of a bed.*]
   That's better . . . Now we can have a quiet, business chat.
ANCHUGIN: Let's have it.
KHOMUTOV: Untie me. Let me go this minute.
ANCHUGIN: First tell us why you came here.
KHOMUTOV: I've told you everything. I don't understand what you want with me.
UGAROV: That's what we're asking you: what do you want with us?
ANCHUGIN: Where does that cash come from? Tell us. Where did you get it?
KHOMUTOV: This is violence, an act of violence. Untie me. Do you hear?
ANCHUGIN: [*turning his fist over under* KHOMUTOV'*s nose.*] If it's a disability pension you're after, I can give you a hand? See?
KHOMUTOV: What for? . . . For wanting to help you?
ANCHUGIN: [*suddenly adopting a friendly tone.*] Come on, pal. You've kept it up long enough. [*Sits down beside* KHOMUTOV. *Confidingly.*] Look, you can depend on us.
UGAROV: Every inch of the way.
ANCHUGIN: We won't turn you in, you needn't worry . . . Now, the money's stolen, isn't it?
UGAROV: So you stole it. So what? Think that's such a big deal?
ANCHUGIN: [*hopefully*] Did you steal it?
KHOMUTOV: [*angrily*] Yes! Yes! Yes! I stole it! Does that make you happy? I stole it! Do you understand?
   [*Silence*]
ANCHUGIN: [*spitefully*] So why get on people's nerves? Setting yourself up as some holy virgin, the soul of goodness! Made you feel good, did it?
KHOMUTOV: [*puzzled*] But isn't that what you wanted? . . . You were trying to get me to say the money was stolen. What are you so het up about?
UGAROV: [*regretfully*] He didn't steal it. It's clear he didn't. There's more to it . . . But what?

ANCHUGIN: Just a minute. [*Takes* KHOMUTOV's *papers out of his jacket and hands them to* UGAROV.] We'll see what sort of fish we've got here.
UGAROV: [*reading*] Gennady Mikhailovich Khomutov . . . Agronomist.
ANCHUGIN: Agronomist?
UGAROV: Yes. And with a name like that he ought to be.*
ANCHUGIN: Look here, Mr Agronomist, how did you come by so much spare cash? . . . What if we take you down to the police station, . . . Fraud Squad . . . and let them look into it?
UGAROV: [*after pause.*] Or maybe you're one of them.
ANCHUGIN: Where'd you get that money? [*Comes up close to* KHOMUTOV.] Will you tell us or won't you?
UGAROV: That'll do, Fedia. That'll do. Don't make things worse. [*Restraining* ANCHUGIN.]
KHOMUTOV: Untie me or you'll answer for this.
ANCHUGIN: I'll give you something . . . [*Tries to break away from* UGAROV.]
UGAROV: Listen . . . Let's untie him. There could be all kinds of things . . . Let him go on his way . . .
[UGAROV *and* ANCHUGIN *wrestle.*]
ANCHUGIN: No . . . He'll tell me the truth first . . . explain everything properly . . .
UGAROV: I tell you we'll let him go . . .
ANCHUGIN: I tell you we won't.
[*They drag each other about the room.*]
UGAROV: Yes, we will.
ANCHUGIN: No, we won't.
KHOMUTOV: Stop that, will you? Stop it . . . Cut it out.
[*The struggle continues, but as they are physically well-matched they eventually tire and fall on the bed . . .*]
ANCHUGIN: [*breathing heavily, to* UGAROV.] Sucker . . . Chump . . .
UGAROV: [*breathing heavily.*] You're a fool, Fiodor Grigoryevich . . .
ANCHUGIN: Shut up, you parasite.
UGAROV: You don't know what you might be letting yourself in for . . . [*Gets up and tries to untie* KHOMUTOV.]

---

*Khomut: the yoke of a horse's harness for ploughing.

[ANCHUGIN *flings himself at* UGAROV. *They sit down on the bed again.*]
You really are a fool.
KHOMUTOV: Well? Now what? . . . What about untying me?
UGAROV: Well, what are we going to do with him?
ANCHUGIN: Nothing . . . He won't get away that easily.
UGAROV: I said: what are we going to do?
[*Brief pause.*]
ANCHUGIN: Call somebody else . . . Invite the neighbours in. Let them decide.
[*He gets up, taps on one wall, then on the other, and goes out into the corridor. Returns, throwing open the door, and stands in the doorway.*] Come in, come in. Lend us a hand, if you can.
[*Enter* BAZILSKY *and* STUPAK, *with wife*, FAINA. STUPAK *is well-fed young man of about thirty. He has a confident air.* FAINA *is no more than twenty.* BAZILSKY *is still absent-mindedly holding his bow. Enter* VASIUTA *behind them.*]
BAZILSKY: What's going on?
STUPAK: What's happened?
VASIUTA: Whatever next?
ANCHUGIN: Sit down, Anna Vasilyevna, and listen. Sit down, everybody. [*To* UGAROV.] Fill 'em in.
UGAROV: Well, my dear neighbours, you see before you a man who's managed to turn us into nervous wrecks in the space of exactly half an hour.
BAZILSKY: Come to the point.
KHOMUTOV: Untie my hands.
STUPAK: Why's he tied up? Is he a criminal, or something?
UGAROV: Maybe he is, or maybe something even worse. Anyway, we got up this morning with a bit of a hangover, if you'll forgive the expression.
ANCHUGIN: The thing is this: a little while ago I put my head out of the window and called out, for a bit of laugh, "Citizens! Lend us a hundred rubles!"
STUPAK: Yes, we heard. Pretty repulsive sort of joke, if you ask me.
BAZILSKY: [*impatiently, to* ANCHUGIN.] Go on.
ANCHUGIN: Well, we had our little joke, then forget all about it. And then this character shows up . . .

UGAROV: Don't know him from Adam . . .
ANCHUGIN: . . . and says, "Was that you asking for money?"
UGAROV: Of course, we needed money. Borrowing three rubles, or even ten from a neighbour is one thing . . .
ANCHUGIN: But this guy pulls out a hundred . . .
VASIUTA: Lord save us!
ANCHUGIN: Pulls it out and says, "If you need it, take it. Do what you like with it."
STUPAK: Impossible.
ANCHUGIN: He leaves this wad here and walks out. [*To* KHOMUTOV.] Isn't that the truth?
KHOMUTOV: Go on.
ANCHUGIN: Well, I ran after him, of course, and dragged him back here to get it out of him straight — how come, why, what's the game? A hundred rubles is no joking matter . . .
UGAROV: After all, it wasn't for our blue eyes, or anything . . .
ANCHUGIN: And he starts preaching at us. Wanted to help you, he says, in all good faith. So we've been trying to get to the bottom of this, but he just keeps on: "I'm giving it to you . . . No thought of gain . . ." Well I ask you! So you, dear neighbours, be the judges.
STUPAK: Er . . . yes . . . Interesting.
UGAROV: Maybe it really is too hard for us to understand. He's only a driver, and my line's keeping my home town in toilet bowls. Maybe we just don't know what life's all about.
VASIUTA: He must be drunk.
ANCHUGIN: Not a bit of it. He's sober. That's the point.
UGAROV: You're not one for fooling around, Mister Musician. You'd know how to talk to him. Have a word . . .
KHOMUTOV: Yes, explain to them, get them to understand . . .
BAZILSKY: Tell me this: is everything they've told us . . .
KHOMUTOV: Yes, it's all true.
BAZILSKY: But . . . Really? A hundred rubles?
KHOMUTOV: Yes. A hundred rubles.
STUPAK: Just like that? For no return?
KHOMUTOV: [*irritably*] Yes. For no return.
STUPAK: Interesting. Makes you wonder, what price charity these days . . .
BAZILSKY: [*to* KHOMUTOV.] Giving these gentlemen a hundred rubles? . . . An odd thing to do . . .

UGAROV: That's the point — very odd.
STUPAK: [*to* BAZILSKY.] Let's not exaggerate. There's no mystery. He's a swindler, pure and simple.
FAINA: [*to her husband.*] Why do you take that attitude? We don't know . . .
STUPAK: [*interrupting*] What don't we know? His motives — he's got good reason for hiding them. Only a crook, a cheat, and a twister could pull a number like that. In other words a swindler.
VASIUTA: Shall I call the manager?
BAZILSKY: Or maybe a doctor? [*To* KHOMUTOV.] You quite sure you feel all right? . . .
KHOMUTOV: Yes. I'm all right. But what's wrong with all of you? Surely it's not that hard to understand. One man hasn't got a bean, another has lots of money. One needs money, another's saving it. So one gives to the other, shares his with him, helps him. What's so odd about that? It's perfectly straightforward.
STUPAK: That's a load of guff. Idealism — if not a swindle.
KHOMUTOV: Look, we all put ourselves first . . . But believe me, we mustn't forget about others. When the time comes we'll pay dearly for being indifferent, for being selfish. That's the truth, I assure you . . .
STUPAK: He's raving. And raving religiously at that. Raving and lying.
KHOMUTOV: [*to* STUPAK.] Ye-es. I understand you. You obviously wouldn't help anybody yourself. But try and understand somebody who does try to help. [*To all.*] Can't you really understand?
UGAROV: We're not as stupid as you think.
STUPAK: Maybe it's popularity you're after? Stocking up with moral capital? That wouldn't be hard to understand.
BAZILSKY: I can't make it out. Nobody in this town goes to concerts except old women and child prodigies, while the educated people, instead of showing any concern for culture, drink vodka and try their damnedest to shock everybody. Why do you do it? What for? You're corrupting people, don't you see? . . . No, I don't believe in your "generosity"! Some sort of dirty dealing more likely. I wouldn't be surprised if something about it appeared in tomorrow's paper.

STUPAK: You wouldn't be a journalist, would you? Out to fill your column? Trying something new?
FAINA: [*to her husband.*] Stop that!
KHOMUTOV: Amazing, isn't it? You do somebody a good turn, and look at the thanks you get.
STUPAK: Less of your stunts. Who do you think you are — chucking hundreds about like this? Tolstoi? Jean-Paul Sartre? Just who are you? Well? . . . I'll tell you. You're a good-for-nothing, to put it mildly.
VASIUTA: What are you doing here — being so fine and noble? Ain't some angel from heaven, are you? God forgive me asking.
BAZILSKY: Unfortunately he's not much like an angel at all. [*To* KHOMUTOV.] You're a poseur, or something very like one.
KHOMUTOV: Thanks a lot. Next time I'll know where to go with my sympathy.
STUPAK: Drop it! Nobody here believes you.
[*Brief pause.*]
FAINA: [*to all.*] But what if he's genuine? . . . What if he really did want to help them? For nothing . . .
STUPAK: [*shouting*] Don't talk nonsense!
FAINA: [*horrified*] Why are you shouting at me?
STUPAK: So you don't butt in where you're not wanted!
FAINA: [*to* KHOMUTOV.] Look, I believe you. I believe you did it for nothing . . .
STUPAK: Idiot! Nothing's for nothing. Never! And don't you forget it!
UGAROV: That's the truth. Nothing's for nothing.
FAINA: [*to all.*] Is that what you think?
VASIUTA: There ain't no other way.
FAINA: [*to* BAZILSKY.] Is that what you think too?
BAZILSKY: What I think's never changed anything in the slightest. [*Stands aside, arms folded on chest.*]
STUPAK: [*to* FAINA.] Don't show everybody how naive you are! [*More gently.*] Please.
FAINA: So whatever anybody does — none of it's for nothing?
VASIUTA: That's right, dearie. None of it. Ain't no doubt about it. Help, sympathy — you don't get 'em for nothing these days. Even love . . .
FAINA: What — love too?

VASIUTA: What about it? Love's all very fine, dearie, but fr'instance, we all know that a husband with a car's better than a husband without one.
STUPAK: [*shouting*] Be quiet!
VASIUTA: Why? Ain't I telling the truth?
[FAINA *sits down on the bed beside* KHOMUTOV.]
STUPAK: [*to* VASIUTA.] What are you doing here?
VASIUTA: I'm talking to her — not you. Let her know where she stands. That's better for you too.
STUPAK: Shut up, old woman!
VASIUTA: What's up with you?
FAINA: What's up with him? . . . The car isn't his. It's mine.
ANCHUGIN: [*menacingly, to* KHOMUTOV.] Watch it, Mister Agronomist. You're upsetting people . . .
STUPAK: [*to* FAINA.] What's the car got to do with it? You ought to be ashamed! [*To all.*] Look, what's going on here? This is monstrous! Here we are at each other's throats — and all because of him! He's provoked all this! He's insulted us! He's slandered us! Spat in our faces! He ought to be put away, put in quarantine! Immediately!
ANCHUGIN: First let him tell us why he came.
[*All except* FAINA *close in on* KHOMUTOV.]
UGAROV: Where'd you get the money?
ANCHUGIN: Why'd you offer it?
BAZILSKY: Isn't it time you told us the real reason?
STUPAK: [*shouting*] Tell us, damn you!
[*Short pause.*]
KHOMUTOV: [*in an injured tone.*] I wanted to help them.
[*Cries of indignation. All except* FAINA *exclaim and shout at once:* "Nut!", "Drunkard!", "Twister!", "Liar!", "I'll break your neck!"]
BAZILSKY: Maniac! Think you're Jesus Christ, do you?
FAINA: [*getting up and placing herself between* KHOMUTOV *and the advancing group.*] Stop! [*Shouting*] Think what you're doing! [*All stop.*]
KHOMUTOV: What do you want me to do? What are you after? . . . Should I tell you I've cut somebody's throat, . . . robbed somebody, . . . murdered somebody?
STUPAK: That can't be ruled out. I'm quite sure we've uncovered

some crime here. We ought to phone the police, and that'd be the end of all this. [*Goes to the phone.*]

BAZILSKY: No. Phone the hospital. It's delusions of grandeur he's got. That's clear. Imagines he's a saviour.

[*Silence*]

STUPAK: [*dialling*] Enquiries? Give me the lunatic asylum's number, please . . . Thank you. [*Dials*]

KHOMUTOV: [*in hoarse voice.*] All right. Untie me . . . I'll explain everything.

[*Short pause.* ANCHUGIN *unties him.*]

[*Slowly*] You've convinced me you're capable of anything . . . But I don't intend to go to a madhouse. I've no time . . . I came here for one week . . . [*Pause*] My mother lived in this town . . . She lived alone and I hadn't seen her for six years . . . [*With an effort.*] And in all those six years . . . I . . . I didn't visit her once. And I didn't do a thing to help her. Not in any way . . . For six years I was planning to send her this money, but I carried it around in my pocket, spent a bit of it sometimes . . . And now . . . [*Pause*] Now she doesn't need anything any more . . . Including this money.

VASIUTA: Lord save us!

KHOMUTOV: I buried her three days ago. And I made up my mind to give the money to the first person I met who needed it more than me . . . You know the rest . . . [*Pause*] Now I hope you understand . . . [*Short pause.*]

ANCHUGIN: Why didn't you tell us earlier, chum?

KHOMUTOV: It's not something you like to admit.

VASIUTA: Lord save us! What a sin . . .

UGAROV: And what about us, eh? . . . It's turned out badly . . .

BAZILSKY: [*to* KHOMUTOV.] Forgive us, if you can . . .

UGAROV: [*softly to* VASIUTA.] Bring us some wine.

[VASIUTA *disappears.*]

BAZILSKY: [*surprised*] This is awful, awful. Something strange has happened to us, . . . made us so mistrustful . . .

ANCHUGIN: [*sitting down beside* KHOMUTOV.] Sorry, pal. Don't be angry.

UGAROV: If we'd only known what it'd lead to . . .

STUPAK: We're sorry, of course. But as it turns out, we're quits. Today I've quarrelled with my wife for the first time. [*To* FAINA.]

Stop sulking. Can't you see, our friend here's had a bad time of it? [*Goes up to her.*] Well, I'm sorry. [*Tries to take her arm.*] Don't sulk.

FAINA: [*taking her arm away.*] Don't touch me, if you don't mind.

STUPAK: What? . . . Not even like that?

[FAINA *says nothing.*]

Come on, let's go. [*Goes to the door. Stops.*] Or do you intend to stay here?

FAINA: Yes I do.

STUPAK: You do? . . . Well, do as you please. [*Exit*]

BAZILSKY: [*to* KHOMUTOV.] Please, you mustn't think we're as inhuman as all that . . . It was something awful that suddenly came over us, I assure you . . . Of course, we should have believed you. We were bound to believe you . . .

[*Enter* VASIUTA *with wine.* UGAROV *hastens to pour it into some glasses.*]

ANCHUGIN: [*to* KHOMUTOV.] You must understand, chum: money's a terrible thing when you haven't got any.

VASIUTA: Devil take the stuff! Where there's money, there's trouble. Never any different.

UGAROV: [*to* KHOMUTOV.] Too bad . . . [*With glass in hand.*] To your mother . . . God rest her soul . . . Forgive us. [*Drinks*]

ANCHUGIN: [*to* KHOMUTOV.] Well then . . . Don't take it too hard. Drink up, chum.

[ANCHUGIN, VASIUTA, *and* KHOMUTOV *slowly drink their wine.*]

FAINA: Give me some too. [*Drinks*]

[*Silence.* BAZILSKY *stands by the door, uncertain whether he should leave or stay.*]

UGAROV: Sit down, Mister Musician. [*Pause. Then to all.*] Well, it's too late to do anything now.

KHOMUTOV: [*with a start.*] No, no! Don't worry about it. Life goes on, as they say . . .

[*Pause*]

ANCHUGIN: [*singing*] "Through densest Siberian forest . . ."

UGAROV: [*to* BAZILSKY.] Give him some accompaniment, Mister Musician.

ANCHUGIN: [*continuing*] ". . . From Sakhalin the convict fled.
        To guide him he'd only the narrowest
        Of trails left by deer and sled . . ."

[ANCHUGIN *and* UGAROV *repeat the last two lines in chorus.* BAZILSKY *suddenly starts accompanying them on his violin. They go on singing: bass and tenor, to the violin.*]